THE RISE AND FALL OF THE SOVIET ECONOMY

An Economic History of the USSR from 1945

The Postwar World
General Editors: A.J. Nicholls and Martin S. Alexander

As distance puts events into perspective, and as evidence accumulates, it begins to be possible to form an objective historical view of our recent past. *The Postwar World* is an ambitious series providing a scholarly but readable account of the way our world has ben shaped in the crowded years since the Second World War. Some volumes will deal with regions, or even single nations, others with important themes; all will be written by expert historians drawing on the latest scholarship as well as their own research and judgements. The series should be particularly welcome to students, but it is designed also for the general reader with an interest in contemporary history.

THE RISE AND FALL OF THE SOVIET ECONOMY AN ECONOMIC HISTORY OF THE USSR FROM 1945

PHILIP HANSON

Longman

An imprint of **Pearson Education**

London · New York · Toronto · Sydney · Tokyo · Singapore · Hong Kong · Cape Town
Madrid · Paris · Amsterdam · Munich · Milan

Pearson Education Limited
Edinburgh Gate
Harlow
Essex CM20 2JE,
England

and Associated Companies throughout the world

Visit us on the World Wide Web at:
www.pearsoned.co.uk

First published in Great Britain 2003

© Pearson Education Limited 2003

The right of Philip Hanson to be identified as Author of this Work
has been asserted by him in accordance with the Copyright,
Designs and Patents Act 1988.

ISBN 0 582 29958 6

British Library Cataloguing in Publication Data
A CIP catalogue record for this book can be obtained from the British Library

Library of Congress Cataloging in Publication Data
A CIP catalog record for this book can be obtained from the Library of Congress

10 9 8 7 6 5 4
08 07 06 05 04

Typeset in 11/13pt Baskerville by Graphicraft Limited, Hong Kong
Printed in Malaysia, GPS

The Publishers' policy is to use paper manufactured from sustainable forests.

CONTENTS

LIST OF TABLES

LIST OF FIGURES

ACKNOWLEDGEMENTS

For sharing information and work in progress, discussing interpretations and pointing me to new sources, I am indebted to Julian Cooper, Bob Davies, Don Filtzer, Mark Harrison, Michael Kaser and Elizabeth Teague. For three months' study time at Kyoto, enabling me to make progress with the drafting, I am grateful to the Kyoto Institute of Economic Research, and to Satoshi Mizobata in particular – and to the University of Birmingham for granting me study leave. Expert editing by Elizabeth Teague, by Helen Hodge and by the series editor, Professor Anthony Nicholls, and Marea Arries' skills in assembling the final text were particularly appreciated.

Philip Hanson
July 2002

EDITORIAL FOREWORD

The aim of this series is to describe and analyse the history of the world since 1945. History, like time, does not stand still. What seemed to many of us only recently to be 'current affairs' or the stuff of political speculation, has now become material for historians. The editors feel that it is time for a series of books which will offer the public judicious and scholarly, but at the same time readable, accounts of the way in which our present-day world has been shaped since the Second World War. The period which began in 1945 has witnessed political events and socio-economic developments of enormous significance for the human race, as important as anything which happened before Hitler's death or the bombing of Hiroshima. Ideologies have waxed and waned, the developed economies have boomed and bust, empires of various types have collapsed, new nations have emerged and sometimes themselves fallen into decline. While we can be thankful that no major armed conflict occurred between the so-called superpowers, there have been many other wars, and terrorism emerged as an international plague. Although the position of ethnic minorities improved in some countries, it worsened dramatically in others. As communist tyrannies relaxed their grip on many areas of the world, so half-forgotten national conflicts re-emerged. Nearly everywhere the status of women became an issue which politicians were unable to avoid. The same was true of the natural environment, apparent threats to which have been a recurrent source of international concern. These are only some of the developments we hope will be illuminated by this series as it unfolds.

The books in the series will not follow any set pattern; they will vary in length according to the needs of the subject. Some will deal with regions, or even single nations, and others with themes. Not all of them will begin in 1945, and the terminal date may vary; as with the length, the time-span chosen will be appropriate to the question under discussion. All the books, however, will be written by expert historians drawing on the latest research, as well as their own expertise and judgement. The series should be particularly welcome to students, but it is designed also for the general reader with an interest in contemporary history. We hope that the books will stimulate scholarly discussion and encourage specialists to look beyond their own particular interests to engage in wider controversies.

History, and especially the history of the recent past, is neither 'bunk' nor an intellectual form of stamp-collecting, but an indispensable part of an educated person's approach to life. If it is not written by historians it will be written by others of a less discriminating and more polemical disposition. The editors are confident that this series will help to ensure the victory of the historical approach, with consequential benefits for its readers.

A.J. Nicholls
Martin S. Alexander

INTRODUCTION

The story of the post-war Soviet Union is a story that ends in failure. The Union of Soviet Socialist Republics, or USSR, disintegrated in 1991 into 15 separate states. The doctrine of Marxism-Leninism ceased to be the official basis of government programmes anywhere in the former Soviet territory. In none of the newly independent states of the former Soviet Union did a communist party have a constitutionally entrenched right to rule.

One measure of the completeness of the Soviet collapse is that now, after a decade of economic distress in most of those countries, nobody seriously expects a return to the communist order. In any history of the evolution of mankind's social arrangements – at any rate, in any history written early in the twenty-first century – the failure of Soviet communism can be treated as total.

What is less obvious now, and easily forgotten, is that as late as 1990 such a collapse seemed impossible. Almost all Soviet citizens and almost all foreign observers conceived the Soviet Union as a fixture. It was widely understood to be in difficulties. Its political and economic arrangements were widely seen as both inhumane and ineffective. But hardly anyone expected the state to evaporate, let alone to do so any time soon. (One notable exception among Western specialists was Alexander Shtromas [see Shtromas 1988 and Chapter 7 below].)

What is even more easily forgotten now is that well into the 1970s the Soviet Union was seldom described as failing. Its economy tended, up to the early 1970s, to grow faster than that of the United States. For a generation or more after the Second World War, the traditional Soviet aim of 'catching up and overtaking' the West was not patent nonsense. In the early and middle 1970s the Soviet Union was judged to have achieved strategic parity with the US (or, more broadly, with NATO). Its nuclear arsenal and conventional forces, in other words, could match those of the West in possible conflicts, whether in Europe or globally. Its influence seemed if anything to be spreading in Africa and Asia.

In the course of thirty years, from the end of the Second World War, the Soviet Union had recovered from wartime devastation and massive loss of life. It had made remarkable strides in military technology. It had broken the US monopolies of, successively, the atomic bomb, the hydrogen bomb and inter-continental ballistic missiles. It also had – though this was not widely known at the time – formidable arsenals of biological and chemical weapons. And the lives of Soviet citizens had at the same time improved immensely. After the death of Joseph Stalin in 1953, higher priority had been given to agriculture, to housing and to manufactured consumer goods, and the new priorities made a difference.

The reign of terror, moreover, had ended. Soviet citizens no longer feared a visit from the secret police in the small hours: provided, that is, they had not engaged in public criticism of the authorities. There were still political prisoners; there was still a *gulag* – the chain of labour camps to which millions of people had been consigned under Stalin, almost at random. But it was possible to live securely if you were prepared to keep your head below the parapet – as almost everyone was.

The story of the post-war USSR is therefore a story of rise and fall. This is true of its political standing in the world. It is also true of its economy – to whose rise and fall between 1945 and 1991 this book is devoted.

This is a work of synthesis, not original research from primary sources. From the mid-1960s, however, I was following Soviet economic developments in real time. Some of the story from then on is based on my own interpretation of contemporary Soviet material – though with the considerable advantage of hindsight. For the late Stalin and Khrushchev periods I have relied heavily on the work of others – mainly but not exclusively Western.

The approach adopted in this book is that of an economist looking back at half a century or so of one country's history and trying to make sense, for non-economists, of that country's economic experience. Perhaps that makes it a work of economic history. If there is, in principle, a methodological difference between economic analysis of the past and economic history, it has never been clear to me what that difference should be.

In contemporary practice, as distinct from principle, the difference is clear. Economics is, as my colleague Somnath Sen has observed, 'a broad church run by fundamentalists', and the fundamentalists see physics as the subject to be emulated: theoretical model, hypothesis, hypothesis-testing with empirical data. Economic history, on the other hand, is a broad church not run by fundamentalists. Cliometri modelling may be prestigious, but it is not mandatory. Discursive narratives and tentative interpretations are permissible. In that sense, at least, this is an exercise in economic history. It is also addressed to the general reader. I have tried to avoid the use of jargon. Where I have failed to avoid it, I have, I hope, explained it.

Inevitably, in an account of Soviet economic experience, numbers loom large – and are controversial. In this book I have made extensive use of recalculations of Soviet data by the US Central Intelligence Agency (CIA). Some readers will find this provocative. Surely the CIA 'got it wrong'? What about the new evidence from the Soviet archives?

The CIA, it can be said with hindsight, got a number of things wrong about the USSR during the Cold War. Its analysts overstated the size of the Soviet economy relative to that of the US, though they did not do so because of a conscious intent to deceive. The late 1970s forecast by some CIA analysts of an imminent fall in Soviet oil production was misleading about the timing of that fall. But the Agency's estimate of changes over time in Soviet total output has not been undermined by new information. This was for gross national product or GNP, for practical purposes equivalent, for the USSR, to gross domestic product, or GDP. Angus Maddison, the leading connoisseur of international growth statistics, has reviewed these figures and pronounced them healthy (Maddison 1998).

During the Cold War somebody had to estimate Soviet GNP if there was to be any chance of understanding what was going on in Soviet society and Soviet politics. The second purpose of such estimates – to inform Western threat assessments by comparing Soviet production potential and the economic burden of defence with those of US – was less well served by CIA economic assessments. But the changes over time in GNP/GDP had also to be quantified, and here the Agency was more successful.

Recalculations were necessary because the Soviet official data for total output were in principle incapable of being compared with Western national income figures and in practice also seriously distorted. The reasons for this verdict on Soviet data are given in Chapter 1.

The CIA's recalculations used methods developed in academic studies by Abram Bergson. Their methodology and a large part of the primary information on which they were based were open to scrutiny at the time. The Agency's figures were indeed scrutinised, and they were criticised from a variety of viewpoints. The US Defense Intelligence Agency (DIA) routinely produced different GNP numbers and higher defence-spending numbers. Other analysts, including the present author, argued that in the 1970s and 1980s the CIA was overestimating the 'real' (inflation-adjusted) growth of Soviet investment (see Chapter 5). Unofficial estimates made in the USSR itself, in semi-secrecy, by Grigorii Khanin made the trajectory of Soviet economic change in the post-war period look somewhat different in shape, but did not present a whole new story. In general the CIA estimates stood up fairly well to these critiques.

The Soviet archives and post-Soviet memoirs appear not to have changed the picture significantly. Soviet officials did not operate with a secret set of numbers that differed from those that were (from 1956 on) published. There were some secrets that were not published: the production of military equipment, non-ferrous metals output, the gold reserves. Otherwise, the officials shared their data with us. Like other members of the Soviet intelligentsia, Soviet officials put less trust than Western scholars did in the reported figures of output in physical terms (tons of steel and the like). Otherwise they were no better informed than we were.

An economist's approach to Soviet history differs from that of a general historian in one obvious way. The focus of this book is in the following questions. Why did the Soviet people produce and consume what they did when they did? How did the economy work? Did the way in which it worked change over time? What were the changes in economic policy? Why were they made, and did they achieve their aims? These matters are unavoidably present also in a general history; they are after all fundamental in any society. But they do not provide the main focus.

This difference of focus may contribute to some differences of judgement. Nikita Khrushchev's period of rule (1953–64) is treated rather favourably here, and not just for his liberalising de-Stalinisation. Yes, a great deal went wrong in the latter part of his time in office and, yes, he was ousted from the leadership. But he de-Stalinised the economy as well as the society: not by reforming the economic system but by drastically changing the priorities set for that system, in favour of the people. That was a profound change, and it endured.

Conversely, any economist finds it hard to be too respectful about Mikhail Gorbachev's achievements as a leader. To his leading Western biographer, Archie Brown, Gorbachev's approach to economic reform was 'open-ended'. In Chapters 7 and 8 Gorbachev's record in economic policy is treated as riddled with avoidable inconsistencies from start to finish. It may have been open-ended, but it was full of holes in the middle, too.

In one respect this book resembles a certain kind of political history: the narrative is divided into chapters according to changes in leadership, albeit with two chapters each for Khrushchev, Brezhnev and Gorbachev. This disgracefully unfashionable approach, like that of a history of England organised around kings and queens, is hard to avoid. New leaders did, time and again, make a difference. None of them, it is true, could do much to alter the dipping trajectory of the Soviet economy. But the sequence of reforms and policy changes, however ineffective these ultimately were, is clearly linked to the changes in leadership.

The Soviet economy rose and fell between 1945 and 1991 above all in a relative sense. From growing faster than most of the capitalist world, the Soviet Union began in the 1970s to cease to gain ground. The absolute gap in conventional measures of economic performance, such as per capita GDP or GNP, began to increase.

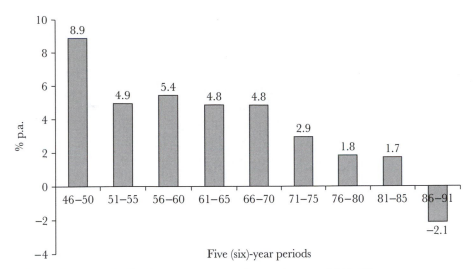

Figure I.1 Soviet GNP: average annual growth rates, 1945–91
Note: Based chiefly on CIA estimates. The data are presented by Maddison as a GDP
series, for comparability with other countries. The CIA originally produced a GNP series;
the practical difference, in the case of the USSR, is negligible, and they are described
here as GNP.
Source: Derived from Maddison (1995).

The most recent retrospective measures of Soviet total GDP, in 1990
dollars, show absolute declines, before 1990, in only three years: 1959,
1963 and 1979 (Maddison 1995, Table C16c). Earlier Western assessments,
in 1970 roubles and in 1982 roubles, show only one or two years of absolute decline before the collapse of 1990–91. (Per capita output shows rather
more declines, but still mainly an upwards movement.) But Soviet economic performance, despite the predominant absolute increase in output,
was deteriorating in comparison with that of the capitalist world.

Relative deterioration was critical in three respects: it threatened the
Soviet Union's ability to match the West militarily; it undermined the self-
confidence of Soviet elites and their belief that their social system could
deliver; and it weakened Soviet citizens' attachment to that system. The
slowdown in Soviet growth is shown in Figure I.1.

In the chapters that follow, I have tried to chart this rise and fall, and
also to suggest reasons for the transition from relative success to relative
failure. The arrangement of the material is chronological.

In this narrative, two things seem reasonably clear. First, the long-run
trajectory of the Soviet economy was little influenced by policy changes
made deliberately to improve it. Like policymakers in Western countries,
Soviet leaders announced all sorts of initiatives which seldom if ever affected

long-term (ten years or more) rates of output growth. Identifying points of change in long-run economic trends is always problematic; insofar as we can identify them, they are seldom if ever explicable as the intended results of policy changes.

Second, Soviet leaders were the directors of a giant firm – what some American commentators called USSR Inc. (see Chapter 1 for an outline of the system). Some acted like chairmen of the board, others like chief executive officers, others again like both. One or two were, or became, more like part-time non-executive directors. The leadership team, at any rate, had formal powers to micro-manage everything, and ultimate responsibility for the economy, in ways that went far beyond the authority of any government in a developed market economy. The record will show, I trust, that each new leader came in with an economic agenda that for a time really did make a difference.

What they could do, and did do, was to change priorities in the allocation of resources and to tinker with methods of centralised economic administration. After Stalin, Nikita Khrushchev shifted priorities in favour of the consumer and in favour of agriculture. No subsequent leader, except Gorbachev briefly in the mid-1980s, tried to shift priorities back towards investment. After Stalin, all, I suggest, were frightened – perhaps unnecessarily – of trying the patience of the Soviet people too far. Leonid Brezhnev (1964–82) removed some of the excessive tinkering of Khrushchev's last years but reaffirmed the post-Stalin priorities. In the mid-1970s he presided over a historically remarkable further downgrading of the priority of investment. Mikhail Gorbachev (1985–91) tried briefly to reassert this, but gave up.

What none of them did was to alter the basic features of the Soviet economic system. Gorbachev might be blamed, or praised, for undermining the system, but he did not do so deliberately. Each of them ran into the limits on economic progress set by a system that took shape during industrialisation in the 1930s.

The view put forward in this book is that the origins of Soviet relative economic decline can be found in the liberalisation of the Soviet social order that followed the death of Stalin in 1953. This is a contentious view and not, I think, one that can be made into a testable hypothesis. Mark Harrison has modelled, using game theory, a story of the interplay between planners and planned, in which the decline of coercion produces an output collapse (Harrison 2001a). His version of events, however, fits, as it is intended to do, the output collapse at the end of the period, in 1990–91. His interpretation of the earlier trajectory is different from mine, and I shall return to these different interpretations in the final chapter.

My own view, in some ways more conventional than Harrison's, is put forward rather tentatively. This is that the erosion of discipline, with effects on economic performance, started earlier and was more gradual, and was one of several factors producing an earlier slowdown. Where we agree is in attributing to a decline in 'plan discipline' a role in Soviet economic failure.

It may be worth adding that no interpretation that stresses the role of coercion entails a favourable view of Stalinism or a belief that economic development under a totalitarian regime of terror could have continued indefinitely. It amounts, rather, to saying that Soviet central planning was an authority-intensive economic system, and that (in my version of events) the erosion of authority made it, gradually, less effective. Liberalising economic reforms time and again introduced internal inconsistencies into the system. If there is a viable halfway-house system between authoritarian central planning with state ownership and capitalist free enterprise, neither the Soviet Union nor any of the East European communist states managed to locate it. (China's comparatively successful reforms may be another story. But they were probably not feasible in more developed economies with political regimes that were already softer by the 1970s than that of Beijing.)

The softening of the political and social regime, as distinct from a softening of plan discipline, also played its part. Not only did managers of production units no longer have reason to fear for their lives or their freedom if they failed to meet a key target. At the same time, as institutions and procedures became routine and – under Brezhnev – managers and planners stayed in post for long periods, networks developed in which a factory manager could and often did conspire with his 'higher authorities', in the ministry supervising his industry, to keep his output targets down and his input allocations up. Then all concerned could report success, without having to exert themselves unduly.

If the undermining effects of reform are one paradox in Soviet economic history, they are not the only one. Another is that the Soviet collapse, when it came, was not the result of a revolt by citizens discontented with their economic lot. In the later chapters of the book it will, I hope, be made clear that the collapse had more to do with high politics than with low economics. The speed with which central planning was abandoned, and capitalism (of a sort) accepted, was indeed remarkable. The alacrity with which old practices were abandoned revealed, certainly, that little confidence in the established economic system remained either in elite circles or in the population at large. But there was no clamour from below for radical change. The notorious patience of Soviet citizens had by 1991 been sorely tried, but not exhausted.

The developments that account for these apparent paradoxes will, I hope, become clear in the later chapters. What is needed before the narrative begins is a brief account of the Soviet economic system that endured, with some modifications, throughout the period covered by this book. Its institutions and procedures had taken shape in the 1930s. A brisk outline of them at the outset will make it easier to follow the fortunes of the Soviet economy after the Second World War. This is provided in Chapter 1, before we embark on the story of post-war economic recovery.

CHAPTER ONE

The Starting Point: the Stalinist Economic System and the Aftermath of War

The inheritance from the 1930s: the Soviet economic planning system

The basic institutions of the Soviet economic system took shape in the First Five-Year Plan (1928/29–32). Subsequent modifications were numerous, but not substantial. Basically, the whole economy was run like a single giant corporation – USSR Inc. As corporations go, USSR Inc. was of exceptional workforce size and was a conglomerate with the most extreme range of activities, yet it was run in a more centralised way than most.

The fundamental difference from a market economy was that decisions about what should be produced and in what quantities, and at what prices that output should be sold, were the result of a hierarchical, top-down process culminating in instructions 'from above' to all producers; they were not the result of decentralised decisions resulting from interactions between customers and suppliers. Producers were concerned above all to meet targets set by planners. They had no particular reason to concern themselves with the wishes of the users of their products, nor with the activities of competitors. Indeed the concept of competition was absent: other producers in the same line of activity were simply not competitors but fellow-executors of the state plan.

Production was controlled by the state. This control was exercised through a layered hierarchy. The central policy-makers were at the top, like a board of directors. Ultimately these top policy-makers were the Politburo of the Central Committee (CC), the inner ruling group of the Communist Party of the Soviet Union (CPSU). Most of the detail and many important matters of substance were decided by the government or, more precisely, those members of the government with economic portfolios. The Politburo and the government (known for most of our period as the USSR Council of Ministers) overlapped in membership.

These top policy-makers relied on key staff units to make their programmes operational: in particular, the USSR State Planning Committee or USSR Gosplan, and the economic sections of the *apparat* (administration) of the Central Committee of the CPSU. The name and precise responsibility of the top planning body changed several times within our period, mainly in Stalin's last years, but for most of the period it was USSR Gosplan.

Reporting to government ministers were the 'branch ministries' – the administrative bodies that supervised particular branches of the economy. (The ministries had been known as People's Commissariats before the Second World War but from 15 March 1946 the bourgeois term 'ministry' was adopted.) Typically – and a little confusingly for diplomatic contacts – a branch minister was not a career politician who had been given a particular industrial portfolio, but a manager who had made his (rarely her) career in the industry he now supervised. The Soviet Minister for the Chemical Industry, for example, had more in common professionally with the Chief Executive Officer of ICI or Dupont than with the President of the British Board of Trade or the US Commerce Secretary.

The branch ministries in turn were typically divided into sub-branch administrations, known as *glavki* (an abbreviation of 'main administrations'). In some branches of the economy there was also a territorial division, with 'All-Union' (USSR-level) ministries replicated at union-republic level: a Ukrainian Soviet Socialist Republic Ministry of the Coal Industry, for example. Finally, at the base of the pyramid, were all the basic management units in the economy: industrial enterprises, state and collective farms, transport organisations, and so on.

The dimensions of this pyramid (Figure 1.1) were not constant. That is to say, the numbers of branch ministries, *glavki* and production units were altered from time to time, and the precise composition of the staff bodies at the top also changed. A reasonably representative set of dimensions for much of our period, however, would be as follows: a Politburo of committee size, around 12–14 people; several thousand staff in the central staff bodies; some 50 or so branch ministries, more than a hundred *glavki*, and close to a million basic production units.

The official description of the economy was that it was a 'planned, socialist economy'. The words 'planned' and 'socialist' could mean all sorts of things. What they meant in Soviet practice was the following.

The economy was planned in the sense that the output produced and the inputs used by every farm, industrial enterprise, construction outfit, transport organisation, service enterprise and research unit were governed by

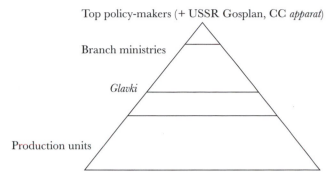

Top policy-makers (+ USSR Gosplan, CC *apparat*)

Branch ministries

Glavki

Production units

Figure 1.1   The Soviet planning system as a layered hierarchy

instructions from above that were part of a single, national plan. There were annual plans, five-year plans and longer-term 'perspective' plans. The annual plans were the most serious operational documents because the national annual plan was made up of obligatory targets and instructions addressed to every production unit – targets that were legally binding. Plans for more than a year were launched with much more public noise, but were less serious. They were by convention identified by their first and final years of operation, so the Fourth Five-Year Plan, for example, was the 1946–50 plan. Outcomes over a five-year plan period usually deviated substantially from plan. The sum of the supposedly component annual plans often differed substantially, too, from the original five-year plan.

The economy was socialist in the sense that private enterprise was, with a few small exceptions, banned. Almost all employment was by the state. Every able-bodied person of working age except full-time students and mothers of very small children was required to be employed in a state entity or in a collective farm, or *kolkhoz*. (The *kolkhozy* are mentioned separately because nominally they were producer collectives, not state-owned enterprises. State farms, or *sovkhozy*, on the other hand, were state enterprises.) In practice the collective farms were controlled by the state and not by members of the collective. Their main practical difference from a state workplace was that the members of the collective farm – the *kolkhozniki* – were not parties to a wage contract with the state; as befitted members of a producer cooperative, they received residual net income from the collective farm's activity. Since the state controlled their output and non-labour input prices and prescribed targets for their production, it indirectly controlled these residual incomes.

All natural resources belonged to the state. The collective farms officially leased land from the state at zero rent in perpetuity. 'Productive assets', that is, the fixed assets of production units other than (nominally) the collective farms, all belonged to the state. Private assets could legally take the form of

11

household contents, houses (chiefly in rural areas and on the fringes of cities; most urban housing belonged to the state), cars, holdings of cash and accounts in the state savings bank, plus the occasional issues of state bonds, the purchase of which was, typically, compulsory.

The planning system covered the state production establishment: that is to say, all the state entities and the collective farms. There were four components of economic activity that were not subject to obligatory annual plan instructions.

First, for most of our period, there was a labour market of sorts. People were not sent under compulsory plan instructions to work at this or that enterprise. They could and did change jobs of their own volition. There were exceptions: prisoners, of course; members of the CPSU (around a tenth of the adult population), who could be directed as a Party obligation to work at particular places but seldom were; and young people graduating from higher and further educational establishments, who were in principle directed to work at particular workplaces for two years after graduation. Some direction of labour continued to be on the statute books for a short time after the Second World War. By and large, however, there was a market relationship between the state as employer and the household sector as a provider of labour services. People needed to be induced by pecuniary and non-pecuniary benefits to work at any particular workplace.

Second, for most of our period households were not allocated rations by the planners but bought what they themselves chose to buy – out of what the state made available. So consumption, like the supply of labour, entailed a market relationship between households and the state production establishment. The market concerned was neither flexible nor competitive. Officially, and for most purposes in reality too, the state production establishment was the sole supplier, and it fixed both prices and the quantities of each item supplied. Unlike the monopolist of the economics textbook, the planners did not fix quantities and let prices adjust, or fix prices and let quantities adjust; they fixed both. The planners lacked both the information and the motivation to fix prices and quantities so that markets cleared. Therefore queues, shortages and occasional surpluses prevailed at established prices for many consumer goods and services.

Third, the Soviet state could not directly plan what foreign partners would buy from it or at what prices they would sell to it. It could plan what would be made available for export and in what quantities, and what it would seek to buy; but it was again obliged to operate on a market basis with foreign trade partners. This was certainly the case in Soviet trade with the West and, on the whole, with developing countries as well. It was less clearly the case in Soviet trade with fellow-members of the Soviet-dominated trading bloc, the Council for Mutual Economic Assistance (CMEA). Even there, however, planning was never effectively supranational, and outcomes depended on inter-state bargaining.

The fourth area where the plan was not in any direct sense the determinant of what happened was the Soviet private sector. This was a mixture of legal, grey- and black-market activity, whose overall size cannot be determined with great confidence. The use by rural and suburban households of small household plots of land was highly regulated and, for part of the period, taxed, and peasants were required to make some deliveries from their plots to the state, but the household plots were legal and not directly planned. For much of our period the 'private plots' produced about a quarter of the Soviet food supply. Much of this was subsistence production: in other words, the food produced on the plot was consumed by the household itself. But some was sold on so-called *kolkhoz* markets. These were regulated but, for most of our period, the prices on them were not directly controlled by the state, and could and did fluctuate as supply and demand conditions altered.

That was the main legal element of private economic activity. There was also a grey area of spare-time repair work by skilled workers or tuition by teachers, whose legal status was never made entirely clear. This grey economy was an area in which ingenuity flourished. When a new block of apartments was fitted out, for example, by a state building trust, one scam was to hang all the doors the wrong way round; the building trust workers would then visit the new occupiers and offer to put things right privately, at a price. Notoriously, medical staff in hospitals often had to be bribed to look after patients properly. By the time the Soviet Union collapsed, there was almost no service that was not susceptible to this kind of corruption.

In the arts, several activities, such as painting and sculpture, were not easily conducted on anything but a freelance basis. Paintings, for instance, were from Khrushchev's time quite freely sold to private patrons at mutually agreed prices. Here the state's main means of control was through admission to the official union of painters (or writers or illustrators or actors). Only practitioners licensed in this way could legally work solely in their chosen field. Anyone who was not in the painters' union, for instance, had no right to a studio and had to have a day job.

Then there was the outright black economy, covering the resale of goods stolen from state sources, extortion, the running of prostitutes, the illegal distilling of vodka and other criminal activities.

In the 1970s and 1980s value added in the private sector (legal plus semilegal plus illegal) may have amounted to around 10 per cent of Soviet GDP. Estimates are discussed later on in this book. The great bulk of production, therefore, really was socialist and planned. State plans were comprehensive, so they necessarily included plans for household consumption, labour supply and foreign trade, but these were not administratively controlled by the state.

The central planning system was a remarkable arrangement. The most remarkable thing about it is that it worked, in the sense that the Soviet economy was for more than half a century a going concern, with output increasing and unemployment minimal. (Officially, the Soviet Union had no unemployment at all. There was therefore no such thing as unemployment benefit. In fact, there was some unemployment, but it was very small.) When one reflects that this system rested on detailed annual instructions to a million or so production units in all sectors of the economy, about the production of perhaps 20 million distinct goods and services, the fact that it functioned at all is impressive. There is no answer to the question, how many different goods and services are produced in a country. The level of disaggregation is almost infinitely adjustable: are 'shoes' a product, or men's shoes, or men's brown brogues, or men's brown brogues size 9, and so on? In the 1960s and 1970s, however, several Soviet commentators referred to a product assortment divided into some 20 million categories, and we can take that as a measure of the range of goods and services that entered into the reckoning of planners and producers, even if much of the planning was done at a more aggregated level.

Who were the recipients of plan instructions? The number varied, probably increasing over time. At the end of 1985, for example, there were 49,400 state and collective farms, 45,691 state industrial enterprises, 42,105 construction organisations, 709,900 retail stores, and so on (*Narkhoz 86*). Shops other than large department stores were grouped into city-wide, product-group management units, so the number of retail plan addressees was smaller than the number of shops. For most of the period we are looking at a total in the high hundred thousands, if not quite a million.

Each of the production management units received large numbers of targets and allocations. In manufacturing, for example, each enterprise was told what to produce (its product-mix), its overall output target (in tons or metres or thousands of roubles); in many cases its targets for main products; its investment plan; its allocation of material inputs from other producers, whether materials, components or sub-assemblies, and exactly how much it was entitled to receive under the plan and from which producer it would receive each item; its labour plan (numbers of employees, total wage-bill); to which producer or distributor its outputs were to go, and in what quantities; moreover, all the prices of inputs and outputs were fixed.

Comprehensive central planning required the drawing up and sending out of this vast number of instructions, including immensely detailed supply plans governing the flows of goods among producers and between producers and distributors. A factory producing a planned quantity of tractors in a given year will require (amongst many other things) specific quantities of particular grades of sheet steel. Therefore the planners had to ensure, not merely that *x* billion roubles' worth of steel of all sorts were produced in the country at large, but that those particular grades and quantities of sheet steel (net of planned inventory changes) were made and that they were sent to this particular tractor plant.

From time to time, when political leaders were allowing reform ideas to be aired, proposals were published for much looser plans, with product detail and inter-enterprise supply left to negotiations between enterprises. These proposals were either ignored or, when implemented, disastrous.

In comparison with a capitalist, market economy, this planning system had certain built-in strengths and certain built-in weaknesses. It possessed great macro-economic stability and a strong tendency to increase output from year to year, and, perhaps inadvertently, it also delivered substantial job security. At the same time, it was doomed to certain information and incentive problems that seem, in the end, to have been fatal.

Strengths of the Soviet planning system

The macro-economic stability stemmed from the fact that the economy was directed from the supply side. The level of economic activity was not the outcome of independent decisions by firms, households and foreign importers, determining aggregate demand, with government monetary and fiscal policies aimed at modifying the outcome so as to steer between high inflation and high unemployment. Planning was 'from resources': labour, materials and production capacities were all there to be (in principle) fully used in production targets set nationally.

In practice, the resources often were under-employed and inefficiently used, but unemployment was still minimal. Officially it did not exist at all; in reality it was almost entirely confined to a very low level of frictional unemployment: people who had left one job and would very soon start another.

Soviet macro-stability, moreover, amounted to more than just continuous low unemployment. Balance of payments crises were avoided by direct administrative control of the import bill (this depended on policy as well as system; in the late 1970s Poland, with the same planning system, contrived to get into balance of payments difficulties after importing heavily on credit; Moscow was more cautious). Inflation was not avoided (see below) but it was repressed, since official prices were controlled, and the price level officially did not change for many years – and in reality was low for most of the period.

National output grew from year to year (albeit at gradually declining rates) because the state ensured that a large share of each year's output took the form of investment goods, which went to increase future production capacity, and because almost all enterprises in almost all years were instructed to increase their output 'from the achieved level'. This may sound a very crude way of securing growth. It *was* a very crude way of ensuring growth. It did not ensure a growth of production of things that people (other than planners) actually wanted. It did not ensure that capital stock growth was accompanied by appropriate rates of technical change and labour-force increase. (See the later chapters of this book.) But it did ensure that in every year, or almost every year, up to 1989 Soviet production at least continued to inch forward, and in the first two post-war decades output grew fast.

In the 1960s to 1980s Czech, Polish and Hungarian economists produced some interesting work on 'socialist production cycles'. This work dealt with Central-East European economies, not with the USSR. It is open to question whether they in fact identified a truly cyclical process even in these economies (Mihalyi 1992). But there is little evidence of macro-economic instability, in the sense of cyclical fluctuations, in the case of the Soviet Union. There was a long-term growth slowdown, but that is another matter.

Job security was an accidental by-product of the system. This was nothing like the prevailing informal contract of 'permanent employment' that operated for a large part of the Japanese workforce until at least the mid-1990s. Labour turnover in the Soviet economy was for most of our period fairly high. But there was security of job tenure in the sense that the holder of a particular job slot could expect to remain in it so long as he or she chose; dismissal on any grounds was rare. This was partly because legislation made it difficult to sack workers. But perhaps more important was the prevailing condition of shortage (see below), which virtually guaranteed that every production unit was constantly seeking to expand its workforce. Managers generally had no interest in reducing their workforces, or indeed in cost-cutting in any form. This Soviet-style job security was associated with inefficiency and did nothing to enhance material prosperity; but it was one of the more comfortable characteristics of the Soviet way of life.

Weaknesses of the Soviet planning system

The Soviet systemic problems with information and with incentives are in the last resort closely connected, but need to be considered in turn.

Information problems are unavoidable in central planning of an economy, so long as omniscience is not available. The scale of the annual-plan information flows to and from an enterprise can be illustrated by a late Soviet example from the 1987 annual plan: the 60 or so enterprises that came under the Ministry of Heavy Engineering. Each received obligatory targets for total deliveries, labour productivity, unit cost and the production of main products: there were 358 main products in all, though any one enterprise probably produced only a modest number of these. There were a further 60 semi-obligatory 'indicators' for which each enterprise received assignments and had to report progress; of these, 40 had to do with the introduction of new technology. Each enterprise could be receiving a plan containing about a hundred performance indicators. A roughly similar targeting process was going on in each of some 60 branch ministries, spanning the whole economy.

The fact that an enterprise had to handle a lot of information flows is not in itself a specifically Soviet phenomenon. Financial and production reporting within a large Western firm might at the time have been similar in scale to that for a Soviet state enterprise. The difference is that in the Soviet case these targeting and reporting flows were part of a vastly larger plan for the entire economy. In consequence, transmitting and implementing Soviet plans required information and incentive arrangements that were different in kind from those familiar in the capitalist world.

Information about a producer's activities had to travel through far more stages in the Soviet system than under capitalism. In the capitalist order, the accounts of publicly-quoted companies would be periodically prepared for shareholders and others; day-to-day operations would require information flows up and down the hierarchy within the firm; strategic decisions would rest on top management information chiefly about the product and capital markets, and the activities of competitors. None of this has to be reported up to central government, let alone for the purpose of receiving detailed instructions *from* central government. Businesses under capitalism bear a burden of taxation and regulation, imposed by government, but that is very different from having every detail of their activity planned from above and reported back up to 'higher authorities'.

The difference is not adequately described by saying that there was 'more bureaucracy' or 'more paperwork' under Soviet socialism. What mattered was that instructions, monitoring and reporting had to pass through more administrative levels, and had to be processed at a central point into a single national plan, which then had to be monitored from a single national command post. That was the source of the information problem specific to central planning, identified at the start of our period by Friedrich von Hayek (Hayek 1945). All things being equal, the incomplete and imperfect knowledge available in society about economic matters is more efficiently used the less it is processed (aggregated, disaggregated, transferred) and the stronger are the incentives of those who do process it to get it right.

In the USSR, there were two devices that made the information problem manageable. First, there was the use of aggregation and disaggregation of data as they moved up and down (respectively) the layers of the planning hierarchy. When annual or five-year plans were being formulated, there was a two-way information flow. Enterprises reported on their current state of play and made requests about their future resource allocations up to their *glavki*. These were mostly aggregated and passed up to the branch ministry level, where they were (again, mostly) aggregated into branch to-tals and passed on to Gosplan. The qualification 'mostly' is needed because some very large investment projects and some of the resulting very large enterprises were treated as, so to speak, separate line items throughout. In the nature of things, however, the planners could accord such special treat-ment to only a small number of top-priority enterprises.

The planners sent aggregate targets downwards. These were disaggregated at successive lower levels until they were split into production targets, re-source allocations and supply plans for individual enterprises. A planning hierarchy without intervening layers, composed simply of central planners at the top and production units at the base, would have been unworkable.

The second way in which the information problem was handled was by iteration. Usually, ministries and their enterprises received draft targets and allocations, about which they then bargained 'upwards'. The normal beha-viour was to seek targets that were as soft as one could get away with: that is, plans in which the ratio of inputs to outputs was as high as could be obtained. The extent to which the branch ministry sided with its subordin-ate enterprises against the central planners was important in this vertical bargaining. Such bargaining was possible because enterprise managers knew more about their production possibilities than did the ministry staff above them, and the latter in turn knew more about their industry than did the central planners.

Various means were used by the central authorities to deal with these biases in the information they received. One was simply to cut input re-quests and increase output proposals by some more or less arbitrary factor. Another was to have special officials whose job it was to oversee (*kurirovat'*) particular enterprises, monitoring what was really going on there. The ef-fectiveness of the latter method was limited, however, both by numbers of available staff to do such detailed monitoring outside the city of Moscow itself, and by the likelihood that the *kurator* would be bribed by those he oversaw.

Incentive problems have already been touched on. Enterprise managers tried to secure easy plans because it was in their interest to do so. The Soviet economy worked on material incentives, like almost all economies at almost all times. Blue-collar workers were paid on a piece-rate basis more widely than was the case in the West. Managers were paid bonuses for meeting plan targets, and these bonuses were typically a substantial component (20–40 per cent) of their annual income. The enterprise managers received from the planners the kinds of targets described above. These are most commonly described in the literature as 'success indicators'. Each enterprise had multiple success indicators, but there was in most of our period one key indicator that was the prime determinant of bonuses. Usually this was some variant of output. In some periods the formal main indicator was production; at other times it was deliveries, and at other times sales. For some branches in some periods cost reductions or profits targets were given priority, but this was unusual. Production, deliveries and sales amounted to almost the same thing in practice. This was after all an economy in which each producer's output was allocated to a designated user under the plan. Only in very peculiar circumstances could it fail to find a 'buyer'.

Soviet managers were not rewarded simply for producing more; they received a bonus if the main annual-plan target was achieved, and no bonus if it was not. If the key plan target was over-fulfilled, the increase in the bonus was proportionally less than the degree of over-fulfilment. A 'low' output target, relative to input allocations, had the obvious attraction that the bonus could be achieved with less effort than if the target was high.

But there was much more to the success indicator system than this. The games played between enterprise managers and their higher authorities were not one-off games but part of a long-running series. Usually, the director of an enterprise – together with other senior managers, who also received bonuses – would be concerned about future years' bonuses as well as the current year's. It was normally the case that, the higher your output in year 1, the higher the target you would be given for year 2. This was precisely because the central planners lacked sufficient knowledge simply to set a maximally taut target each year, and had to fall back on extrapolating 'from the achieved level'. The lower the achieved level, from this point of view, the better.

It was in Hungary, not in the USSR, that the workings of this system were subjected to empirical study – or at any rate to empirical study that saw the light of day (Kornai 1958). Kornai took data for Hungarian light industry enterprises' fulfilment of annual plans. He showed that percentage fulfilment clustered either substantially below 100 per cent or narrowly above it. This he attributed to the ratchet effect, or planning from the achieved level. If your enterprise was clearly, by November, say, not going to meet its target, you were doomed to lose this year's bonus. To miss it by a clear margin (as long as that margin was not so large as to arouse suspicion) was then better than missing it narrowly: it should ensure that next year's target was that much easier. By the same token, large overfulfilment this year would bring some reward, but this would be traded off against a correspondingly higher target next year.

Therefore, once assigned their plan targets for the year, enterprise managers responded to them in ways that differed substantially from output maximisation. Moreover, in the plan-formulation stage they had the strongest possible interest in negotiating for an easy target in the first place. Therefore incentives were built into the Soviet system to moderate the growth of output, even while the central authorities could almost guarantee that there would be some growth. And the pressures from below, during plan formulation, were constantly to use resources wastefully rather than to economise. This was because, once an enterprise had been allocated whatever labour, capital and materials it could secure for itself in its annual plan, those inputs were, from the managers' point of view, free goods. Their costs were built into the plan. If unit cost exceeded the centrally fixed price of output, the enterprise would receive subventions to cover this notional loss. And if production targets could be achieved with fewer inputs, the managers had nothing to gain from economising on those inputs. You never knew what you might need for next year's plan, and you gained no personal benefit from cutting the inputs you used. Soviet managers were in a position familiar to anyone assigned a budget within a hierarchical organisation: use it or lose it.

If output had been of a single, homogeneous good, the previous four paragraphs would cover the incentive problem. But in a world of multiple products, multi-product production units and changing technologies, there were further ramifications. Bonuses attached to a global output target could be most easily obtained by concentrating on the easiest products in your product range. (Threshold bonus-qualification requirements for a certain product-mix were used by the planners to try to offset this, but such refinements were often overlooked in practice.) If your output target was measured by weight, you had an incentive to make your products heavier than necessary; if by length, then narrower, and so on. The household customers for consumer goods or the industrial customers for materials and equipment seldom had much influence. The military were the big exception. They had permanent representatives, the *voenpredy*, in defence-sector plants, checking and if necessary rejecting products. All that other end-users had going for them were the compulsory quality standards, largely derived from the German DIN standards. These were in practice routinely flouted. An assignment to produce for export was regarded as a form of punishment, since foreign customers could be picky. There was, in short, a built-in quality and product-mix problem.

What perhaps proved most damaging for the Soviet economy in the long run was that the incentives for Soviet producers to introduce new products and processes, even when instructed from above to do so, were minimal. Indeed, producers were on balance motivated to avoid innovation. Any substantial change in products or processes tended to disrupt current production (of established products), and it was current production alone that brought bonuses. Technological innovation came about, broadly speaking, in three ways: by centrally planned investment projects that built new plants with new technology embodied in them (a process of dwindling importance once an industrial base had been built); by the necessarily narrowly focused attention of the leadership on some particular issue, as in Khrushchev's drive to upgrade the chemical sector; and by the competitive pressure of the arms race, transmitted to Soviet weapons producers by the exceptional customer power of the military.

The preceding sketch of the Soviet planning system and some of its key features is no more than that – a sketch. In subsequent chapters we shall look more closely at how these characteristics of the system showed up in Soviet economic performance. We shall also see how they became in periods of reform a subject of public debate, and how the system was modified in attempts to remedy weaknesses. What we now know is that the weaknesses in the Soviet system of central planning persisted, and were never successfully dealt with.

The aftermath of war

At the end of the Second World War, the Soviet people were exhausted and ill-nourished, but full of hope. The Soviet economy was badly battered, but capable of rapid recovery. Output did indeed recover. Until Stalin's death in 1953, however, people's hopes for substantial material improvement were disappointed.

That there was an expectation of change is not a matter of mere speculation. Many observers commented on it. As in post-war Britain, there was a widespread belief that life had to become easier than it had been in the 1930s. In the Soviet case, the pre-war decade had been tainted not by high unemployment and highly visible inequality but by a reign of terror, along with material wretchedness for almost everyone, all accompanied by official propaganda that sought to obscure reality. In the nature of Soviet things, this view was not recorded in anything that got past the censor at the time. But many foreign observers, as well as Soviets writing 'for the drawer', were struck by its prevalence.

One view, perhaps a view more characteristic of intellectuals than of most Soviet citizens, was that the war itself was in some ways a liberating experience.

And when the war broke out, its real horrors, its real dangers, its menace
of real death, were a blessing compared with the inhuman power of the lie,
a relief because it broke the spell of the dead letter.

Boris Pasternak, writing in the 1950s, put these words in the mouth of his
character Nikolay Dudorov, reflecting late in the war on what had been
happening to his countrymen (Pasternak 1958, p. 495).

The Yugoslav writer and politician Milovan Djilas, who served in the
Yugoslav Military Mission to the USSR towards the end of the war, wrote
of what seems to have been a very widespread belief in the Soviet Union at
that time (Djilas 1963, p. 40):

> As I look back, I can say that the conviction spread spontaneously in
> the USSR that now, after a war that had demonstrated the devotion of
> the Soviet people to their homeland and the basic achievements of the
> revolution, there would be no further reason for the political restrictions
> and for the ideological monopolies held by little groups of leaders, and
> especially by a single leader.

Edward Crankshaw, who served in the British Military Mission in Moscow
during the war, wrote later: 'Every Russian fervently believed that Stalin's
first act after the war would be to convene a new Party Congress and
announce a new deal' (Crankshaw 1959, p. 34).

The damage of all kinds done by the war was, of course, immense. By
the end of the war the Soviet Union had lost some 27–28 million people
over and above deaths that would have occurred over the same period in
conditions of peace (Barber and Harrison 1991, p. 206). Another 25 million
had lost their homes (Nove 1992, p. 295). Other physical assets had been
destroyed. The number of state and cooperative retail outlets, for example,
was down by about 40 per cent (Hessler 2001, p. 447). At the end of 1945
the capital stock, thanks to substantial rebuilding and new building of factories during the war, was only 20 per cent less, on official estimates, than it
had been in 1940 (*Narkhoz 87*, p. 43). Still, it was substantially down, and
even more tilted towards arms production than it had been before the war.

At the same time, the scope for an improvement in people's welfare,
once the war had ended, was very great.

To begin with, it was reasonable to expect that priorities could be shifted
towards things that people wanted. Between the late 1920s and the start
of the war in 1941 the country's productive capacity had been built up
rapidly. This was done, however, with a degree of priority for both military production and industrial investment that squeezed household consumption and agriculture mercilessly. No peacetime free-market economy

has ever developed in this way. It is true that Japan and some other Asian late-industrialising economies have matched Soviet shares of investment in national income. Their high investment shares, however, have been based on high voluntary savings by the population, not on savings extracted by coercion. And, with the exception of Japan in the 1930s, they have not been combined with a massive diversion of resources to a military build-up.

Still, by 1945 even a reversion from wartime to 1930s priorities promised some improvement in daily life. During the war, the Soviet economy had been subjected to even more intense and more sudden pressures. Land, labour and production capacity were lost for a time to the advancing German army. In 1941–42 the workforce under Soviet control fell from 88 million people to 53 million (Barber and Harrison 1991, p. 147). A third of the 1940 capital stock was destroyed (*op. cit.*, p. 137). With a large part of the remaining civilian-goods capacity being switched to military production, the reduction in food and consumer-goods supply – which had been niggardly enough to begin with – was drastic. Even in 1944 food production was still less than in 1940 (*op. cit.*, p. 188).

That the economy could adjust, if its rulers wished, was clear. Two developments during the war had shown the resilience, for all its distortions, of the Soviet production system: the strong growth of urgently needed weapons production after the devastation of 1941–42, and the remarkable evacuation of a large part of that arms industry eastwards, out of the path of the German invasion. John Barber and Mark Harrison, in their study of the Soviet wartime economy, quote an estimate that as much as 8–10 per cent of the 1940 net capital stock was shifted (p. 130). They describe the evacuation as unplanned, in the sense of being ill-coordinated, but they also note that labour productivity in munitions production may have doubled between 1940 and 1944 (p. 177).

It is true that total war is a state of affairs in which, under exceptional pressure, rapid resource shifts and steep jumps in productivity in the manufacture of arms have occurred in several countries. But the Soviet production system, which might have been thought of as especially rigid, had at least shown that it, too, was capable of swift and drastic adaptation.

There were other grounds for anticipating that a strong improvement in living conditions was possible. For one thing, the number of people to feed and clothe was – albeit for the grimmest possible reasons – reduced. For another, there had been substantial injections of assistance from the Western allies, mainly the US. Barber and Harrison (p. 192) estimate that US Lend Lease and other assistance may have been about 20 per cent of Soviet net material product in 1943–44. This was not only armaments, but jeeps, trucks and food as well. Indeed, of a cumulative total of $9.5 billion of US

Lend Lease supplies (in the prices of the time), $5 billion were non-military items (Holzman 1963, p. 291). Sutton (1971) provides evidence that this should not be seen merely as a one-off resource transfer; embodied in much of the equipment the Soviet authorities received were technologies not previously used by them and capable of raising labour productivity. By copying ('reverse engineering') they could and did incorporate a good deal of this technology into their own domestic production later on.

In the event, supplies of food and other consumer goods did improve between 1945 and 1953. Food rationing was ended in December 1947, ahead of most European countries. But the Stalinist regime did not relax. The priorities of the 1930s were not appreciably changed. The coercive political regime remained in place. One consequence was that improvements in material welfare from the depths of wartime were slow in coming.

Alec Nove described the post-war Stalin years (1945–53) as 'an oddly shapeless period' (Nove 1992, p. 294). He pointed out that policy and organisation seemed frozen in a pre-war mould; Stalin made few public speeches; no Party congresses were held, and even Central Committee plenary meetings were rare. 'At no time, before or since, were Soviet publications more empty of real matter' (*ibid.*). Archival research has filled in the picture. The Politburo practically ceased to function after October 1946. It was replaced by small kitchen cabinets with no established rules for decision-making (Gorlizki 2001, pp. 291, 296).

It is now clear that Stalin took a much less active role in the drawing-up of the Fifth Five-Year Plan (1951–55) than he had with pre-war plans. He remained the final arbiter, however; top secret drafts were sent to him (Tikhonov and Gregory 2001). The plan, it seems, was put together largely by the functional agencies: Gosplan, Gossnab (the centralised supply agency) and the Ministry of Finance. The branch ministries, which would have to implement it, had little input (*ibid.*).

Stalin's influence on the economy remained great, even though he took, in his last few years, a less active role in policy. His presence acted as a brake on innovation – whether in priorities or in organisation. Years later, Nikolai Baibakov, who was Minister of the Oil Industry in Stalin's last years, and later head of Gosplan, put it like this: 'We took very few decisions because we answered with our heads for each point of a decision' (Baibakov 1993a).

Featureless the period may have been, but an economic story can be picked out. There was a rapid recovery in total production, but with little to satisfy the heightened expectations of the Soviet people. Consumption levels moved back only slowly to 1940 levels, while military priorities stayed high. One result of this was that, below the surface, tensions and discontents also grew. The discontents were to do not only with continuing poverty, but with the continuation of repressive rule as well. The importance of these discontents became clear to the wider world only after Stalin's death.

Post-war recovery:
the Fourth Five-Year Plan, 1946–50

Official Soviet statistics show national income produced almost doubling between 1945 and 1950, with the latter year's production almost two-thirds above the level of 1940 (see Table 1.1). That is a rapid recovery by any-one's standards.

Unfortunately, these figures are unsatisfactory in two ways. The Soviet concept of national income, often referred to in the West as 'net material product' (henceforth), excludes most of the service sector and also subtracts estimated depreciation of capital. It is therefore not comparable with what are now the standard international measures of aggregate production: gross national product (GNP) or gross domestic product (GDP).

In addition, Soviet growth figures were deployed as propaganda. They were notoriously exaggerated. In the late Stalin period, in particular, the basic physical (tonnage) figures of the grain harvest were inflated. The 'volume' of total output was reckoned in prices of a remote base year, which in any growing economy would give a favourable picture of the rate of expansion; new products at new prices were included in 'constant-price' measures of the change of volume, inflating the increase. And so on. A minor Western academic and, later, government industry developed that was devoted to recalculating Soviet output levels, relative to those of other countries, and growth rates over time, to make them comparable with normal international practice. The basic concepts and methods used in these recalculations were developed by Abram Bergson of Harvard. They later became the foundation of Central Intelligence Agency (CIA) estimates that were published and widely used. (For the methodological and data problems involved, see Bergson 1961.)

Even the Western recalculations for this period, in fact, show an impress-ive recovery of output. The estimates by Moorsteen and Powell, for GNP in 1937 prices, show the 1940 level being reached again by 1948 (an increase of a quarter in three years). They put the level in 1950 about one-fifth above the pre-war level, and the level in the year of Stalin's death very nearly 50 per cent above 1940.

The official framework for this recovery was the Fourth Five-Year Plan. It set a 1950 target for NMP that was two-thirds greater than the 1945 level

Table 1.1 *USSR post-Second World War economic recovery: some selected figures (selected years; index numbers and natural units as indicated: P = plan; A = actual)*

	1940	1945	1950P	1950A
NMP	100	83	138	164
Industrial output	100	92	148	173
Agric output	100	60	127	99
Coal (m tons)	165.9	149.3	250	261.1
Steel (m tons)	18.3	12.3	25.4	27.3
Cotton fabrics (m metres)	3,900	1,617	4,686	3,899
Leather f'wear (m pairs)	211	63	240	203.4
Grain (m tons)	95.6	47.3	–	81.2
Labour force (m)	31.2	27.3	33.5	39.2
Memorandum items				
GNP est	100	79.4		121.4
Population (m)	196.5	166		180.1
GNP per cap (index)	100	93.9		132.5
Grain per cap (kg)	48.7	28.5		45.1

Notes: The grain figures are Soviet official gross harvest figures, but as provided after Stalin's death. Inflation of the harvest figures was one of the lesser charges levied against him by Khrushchev.
Sources: Rows other than memorandum items: Soviet official figures as cited by Nove 1992, p. 298; GNP: Moorsteen and Powell 1966, pp. 622–4; population figures are mid-year, from Maddison 1995.

and almost two-fifths higher than 1940. The official outcome, noted above, was an even larger increase than that. The Western recalculations give a somewhat more modest, but still impressive picture. A selection of key figures for this plan period is given in Table 1.1.

These figures illustrate some standard characteristics of Soviet planning that were discussed in the first section of this chapter: the unreliability of five-year-plan targets as guides to actual outcomes, for a start. They also bring out some striking features of the early post-war period.

The system encouraged a wasteful use of capital, labour and materials, because the enterprise managers' incentives were to keep input-output ratios higher than they could have been (see the sketch of the planning system, above). The system also tended – new investment apart – to encourage a rigidly maintained composition of output, since every production unit was pushed forward from the achieved level, changes in consumer demand were at most grudgingly and belatedly acknowledged by the planners, the introduction of new products and processes could come only from a high-level initiative, and central policy-makers and planners could at best introduce such initiatives only for a narrow range of items – usually military items.

Even with such a rigid economic system, the limits to the central planners' information were such that output levels 'planned' for the last year of a five-year plan were usually wide of the mark. Moreover, they were wide of the mark in ways that became familiar to all involved: targets for producer goods in general and investment items in particular were usually over-fulfilled; targets for consumer-goods and agriculture were usually under-fulfilled. There were priorities in the plan as written. There were also unwritten rules that guided implementation. If steel, say, was in shorter supply than originally planned, it was the production of bicycles that would lose out, not that of tanks or machine-tools.

For 1946–50, this pattern can be seen clearly in the differences in the 1950P and 1950A columns. Soviet plans also included a division of industry into Industry Group A (producer goods) and Industry Group B (consumer goods). This is too silly a categorisation to be included in a book for grown-ups, so it is omitted from Table 1.1. It was however made much of in Soviet plan presentation and, after Stalin, in policy debates. Setting a higher growth rate for Industry A than for Industry B was ideologically approved and was what normally happened. We shall see later that from time to time in the years after Stalin's death a daring deviationist proposed that Industry B should be targeted to grow faster than Industry A. More often, a narrowing of the gap between the growth rate targets for A and B sent pro-consumer signals, and a widening of the gap sent the opposite message.

As a guide to real priorities the distinction means very little. Industry is only part of the economy, though Soviet discourse often used the two as though they were interchangeable. Soviet industrial output figures were for gross output – the sum of each reporting unit's turnover, without netting out the double counting: deliveries from the flour mill to the bakery or from the steelworks to the truck factory. They were not industrial value added or industrial sales to final demand (consumption, investment, government and exports). Therefore A was bound to be a much larger part of industry than B, since the latter amounted roughly to just the final stage of consumer-goods production. Steel was Industry A even if some of it went into domestic refrigerators. And any vertical disintegration of the process of production – splitting stages in the production process into a larger number of reporting units (enterprises) – would produce a rise in A relative to B, regardless of what was happening to the final end-use pattern of production.

Anyway, even by more sensible measurements, the Fourth Five-Year Plan as printed sent out firmly non-consumerist signals. As implemented, it sent the same message even louder and clearer. This can be seen in Table 1.1. Coal and steel pull well clear of their 1950 targets and their 1940 levels. Cotton fabrics and footwear do neither, and officially measured farm output falls just short and the grain harvest well short of the 1940 level.

One other feature of the 1946–50 plan deserves comment. The labour force, as Table 1.1 shows, increased over the period by almost twice as many people as had been planned. It should be explained that these figures are for the state labour force. They exclude the *kolkhozniki*, or collective-farm workers. The latter were nominally members of producer cooperatives, not state employees. More will be said about their situation in the section on agriculture, below. A large part of the 92 per cent error in the plan for the increment in the state labour force was the result of people moving from the collective farms to the state labour force. Part of this, in turn, was a flight from famine-stricken rural areas in 1946–47 (see below). The fact that millions fled a starving countryside, however, does not explain how industrial and construction enterprises, with supposedly fixed plans for labour inputs, could take them on to their payrolls. The answer has to do with unintended side-effects of the planning system.

Soviet planners targeted output – usually measured in physical terms (tons, square metres) above all else. There were plans for inputs as well, of course. There had to be, since every production unit had an annual plan telling it not only 'how much' to produce, but which particular products to produce, which particular materials and components were allocated to it from other producers, and to which other producers or distributors to send its output. Along with the plan for material inputs, it had a labour input plan: numbers and grades of workers, and a cap on the total wage-bill. But meeting the output targets was what earned plan-fulfilment bonuses for enterprise directors. It was also what each branch ministry and Gosplan itself treated as top priority. Material input plans were hard to alter in mid-plan (mid-annual plan, that is), because the steelworks' input plan was in part the coal mine's output plan, and so on. But labour supply was not controlled in the same piecemeal way. And through most of Soviet history if you, an enterprise director, could meet your plan target by taking on more than your planned labour supply, the higher authorities generally did not penalise you for doing so.

Labour was for the most part wastefully used, since the cost of it did not concern the enterprise managers. There was no incentive whatever to economise on the amount of labour included in your plan. For most of the Soviet period, though not all, there was also little to deter managers from hiring more labour than planned, if only they could find live people to hire. The financial plan and the labour plan would be exceeded with the blessing of the authorities as long as a halfway plausible story could be put forward that you needed the extra workers to meet your output target. And the more workers (for most of the Soviet period), the better. Managerial basic salaries were linked to size of workforce. Material supplies arrived irregularly and unpredictably, so periods of slack alternated with periods of frenzied activity, the latter coming particularly just before the end of reporting periods – months, quarters. And the manager never knew when the local Communist Party boss might suddenly commandeer workers from his enterprise to repair a local road or perform some other local chore.

With such processes at work at enterprise level, it is not so surprising after all that the state labour force in 1950 was almost one-fifth higher than it was 'planned' to be. The labour-force figures in Table 1.1, at first sight baffling, provide clues to a fundamental characteristic of the Soviet system: it was a shortage economy in the sense that demand for all inputs tended to exceed supply at the controlled prices; therefore there was constant inflationary pressure, largely repressed (since most prices were controlled); and there was built-in full employment, in the sense that the tiny number of people of working age who were not employed at any one time, students, invalids and prisoners apart, were simply between jobs, and usually for a short time only.

Several other features of the 1946–50 plan are specific to the period. The loss of population during the war had been so large that per capita total output was not much lower in 1945 than in 1940. A large part of that total output, admittedly, was warships, fighter planes and other weapons or weapon-systems. The material conditions of everyday life in 1945 were miserable. But the wartime loss of population also meant that per capita production of food and consumer goods in 1950 fell only a little short, or for some items was slightly above, the levels of 1940.

The rapid growth of production after 1945 was characteristic of other severely war-damaged economies – Germany's, for example. The destruction of large proportions of a nation's production facilities can generally be made good rapidly so long as the necessary production skills and knowledge have not been lost. Capacities switched to military production can more readily be switched back to civilian output than capacities originally designed for strictly military purposes.

It is also the case, in post-war catch-up periods in general, that technologies are available for use in civilian production at the end of a major modern war that were not available before the war. Partly, this is because there is a backlog of new product and process ideas that were not exploited during the war. Partly, it is because technologies developed for military purposes in the course of the war often have civilian applications that can, in peacetime, be developed.

In the case of the post-war Soviet Union, these technological influences probably worked in a rather distinctive way. In the first place, the Soviet Union was engaged in catching up the advanced nations' technology before the Second World War, and still had much catching-up to do. To some extent, therefore, there was a return to business as usual in that respect: copying, reverse-engineering (working back from somebody else's product to your own design) and industrial espionage.

But where those arm's-length, unilateral methods had been supplemented in the early 1930s by the buying-in of complete plants and the employment of foreign engineers, the war had seen a different form of cooperation – Lend-Lease deliveries of goods from the US, in particular. Many of these items, such as trucks and Caterpillar tractors, were reverse engineered to produce Soviet equivalents. Assessments of the aggregate importance of this particular technology transfer are well-nigh impossible, but Andrew Sutton (1971) provides a wealth of persuasive detail suggesting that the overall effects were quite large. By the same token, the ending of Lend-Lease in August 1945 must have had a dampening effect on subsequent modernisation.

Another distinctive feature of Soviet post-war modernisation was the import of complete plants from Soviet-occupied ex-Axis countries as a form of reparations. The dismantling and shipment of production units from the Zeiss works at Jena in Soviet-occupied Germany is a particularly well-known example, but there were many more, from Hungary, Bulgaria and Romania as well as Germany. East (Soviet-occupied) Germany appears to have lost an appreciable amount of capital assets in this way. Its post-war starting-point was set back by these reparations, in comparison with that of West Germany, even though the pre-war per capita capital stocks of the two regions had been similar (Gregory and Stuart 1995, p. 219). The labour of German prisoners-of-war was also extensively used, including on some of the better-made buildings of the time.

All in all, the rapid Soviet post-war recovery was not mysterious. It was nonetheless impressive, so far as total production was concerned. So far as food, housing and manufactured consumer goods were concerned, it was much less satisfactory.

Priorities and the defence sector

The way in which Soviet priorities worked has been touched upon already. Priorities were embodied in the growth targets in the plans, both five-year and annual. There were also rules of thumb that were known to all planners and officials, and which guided the implementation of a plan. They all understood, in the Stalin period, that housing construction and maintenance, textiles, clothing, food-processing and agriculture were at the bottom of the priority list. Later on, the formal plan priorities did change. The rule of thumb, which had become a matter of custom and practice, did not change so easily.

The highest priority was not mentioned in the plan targets at all. This was arms production or, more broadly, resources allocated to defence. The importance of the defence sector is hard to exaggerate. Yet many descriptions of the Soviet economy focus on industry and agriculture, investment and consumption and contain little or nothing about the defence economy.

A brief digression on the choice of words: 'defence' is used deliberately here, rather than 'the military', because there is little evidence of a grand Soviet plan of aggression, whether under Stalin or later. Soviet leaders, from Lenin to Chernenko (1984–85), feared the West; Gorbachev, in power from 1985 until late 1991, was the exception, and he proved fatal to communist rule. His predecessors all rightly feared for their own power. They had never received a popular mandate to govern their country, and were careful not to risk seeking one. The West was comparatively wealthy and comparatively free. Soviet citizens had, with a few privileged exceptions, to be protected from experiencing it. Those who had done so without authorisation – like many of the Soviet soldiers taken prisoner in the Second World War – were likely to be sent to the camps so they did not contaminate others. Catching up economically with the West was necessary for survival as well as prestige. Meanwhile, it was necessary to defend Soviet rule against a Western military alliance that not only had far more resources but was also ahead in most military technologies most of the time.

In short, the Soviet leadership's stance towards the rest of the world was characteristically fearful, defensive and risk-averse. The word 'defence' is not a euphemism.

The Soviet defence effort was itself defended by extreme secrecy. Branch ministries concerned primarily with military production were not mentioned in plan documents or plan fulfilment reports. Did anything published about the engineering sector ('machine-building and metal-working', in the usual translation) include defence production as well? (The answer was that sometimes it did and sometimes it didn't.) Was the economic activity concerned with final-stage assembly of armaments included in net material product and gross industrial output at all? How much of the research, development, testing and evaluation (RDT&E) was military, and how much civilian? What did the solitary Soviet budget line 'defence' mean? Did it bear any relationship to the defence effort as measured in other countries? How large was the Soviet defence burden (resource allocation to defence as a share of GNP, in prices adjusted to approximate factor costs)?

How large was it compared with the US equivalent (the two usually being compared in US dollars)? In the West academic analysts and government researchers grappled with these questions, often coming up with sharply conflicting answers. In Washington, notoriously, the Central Intelligence Agency and the Defense Intelligence Agency regularly confronted one another (and Congress) with radically different assessments. Meanwhile, the US defence budget was published in stupefying detail. If the detail was not sufficient to prevent gold-plating by defence contractors and the perpetuation of rejected weapons programmes under different names, it was still, by Soviet standards, quite shocking.

If the Soviet economy by the early 1950s was (in US dollar prices) about a quarter to a half the size of the US economy (Bornstein 1959), and even smaller in relation to the whole of NATO, its defence developments in the late Stalin period were remarkable. Initially, the US monopoly of nuclear weapons was offset by Moscow's maintenance of a very large standing army, ready to roll into Western Europe if nuclear weapons were used or threatened against the USSR. When, in August 1949, the Soviet Union tested its first atom bomb, breaking the US monopoly, the conventional forces were not reduced.

In the midst of post-war civilian recovery, the Soviets put a huge effort into 'catching up' militarily. We now know, for example, that early in the post-war period a new biological weapons facility was built near Sverdlovsk (now known once more as Ekaterinburg), based on designs taken from a Japanese biological weapons programme (Rimmington 2000, p. 24). We also now know in some detail how the Soviets developed their first long-range bomber, the Tu-4. Stalin in 1945 ordered a crash programme to produce exact copies of three B-29 Superfortresses that had made forced landings on Soviet soil in 1944 and had been impounded (the US refused to supply B-29s under Lend-Lease). This required the copying of 105,000 components, using resources from 64 design bureaux and over 900 factories and research institutes. By 1950 the Soviet Union could deploy 281 Tu-4s (Hardesty 2001).

The most salient example, however, was the development of nuclear weapons. The speed of the Soviet development, first of an atomic bomb, then of a hydrogen bomb, and later of intercontinental ballistic missiles as delivery systems was constantly underestimated in the West (see Figure 1.2).

It has always been difficult to square Soviet defence achievements with even the most carefully researched assessments of the size of the Soviet defence effort in an economic sense. Here is an example.

For the year 1955, six years after the first Soviet A-bomb test, the Moorsteen and Powell estimates make the Soviet economy 60 per cent larger than in 1949. For that year, 1955, Bornstein makes the following

6 August 1945	US drops A-bomb on Hiroshima
1 July 1946	US Bikini Atoll A-bomb test
17 May 1948	US announces completion of another test
6 July 1948	CIA Top Secret memo to President Truman says earliest date by which USSR could possibly complete its first A-bomb test is mid-1950
1 July 1949	CIA Top Secret memo repeats same time-scale for USSR first A-bomb test
28 August 1949	First Soviet A-bomb test
23 September 1949	Moscow Radio announces USSR has A-bomb
27 September 1949	CIA Top Secret memo gives 28 August 1949 as date of Soviet A-bomb test
October 1952	First UK A-bomb test
	First US H-bomb test
August 1953	First Soviet H-bomb test

Figure 1.2 The Soviet Union and the development of nuclear weapons
Sources: main dates from Hersey (1986) pp. 3, 175, 179, 183; CIA memos from *CIA 1946–76*.

estimates of the economic size of the Soviet defence effort, defined exactly as it would be in US statistics for the US. The defence 'burden' is the share of resources going to defence, as represented by defence spending and GNP in prices approximating factor cost: 13.0 per cent for the USSR, against 10.2 per cent for the US. In this comparison, each country's burden is measured at its own prices. When the two defence efforts are compared directly, the Soviet defence effort is 75.3 per cent of the US when both are priced in roubles, and 94.3 per cent of the US when both are priced in dollars (Bornstein 1959, pp. 380, 385).

There are conundrums in these calculations, as Bornstein and other analysts were well aware. It was always difficult for economists to square the backward state of the Soviet economy with the military prowess of the USSR. If the Soviet Union's economy was in dollar terms a half or less the size of that of the US, and it was allocating a not enormously larger share of its resources to defence, how could its defence effort come anywhere near matching that of its opposing superpower? This was something that was endlessly debated amongst Western policy analysts during the Cold War.

Of course, the estimates of the Soviet 'defence burden' (13.0 per cent of GNP in 1955, according to Bornstein 1959, p. 380) could not be fool-proof, but they were the best that could be made at the time from the available data, and they were consistently much larger than the Soviets' own official 'defence' spending figures. Even so, the outcome in military capabilities looked remarkable. Were resources being used much more efficiently in the Soviet defence sector than in the civilian economy? Were there, on the contrary, hidden inputs into the Soviet defence effort that even the most careful analysis could not detect? We shall come back to these questions in later chapters.

For the present, it is enough to note that in the early post-war period, around 1949, when the CIA was putting Soviet total output at about a quarter of US, and production of food and consumer goods in the USSR was still not back to 1940 levels, the Soviet Union was catching up the United States in nuclear and other weaponry, and doing so at a remarkable speed. The defence priority worked. What the opportunity cost was to Soviet society is a difficult question, which careful, professional assessments of GNP shares may not fully answer. In 1952 the US Central Intelligence Agency estimated Soviet defence spending at about a fifth of GNP ('Soviet Bloc Capabilities Through Mid-1953', National Intelligence Estimate 64, 12 November 1952, declassified 1979, in *CIA 1946–76*). This was very high by international, peacetime standards. Much later, in the 1970s and 1980s, the Agency's assessments of the Soviet defence 'burden', which by then were openly published, were more likely to be criticised for being too low than too high.

Agriculture

Under Stalin, the food supply available to the Soviet population depended entirely on the Soviet farm sector. Food was not imported until Khrushchev's time. Indeed, the USSR had maintained some food exports in the early 1930s, when large areas of the Soviet countryside, chiefly in Ukraine, were suffering a famine in which millions died (Dalrymple 1963; Conquest 1986; Wheatcroft 1990). Grain was of fundamental importance. The Soviet diet was heavily and directly dependent on grain and potatoes until well into the 1950s. Livestock also relied more heavily on grain as fodder than was usual in other countries. Preparations for each year's harvest, and estimates of its size, were headline items in the Soviet media almost throughout Soviet history, even though, from 1963 onwards, domestic food production was supplemented by net imports (i.e. imports less exports).

The farm sector still loomed large in employment. Even in the late 1950s more than half the population lived in rural areas, and almost a third were members of collective-farm households (1959 census data from *Narkhoz 61*, pp. 8, 27). These shares were declining over time. In 1950, 61.6 per cent of the population lived in rural areas and 55.7 per cent of the labour force worked in agriculture (Eason 1963, pp. 72, 77). In every respect, agriculture was a large part of the economy.

In the immediate aftermath of war the state of domestic agriculture was calamitous. Millions of peasants had fought and been killed in the war. Many who survived took the opportunity to improve their lives by returning, not to their home villages, but to new lives in the towns. Many who had been captured by the Germans were put in prison camps because they had been contaminated by contact with the outside world. At the end of the war there were 13 million more women than men working in the *kolkhozy* (Barber and Harrison 1991, p. 207).

During the war, the *kolkhozy* had been supervised less minutely than before. The authorities were interested in the quantities of farm products that could be procured by the state to feed the cities and the war effort, but less concerned with just how the farms operated. Some land was used by individuals, over and above the small household plots already allowed, and by non-farm organisations, primarily for purposes of subsistence. In the optimistic mood that prevailed towards the end of the war, there were rumours that the *kolkhoz* system would be relaxed or abolished. It was, on the contrary, tightened again. On 19 September 1946 a decree laid down that land appropriated from collective farms during the war had to be returned to them, that detailed, crop-by-crop sowing plans had to be drawn up by each farm. The machine-tractor stations (which provided equipment for use by farms in a district and were compensated in kind, thus serving as part of the procurement system) were given a stronger supervisory role (Nove 1992, pp. 304–5).

The same system was extended to the territories acquired on the eve of war under the terms of the 1939 Molotov-Ribbentrop agreement: the Baltic states, Western Belorussia, Bessarabia and western Ukraine. Their agriculture was collectivised under a decision of 21 May 1947. As in the original collectivisation of 1929–31, recalcitrant farmers found themselves relocated to Siberia. Years later, in the 1960s, the Moscow intellectual Andrei Amalrik noted the presence of Latvians in the remote district of Tomsk region to which he, too, had been exiled (Amalrik 1970).

Organisation, then, was not liberalised. Nor were incentives to the farm population strengthened. The collective farms were at this time still the dominant form of Soviet agriculture (conversion of some of them to state farms, and the creation of new state farms, came later, under Khrushchev). The collective-farm peasants, or *kolkhozniki*, were remunerated from the farms' residual net income, and not by a contractually fixed wage (see above). Therefore peasant incomes depended in part on what they could produce on their private plots, and in part on the net income of the *kolkhoz*. The latter depended on production quantities and the prices of inputs and outputs, set by the state.

The *kolkhozniki* were paid for their work on the collective farm in so-called 'work-days' (*trudodni*). The completion of a particular task, such as the ploughing of a certain number of hectares, was rated as so many work-days, and each member of the collective chalked up a certain total of work-days over the year. The net income of the collective farm was shared out in proportion to members' cumulated work-days – usually paid at this time entirely in kind.

In the late 1960s Andrei Amalrik, exiled to a farm in the Tomsk region, observed the work-day system from the sharp end. The work-day unit was in his experience 'an arbitrarily defined unit'. Referring back to his co-workers' memories of the late Stalin period, he says, 'The half-literate accountants used to put down check-marks corresponding to the number of labor-days earned' (*op. cit.*, p. 159). At that time, he noted, in that particular farm, a *kolkhoznik* might have to be credited with 500 work-days to get a sack of grain or three sacks of potatoes for his year's work (*ibid.*).

The problem for the *kolkhozniki* after the war, as it had been in the 1930s, was that farm output was extracted by coercion from the farms, at prices that were unchanged while other prices rose steeply. For two years after the Second World War the procurement prices remained unchanged. As late as 1952 the price paid for compulsory deliveries of potatoes was less than the average cost of getting them to the collection point (Nove 1992, p. 307).

In practice, this meant that incomes from collective-farm work were either very small or non-existent. The peasants fell back on subsistence production from their private plots. The collective farm chairman, who had to meet the state's sowing and procurement targets, had typically to coax, threaten and otherwise drag the members of his collective to work on the *kolkhoz* fields. Milking one's own cow, picking mushrooms, illegally distilling moonshine vodka (*samogon*) – almost anything was more attractive than working to accumulate *trudodni* that might be worthless. The tribulations of one such farm chairman, caught between ignorant but demanding higher authorities and reluctant workers, are vividly described by the rural writer Fedor Abramov (Abramov 1963). As with Amalrik's testimony, this account is of a later, less harsh period, after Stalin's death; the circumstances of farm life in the late 1940s and early 1950s must have been worse still.

One rough-and-ready estimate of the reality of work-day earnings in the late Stalin period can be made as follows. Nove (1992, p. 307, citing a Khrushchev 'revelation' from 1958), quotes a figure of average collective-farm cash earnings per *kolkhoz* household of 623 roubles in 1952 (these are 'old' roubles; the rouble was re-denominated in 1961, when the new rouble was made equal to 10 old roubles). If we apply to that rouble figure the purchasing power conversion rate used by Bornstein for household con-sumption in 1955 (Bornstein 1959, derived from Tables 1 and 3), this is equivalent to $78 (in US 1955 prices). That amount is per annum per household. It covers only income in cash, not in kind, and the latter still predominated. But the monetary value of the total income from the collective would still have been very small – and smaller in the late 1940s than in 1952. Nove (*op. cit.*, p. 308) estimates that in 1948–50 it took on average 60 *trudodni* to earn 1 kg of butter.

Had the household plots been left alone by the authorities, the peasants would have been substantially better off than this, as a result of supplementing their earnings from the collective by their subsistence production, plus perhaps some sales, from their own small plots of land. Indeed, the household plots really did enable them (most of the time) to survive. By the same token, however, if the state had not taxed or otherwise impeded household-plot production, the peasants would have had even less incentive to work on the collective land. The Stalinist state was always more interested in concentrating peasant effort on collective work, since the collectives were larger, fewer and more easily monitored than small household plots. To divert effort from the latter to the former, the household plots were subjected to compulsory product deliveries to the state and to taxation based on numbers of livestock held. Livestock holdings per 100 *kolkhoz* households were substantially lower in 1952 than they had been in 1940 (Nove, *op. cit.*, p. 309, citing *Kommunist* 1954 no. 1; see also Nove 1953).

All of this meant that life in the rural parts of the USSR continued to be harsh in the extreme. Food supplies were poor everywhere, except for the more or less privileged party and state officials. Djilas records Stalin, Khrushchev and their entourages eating sumptuously even in 1945 (Djilas 1963, p. 97). But the Stalinist practice of 'taking grain' from the peasants continued much as it had in the 1930s. That is to say, the procurement organisations were set high collection targets, and scooped up much of what was available in the countryside. As before the war, industry and the cities had priority. As a result, food was often in shorter supply in farming areas than in the cities.

If the weather was poor and harvests suffered, it was the countryside that bore the brunt of the resulting privation. A poor grain harvest in 1945 (47.3 million tons), followed by an even poorer one in 1946 (39.6 million tons) produced famine in Ukraine, Moldavia and some neighbouring parts of Russia in 1946–47. Nikita Khrushchev, the future Soviet leader, was at that time in charge of the government in Ukraine. In his memoirs he recalls the following.

By now [summer 1946], as I had predicted, famine was on the way. Soon I was receiving letters and official reports about deaths from starvation. Then cannibalism started. I received a report that a human head and the soles of feet had been found under a little bridge near Vasilkovo. . . .

(Khrushchev 1971, p. 205)

After describing further horrors, Khrushchev gives his version of the political consequences. He was talked into appealing to Moscow for help for Ukraine (he admits his reluctance, because of his fear of Stalin), trying to ensure that a rationing system would be instituted for Ukraine. The idea was to circumvent Stalin, who was on holiday, and get action without involving the leader himself. But Foreign Minister Vyacheslav Molotov and secret police chief Lavrentii Beria forwarded his request to the leader at his holiday dacha on the Black Sea, and Khrushchev was scolded by Stalin. He was accused of giving in to local Ukrainian interests who were exploiting his 'sentimentality' in an effort to get him to 'give them all your [i.e. Ukraine's] reserves'. Stalin, meanwhile, was insisting on Soviet grain deliveries to Poland and East Germany, to consolidate the new Soviet bloc (*op. cit.*, pp. 204, 206). Thus the gruesome history of the 1932–34 Ukrainian famine was repeated, though mercifully on a much smaller scale.

Zima (1996, pp. 168–9) estimates that in the 1946–47 famine about one million people died of starvation and famine-related diseases such as typhus and dysentery, and that about five million people fled the affected areas. As Filtzer (1999, p. 1020) points out, it is not clear how Zima arrives at these numbers. Still, Filtzer presents evidence that is consistent with them. Ellman (2000) estimates officially recorded deaths from July 1946 to September 1947 as exceeding what might normally have been expected by 1.2 million, with the rate of registered excess deaths highest in Moldavia (pp. 612–13). He considers various plausible assumptions about the extent of rural under-registration of deaths and concludes that the range of reasonable estimates of deaths resulting from the famine is 1.0–1.5 million (p. 615).

This famine, often referred to as the 1947 famine, but extending from summer 1946 into early 1948, was, as Ellman notes, the fourth and last in Soviet history. In assessing its causes, he addresses a controversy about the origins of famines in general: to what extent are they the result of a general decline in food availability in a country or region, and to what extent are they the result of 'entitlement' to food being withheld from part of the population when overall per capita food supplies are unchanged (see Sen 1981)?

His conclusion is convincing: there was a drop in food availability in the Soviet Union in 1946–47. When the grain harvest rebounded to 65.9 million tons in 1947, the problem was brought to an end. At the same time, the priorities and practices of the Soviet state were such that the famine was allowed to destroy many lives that could have been saved. Government policies were not – or not significantly – modified to counter the famine. Priorities for taking large quantities of grain away from the countryside at very low prices were maintained, the saving of lives had a low priority, the population was not allowed to retain substantial food reserves of their own

Table 1.2 *USSR net agricultural production per head of population, 1940 and 1950–53 (selected products, kg)*

	1940	1950–53 average
Grain	238.4	247.9
Potatoes	194.6	172.8
Green vegetables	50.1	41.2
Milk	144.2	144.8
Meat	24.5	27.5
Eggs (units)	58.9	68.0

Source: Johnson and Kahan 1959, p. 210.

and private trade was tightly restricted (Ellman 2000, p. 620). Policies and priorities did not change after 1947; the weather did. It was only under Khrushchev that priorities were altered, so that such famines could not occur again.

Despite the harsh treatment of the rural population, farm output gradually recovered from its desperately low levels of 1945–46. By the early 1950s it was around the level reached in 1940. Table 1.2 contains estimates that approximate the food supply available (ignoring exports) to the population. 'Net output' is farm production net of internal usage in production, such as seed grain, seed potatoes, fodder fed to livestock and the like.

The end of food rationing (December 1947) may, for all the limitations imposed by Stalin's priorities, have marked a turn for the better in the lives of Soviet citizens. Hessler (2001) suggests that in every year between 1916 and 1949 a significant number of Soviet people starved, except in 1926, 1927 and (prisoners apart) 1938; from 1949 on, starvation does not seem to have reappeared. One indicator of improvement, she notes (p. 451), was the fall in market prices for food in 1948. She goes on to argue (p. 464) that the end of starvation was not initially the result of a change in policy but of better weather. It was post-Stalin policies that secured the improvement.

In a long-term, comparative perspective, the state of Soviet agriculture towards the end of Stalin's life, though better than in the aftermath of war, was still extremely poor. Johnson and Kahan (1959, p. 222) offer the following comparative estimates relating to the territory occupied by the USSR after the Second World War. In 1913 meat production per head of population on that territory had been 58.1 per cent of the US level. As late as 1958 it was only 48.0 per cent. Milk production per head of population had been 72.8 per cent of the US level in 1913. In 1950 it was only 51.6 per cent of the contemporary US level, and in 1953, 52.1 per cent.

This was one important part of Stalin's legacy. His successors set about changing it for the better. Indeed, they had attempted to do so even before Stalin's death. In February 1953, a draft party-state resolution was prepared, under which state procurement prices for farm products would have been raised. But it was not adopted (Zubkova 2000, p. 78).

Economic organisation and policy more generally

So far in this chapter we have devoted particular attention to military priorities and to agriculture in Stalin's last years. Both were of the greatest importance, yet they represent the opposite extremes of Stalinist economic policy-making: a high-priority military sector that achieved a great deal in this period, and a low-priority farm sector that was ruthlessly exploited for the sake of industry and, as a result, performed poorly, exhibiting only a sluggish post-war recovery. Between them lay most of the rest of the economy: civilian industry, transport, construction and services (see Table 1.1 above for some data on output of selected products). Within that civilian sector, the production of investment goods and intermediate products (coal, steel, electricity) had higher priority than the production of consumer goods and, within investment, there was little construction of housing.

In all these respects the period 1945–53 was a continuation of the Stalinist pre-war economy of 1928–41. For significant changes to occur in the composition of output and the character of the economy, there would have to have been substantial changes in organisation, policy, the operating environment or some combination of these. Such changes as there were, however, were not substantial.

The organisational changes that did occur were minor. Some changes were simply a return from special wartime arrangements. In September 1945 the State Defence Committee was abolished and peacetime government entities restored. People were allowed from mid-1945 to take holidays again. Formal restrictions on job-changing, which had in fact been introduced before the start of the war, were lifted. They had not been very effective in practice.

Other changes were more or less trivial. The 1946 re-labelling of People's Commissariats as Ministries, was just that: a change of labels. There was at first a growth in the number of branch ministries and then some reduction again through mergers. The status and responsibilities of USSR Gosplan were tinkered with. In December 1947 it became a Committee instead of a

Commission. Responsibilities for organising inter-enterprise supply flows were hived off to the State Committee for Material-Technical Supply (USSR Gossnab), though Gosplan retained oversight of supply planning and direct control of some key products. In August 1948 the compilation and processing of statistics were removed from Gosplan and transferred to a separate organisation, the Central Statistical Administration of the USSR.

In 1949 Nikolai Voznesensky, an economic administrator who was both a Politburo member and head of Gosplan, was removed from his posts and a little later shot. This probably had little to do with economic policy and much to do with palace politics. He was one of a group of leading officials from Leningrad who were purged at the time, and he may have suffered because he had earlier tried to shift resources away from departments controlled by Beria, the head of the secret police (Khrushchev 1971, pp. 220–22).

In general, the character of the economic system was unchanged. To put it another way, there was no systemic reform of even the most modest kind. Nor was there any encouragement at all for discussion of reform. No economic statistics were published except for plan figures for percentage increases, usually from some undefined base. Economists who said anything interesting were rebuked, and quickly resumed the habit of silence. Stalin, in his last published work, *Economic Problems of Socialism in the USSR* (1952), explicitly stated that economic policy was not for economists to discuss.

Systemic reform provides analysts with a good deal of intellectual enjoyment. Throughout Soviet history, therefore, reform and discussion of reform always generated a great deal of Western comment. Reform, however, is not the only way to alter economic outcomes. Changes in policy – for example, in priorities – can produce substantial results, as Khrushchev's rule was to demonstrate. The effects of policy changes are also more predictable than changes in the rules of the economic game. Even policy changes, however, were minimal in this period.

The continuation of military priorities, albeit in a less extreme form than in wartime, has already been discussed. So has the maintenance of a low priority for agriculture and the consumer generally. One policy act is worth mentioning, not because it represented any change in direction, but because it had long-term effects on popular perceptions.

On 14 December 1947 there was a confiscation of currency, reducing the population's liquid assets. Cash roubles were surrendered for new notes in a ratio of 10 to 1. This was not a re-denomination, such as occurred in 1961, but simply the removal of a large chunk of cash from circulation. Accounts in savings banks up to 3,000 roubles (equal to about six months' average wages) were not affected, but amounts in excess of 3,000 roubles were (Nove 1992, pp. 316–17). At a time when real incomes were still well below the level of 1940, this was a harsh act. It was, however, synchronised with the abolition of rationing, and had the useful effect of lessening the shortages (excess demand at controlled prices) that followed once quantity demanded was no longer limited by rationing.

The currency reform was followed, however, by a policy of reducing retail prices each year from 1948 to 1954. So the initial effect of the monetary confiscation, reducing aggregate monetary demand, was at least partly offset later by price reductions, reducing aggregate supply at established prices. The welfare effect of the price reductions, however, was limited and may even on balance have been negative. The price cuts were introduced in what was already a regime of shortage. They simply increased the pressure of repressed inflation. In the terminology used in Britain at the time, the 'inflationary gap' was first reduced by monetary confiscation and then widened again by cuts in administered prices.

This so-called currency reform seems to have stayed in Soviet folk memories for the rest of Soviet history. Later moves, such as the re-denomination of the currency in 1961 and various manoeuvres with the currency in the Gorbachev period, were viewed with understandable distrust. Rumours of any kind of monetary reform regularly produced panic buying in later years, exacerbating inflationary pressure.

It is tempting to speculate, however idly, that the stagnation of economic policy in 1945–53 was connected with the ageing of Stalin himself. Djilas (1963, p. 118) comments on the sharp loss of vigour and mental agility that he observed in the Soviet leader between 1945 and early 1948. Certainly, no major change in policy could have been made without Stalin's approval. It is equally clear that the major contenders for the succession all proved, on Stalin's death, to be nurturing plans for radical shifts in economic policy (Service 1981; Zubkova 2000). Elena Zubkova has pointed out that both Malenkov and Khrushchev, and indeed the Politburo as a whole, supported measures to improve the wretched living conditions in the villages by reducing agricultural taxes and raising procurement prices, almost as soon as Stalin was out of the way.

On the other hand, in 1945–53, Stalin simply presided over a resumption of the organisational arrangements and resource allocation priorities that had been maintained in the 1930s. Those arrangements and priorities had built up Soviet coal, steel, electricity and munitions capacities sufficiently for the country, with some important help from the West, to prevail in the war against Germany. For a leader who expected another war in 15– 20 years' time (Djilas, *op. cit.*, p. 91) this may have seemed simply to be a winning strategy that should be adhered to. At all events, the Soviet economy remained even in peacetime what the Polish economist Oskar Lange called 'a *sui generis* war economy'. Yet even under this unaltered economic regime, there were people seeking to live in ways that, materially, the Stalinist order could not deliver – or at any rate, not legally.

Living conditions and the first stirrings of acquisitive dissent

From the low point of the war, the material circumstances of the Soviet people did recover. Even if per capita food supplies had not returned to 1940 levels by 1950 (see above), they had certainly improved from 1945 levels. Much the same could be said of the supplies of non-food consumer goods. There was some construction of housing: just over a million apartments, for example, in 1950 (*Narkhoz 22–82*, p. 427). If one considers, however, that there had been extensive destruction of housing during the war, that urbanisation was continuing, and that most people in cities still lived in 'communal' (multi-household) apartments, the rate of housing construction was extremely modest.

There were other ways in which life improved. Official figures showed that during the war itself the numbers held in prisons and prison-camps declined, from 2.3 million in June 1941 to 1.45 million at the end of 1944 (Barber and Harrison 1991, p. 169). Recent archive research confirms this general picture (Kokurin and Morukov 1999–2000). Numbers apparently did not subsequently return to pre-war levels. There were fears that towards the end of his life Stalin was preparing another wave of mass arrests. If this was so, he died before initiating it.

Two Western studies of changes over time in Soviet consumption levels, though differing in method and in some of their conclusions, concur in showing a clear recovery in Soviet real incomes, albeit a slower recovery than that in total output. Table 1.3 selects the relevant numbers from these studies.

Filtzer (1999), focusing on earnings in the state sector (roughly, non-agricultural plus state-farm pay) estimates that real wages returned to 1940 levels only in 1949. His calculations also imply that per capita labour incomes in farm households got back to 1940 levels only in 1950. He points out that one way in which the government handled the 1946 harvest failure was by removing many people from the rationing system and raising ration prices (in September 1946). Urban real incomes got worse before they got better.

While this modest improvement was taking place, and despite the repressive political regime, black markets thrived. What was traded on them indicated the gaps between, on the one hand, what the system provided

Table 1.3 *Soviet real incomes and consumption levels, 1937–55 (1937 = 100; Jasny and Chapman estimates compared)*

	Jasny (per capita real incomes in 1927–28 prices)	Chapman (per capita private consumption in adjusted year 1937 prices)
1940	86	96
1944	–	66
1948	74	–
1950	97	114
1952	113	–
1955	135	159

Sources: derived from Jasny 1961, p. 447 and Chapman 1963, p. 238.

and on what terms, and on the other hand, what many people wanted, and on what terms. The examples that follow are, in the scornful phrase of social scientists, 'merely anecdotal'. But they are also, like the merely anecdotal swallows whose arrival heralds a change of season, clues to the future.

The term *stilyaga*' was used in Russian from 1948 (Kozlov 1998, p. 76). It referred to a young man who was style-conscious and who dressed in ways that were supposed to ape Western fashion. In Soviet official discourse of the late 1940s and 1950s, *stilyaga* carried some of the moral overtones of the then-current British word 'spiv'. But whereas 'spiv' denoted someone who made a good living on the black market and dressed in a colourful, pseudo-American way, a *stilyaga* was identified by his clothing and other tastes alone. He was more likely to be a buyer than a seller on the black market.

It is hard now to imagine people visibly flouting convention under Stalin, but it appears that a small but dedicated community, at least in Moscow, did. Aleksei Kozlov, who was one of them and who was later to become a leading jazz musician, recalls how in 1952 he discovered 'Broadway', or, rather 'Brodvei'. This was the name given by insiders to the left-hand side of Gorky Street (going towards Red Square) from the Pushkin statue down to the Manezh. (Gorky Street is now Tverskaya Street.) Here, improbable as it may seem now, while Stalin still ruled, young men paraded in what they fancied to be American-style narrow trousers and pork-pie hats. The trading and improvisation required to achieve the 'Brodvei' look were a way of life in themselves (Kozlov 1998, pp. 73–9).

Kozlov goes on to describe how American music (jazz) was also part of this way of life, and how officially unobtainable records, including those by Soviet musicians from an earlier era, were in fact obtained. He later realised that the fascination with things American was not unique to the post-war

Soviet Union, but widely shared throughout Europe. What was specific to communist countries was that fads and fashions not officially approved were simply not provided for by the legal economy.

Other memoirs, usually in passing, refer to black markets of a very different sort. The soprano Galina Vishnevskaya describes her recovery from tuberculosis in 1951–52, when she was living in Leningrad.

> Streptomycin had just appeared in Russia, but it was not available in drugstores. You could only get it on the black market at outrageous prices. . . . Once a week, Mark [her husband] went to the airport, where a black marketeer would come from Moscow, bringing little vials of the antibiotic at 30 roubles a gram – my fee for a single concert. And I needed 120 grams; that is, 3,600 roubles.
>
> (Vishnevskaya 1984, p. 79)

Evidently, many of the black-market or second-economy phenomena that have been more extensively studied for later periods of Soviet history were present even under late Stalinism. It is likely that the Stalinist regime constrained second-economy activities more tightly than did later, softer Soviet regimes. The risk premium in black market prices must have been higher in 1950 than in 1975. But officials throughout the system would have been aware that there was a hunger, backed by money, for goods and services that the official system did not provide.

Economic relations with the outside world

On the eve of the Second World War the USSR had become an almost autarkic economy, with merchandise exports equivalent to half a per cent of national income (Holzman 1963, p. 290). After the war, two things had changed. The Soviet Union had acquired – largely but not wholly through force of arms – a group of allied, socialist states in East and Central Europe. It was also initially on good terms, at any rate formally, with its wartime military allies. It was quite widely believed in 1945–46 that closer economic cooperation with the West was possible.

Of these two changes, only the first lasted beyond 1947. Even before the war ended, the Soviet government had opted in 1944, after prolonged equivocation, not to become one of the founding member-states of the International Monetary Fund and the World Bank. Thus the USSR kept its distance from the international financial institutions that formed an important part of the post-war international economic order. How near Moscow came to joining in those arrangements is, on the available evidence, unclear. It is also open to debate whether its doing so would have compromised their functioning. A centrally planned, state-trading economy – and one, moreover, whose international reserves were a state secret – might have tested the Bretton Woods institutions to destruction. A case can however be made that Soviet policy-makers in 1944 seriously considered Soviet participation in international financial institutions and that, had this come about, subsequent Soviet economic outcomes might have been different (see Axelrod 1994).

A few years later there was another crucial act of economic distancing from the Western allies. At the Paris conference of June-July 1947 the Soviet Union declined to participate in the US Marshall Plan. In other words, it rejected assistance that, according to most subsequent analyses, had substantial positive effects in Western Europe (De Long and Eichengreen 1992) Moscow advised its allies to reject Marshall Aid as well, and the Central and East European leaders knew better than to reject Soviet advice. By this time, with East-West political relations deteriorating, any other decision would have been against the run of play.

For the USSR, this parting of the ways only underlined the political desirability of closer economic links with its newly created socialist allies: East Germany, Poland, Czechoslovakia, Hungary, Bulgaria, Romania, Albania and Yugoslavia. In practice, the Soviet economic bloc quickly came to be made up of the USSR and the first six of these countries. The last two were comparatively independent. Their communist leaderships were home-made and did not owe their power to the Soviet Army. Accordingly, while communist rule was being established in the other Central and East European states, Albania and Yugoslavia contrived to be both more convincingly communist and less biddable than the others. In 1948 there was an open break between Belgrade and Moscow, and Tito's Yugoslavia developed as a non-aligned socialist country, more open than the Soviet bloc to the Western world economy. Much later, after siding with China in the Sino-Soviet split, and then splitting with China, Albania became an outpost of unreconstructed Stalinism, and the twentieth century's most isolated and trade-free small economy – with Burma/Myanmar a close second.

Already in 1946–47 Stalin was concerned to demonstrate that Poland and East Germany could benefit from trade with Moscow (Khrushchev 1971, p. 205). After the Soviet Union and its allies opted out of the Marshall Plan, the USSR signed credit agreements with Yugoslavia (before the Stalin-Tito break), Bulgaria and Czechoslovakia. In June 1948 reparations due from former Axis countries Romania and Hungary were halved by Moscow; two years later East Germany received the same treatment (Nove 1992, p. 322).

Finally, in early 1949, the Soviet economic bloc took organisational shape when the Council for Mutual Economic Assistance (CMEA, sometimes referred to as Comecon) was formed. Its headquarters were in Moscow. Trade flows amongst its members were concentrated on 'radial' flows between the USSR and each of the other members (and thus concentrated to a greater degree than could have been predicted simply from the Soviet Union's larger economic size). Settlements were primarily bilateral. But whatever the special character of this trading bloc, the Soviet Union was no longer on its own in the world economy. It had trade partners whose political interests needed no longer to be treated with extreme suspicion. Two of them – East Germany and Czechoslovakia – were comparatively highly developed, and might serve as unthreatening sources of advanced technology.

At the same time, when Stalin died, the Soviet economy was still comparatively small and backward. It did not loom large in the world. Contemporary estimates by the CIA put its output in 1949–51 at around a quarter of the US level (*CIA 1946–76*). Its newly acquired allies, though some of them were more highly developed than the USSR itself, were small-to-medium-size countries. Moreover, the bloc as a whole was keeping its distance from the international trade and finance arrangements of the Western world, under which a quarter-century of sustained growth, trade and international investment had begun. And the leaders of this comparatively backward and semi-isolated country aspired to match the Western world militarily. Under Stalin this ambition was pursued relentlessly, with little concern for the material welfare of the Soviet people. Any relaxation of political control would raise the question whether these priorities could be maintained.

CHAPTER TWO

Khrushchev: Hope Rewarded, 1953–60

Alone among Soviet rulers, Nikita Khrushchev left the Soviet Union better off than when he became its leader.

(Taubman *et al.* 2000, p. 1)

Substitute 'a better place' for 'better off', and that claim is defensible. Replace 'better off' with a narrower and more pedantic term – 'with higher per capita consumption levels', for example – and it is not. The average Soviet citizen was substantially better fed, dressed, housed and otherwise catered for in 1991 than in 1917. For all the Soviet Union's comparative economic failure, there was in absolute terms a great deal of 'material progress', as the Victorians called it, over a large part of Soviet history. This did not occur solely on Khrushchev's watch.

Khrushchev did indeed preside over a marked increase in prosperity between March 1953 and October 1964: that is, between Stalin's death and his own removal from power. But what is unique about the Khrushchev period might be summed up in another Victorian phrase: it was a time of 'moral and material progress'. That quaint old phrase begs many questions. Still, Nikita Khrushchev was the only Soviet ruler to whose time in office it is remotely applicable. And even that, benign, period is more impressive in the early years; the last few years, when troubles multiplied, are dealt with in the next chapter.

So far as the economy was concerned, this was a period of strong growth combined with a major shift of priorities in favour of the consumer. Khrushchev presided over a major switch of resources towards agriculture, improved incentives for food production, the launch of a badly needed housing programme, a shortening of the work-week, a large cut in the armed forces and an easing of the priority for heavy industry. This material improvement was accompanied by an ending of the arbitrary reign of terror, an easing of censorship and a controlled opening to the outside world. What all these improvements were not accompanied by was any serious reform of the economic system.

The economist Andrei Belousov (2000) has treated the period 1950–70 as one of 'modernisation of the Soviet industrial system'. That sounds somewhat like reform, but his account shows that what he chiefly has in mind are changes in priorities. He argues that the aim of raising the living standards of the Soviet population had now become important, along with military competition with the West and integration with the new economic partners in Central and Eastern Europe. The rise in the priority of consumption had consequences for agriculture, for consumer-durables production and for housing, which he traces. The terms he uses in telling this story are different from those used here, but the story itself does not seem fundamentally different.

The Khrushchev period is at the heart of the post-war Soviet economic story. Stalin had built an economic system that was authority-intensive. It extracted rapidly increasing amounts of work and capital from a cowed population. It extracted the work through a rising labour-force participation rate, with an element of forced labour. It extracted the capital through forced saving. This forced growth of inputs propelled output, in what later came to be termed 'extensive growth'. The Khrushchev period is the prelude to the failure of the extensive growth strategy – with hints of that impending failure detectable (with hindsight) in the last few years of Khrushchev's rule.

Extensive growth is a growth of output stemming largely from a growth of inputs of labour, capital and land. Intensive growth, in contrast, stems chiefly from a growth in the productivity of those inputs – from increases in the combined productivity of land, labour and capital. In any statistical analysis aimed at accounting for a country's economic growth, the separation of this total factor productivity growth from the growth of combined inputs is in practice rather tricky. What is clear in the Soviet case is that when the sources of extensive growth – increments of capital and labour inputs – slowed, the Soviet economic system proved incapable of generating faster productivity growth to offset that deceleration.

This did not become apparent during the Khrushchev period. Between 1953 and 1964 policy changes brought a considerable increase in prosperity without, initially, a loss of momentum in the growth of total output. Some early symptoms of the slowdown can be detected in the last years of the Khrushchev period. But growth picked up again in the late 1960s, and it was only in the 1970s that it was clear that Soviet economic growth had entered a period of prolonged deceleration. A large part of that slowdown was attributable to demographic and geographical factors beyond the reach of policy-making (see the chapters on the Brezhnev period). But the humane softening of the system that occurred under Khrushchev's rule probably contributed to the later slowdown. He weakened the social control on which an authority-intensive economic system depended.

In eschewing economic reforms, however, Khrushchev did the right thing. Subsequent attempts at reform within the confines of a centrally planned, socialist economy only made things worse (Kontorovich 1988 on the 1965 reforms; Hanson 1992 on Gorbachev's reforms; Tompson 2000 on judgements on Khrushchev in this light). What Khrushchev's period in office showed was how effective changes in policy could be, in the absence of changes in system. That this is in general likely to be the case was well argued by Antoni Chawluk (1974). Khrushchev's years in power illustrate it rather well.

What this period also showed, however, was that policy changes, too, have their limitations. Developed countries exhibit remarkably stable trend rates of growth (about 2.25 per cent per annum for the UK in the twentieth century) that seem impervious to policy changes. In any case, Khrushchev's policy-making was a mixed bag. His changes in priorities were, broadly speaking, beneficial to Soviet citizens. At the same time, his launching of campaigns for particular choices of technology (more maize, more silage, the ploughing up of the Virgin Lands, chemicalisation) were often mistaken from the start or overdone or productive of damaging side-effects – or sometimes all three.

Still, Khrushchev made a difference. For Soviet people that difference was beneficial: he shifted resources away from the Stalinist priorities of the military and of investment for the sake of investment – what Peter Wiles (1962) called the 'solipsistic enclave' of machine tools to produce machine tools to produce machine tools *ad infinitum*. He also made plenty of mistakes, both economic and political, and these brought him down. But his successors, however grey and repressive their regimes, never reverted to full-blown Stalinist priorities or methods of rule.

Policy-making and power

Khrushchev, like other Soviet leaders, took time to get a grip on power. When Stalin died in March 1953, the most likely successor seemed to be either Georgiy Malenkov or Lavrentii Beria. Malenkov, once Stalin's private secretary and latterly expected by many to be his successor, initially inherited Stalin's posts as party leader (party first secretary) and head of government (prime minister), but in the reshuffle in September Khrushchev acquired the post of party first secretary. Beria had the secret police. In June 1953 the other leaders ganged up on Beria and arrested him. He was executed in

December. From June 1953 to January 1955 Malenkov continued as head of government, but Khrushchev and the party apparatus gradually gained the upper hand. Then Malenkov resigned as Prime Minister, leaving Khrushchev apparently the strongest individual in what many still saw as a collective leadership. From mid-1957, Khrushchev is generally agreed to have been in sole command (Crankshaw 1959, pp. 43–8; Zubkova 2000, pp. 67–8).

Khrushchev was visibly dominating economic policy from early 1955. But the shift in priorities in favour of the consumer would probably have come even if Beria or Malenkov had won the leadership battle (see Chapter 1). For a time, in 1953–54, it was Malenkov who publicly espoused pro-consumer policies. He even advocated that industry group B (consumer goods) should grow faster than industry group A (producer goods). (On the largely symbolic nature of these categories, see the previous chapter.)

The poet Yevgeny Yevtushenko, writing about the immediate aftermath of Stalin's death, dealt contemptuously with Malenkov: '. . . a man with a womanish face and studied diction who addressed [the people] on the coming improvements in food, tailoring and haberdashery' (Yevtushenko 1963, p. 101). The people, Yevtushenko went on to say, had never reduced living to mere consuming; but the poet may by 1963 have forgotten the priorities of the poor. When, at the August 1953 session of the USSR Supreme Soviet, Malenkov spoke of turning the economy's face towards the people, he was espousing a radical change.

Khrushchev at first spoke publicly for the old, Stalinist priorities. But once he had bested Malenkov and grabbed power, he, too, adopted consumerism. Zubkova (2000) offers an intriguing counter-factual speculation: if Khrushchev, instead of ousting Malenkov, had allotted him a role as second-in-command, Malenkov's cooler, less impulsive approach to policy-making would have complemented Khrushchev's vision and energy, and perhaps saved him from many of his mistakes. After all, she argues, their policy objectives were similar, and Malenkov's actions implied that this was an arrangement he would have accepted. Well, we shall never know. At least her assessment of Malenkov is more adult than Yevtushenko's. And, whatever might have been, Khrushchev had the main responsibility for economic policy from early 1955.

Khrushchev's initiatives

The major changes in economic policy that Khrushchev pushed through were the following: drastically improved incentives for agriculture; the extension of cultivated land by ploughing up the 'Virgin Lands' of northern

Kazakhstan and southern Siberia; campaigns to change cropping patterns; the territorial decentralisation of economic management; the initiation of large-scale imports of machinery and know-how (specifically to upgrade an extremely backward chemical industry, though this practice was later extended to more branches of the economy); the development of foreign trade more generally; the first large-scale importation of food; a wage reform, with the introduction of a minimum wage and a shortening of the working week; the start of a major programme of housing construction; the publication of official economic statistics; and freer public discussion of economic matters (economists were released from their intellectual straitjackets and allowed out into an intellectual prison yard; this was quite safe, since policy-makers paid no attention to what they said).

There was also a change in military priorities that had economic repercussions: cuts in conventional forces alongside an enhanced space and missile effort.

The outcomes were patchy. Khrushchev's maize and other crop campaigns were micro-management from on high at its worst, and ended badly. His territorialisation of economic management proved unworkable. The Virgin Lands campaign was a costly short-cut to raising grain production, with results that fluctuated dramatically from year to year. The rest, however, was in broad terms, and within the limits imposed by the system, humane and liberal. And on the whole these measures brought improvements in the material welfare of the Soviet people.

As Michael Ellman has written, '. . . one could say that Khrushchev introduced, and Brezhnev maintained, an anti-famine political contract in the USSR' (Ellman 2000, p. 620).

Agriculture

Of all the changes in economic policy that followed the death of Stalin, none mattered more than those affecting the farm sector. The importance of the Soviet farm sector for Soviet consumption levels is hard for people living in prosperous, open economies to grasp. Soviet real incomes were always substantially lower than real incomes in Western Europe. They were very much lower in the early 1950s. Food therefore bulked large in total consumption. And the available food supplies came almost entirely from domestic production. It was not until 1963–64 that Moscow turned to imports of food on any substantial scale. (Previously, imports had been restricted to small quantities of tropical products like cocoa beans.)

CIA calculations put food at more than half of total consumption in the 1950s (derived from Pitzer 1982, Table A-6; measurement here is in 1970 factor cost). 'Consumption' here includes state provision of health and education. At contemporary established prices (given the subsidisation of housing), food would have been around three-fifths of household spending. The order of magnitude, in resource costs rather than established prices, of food consumption and agricultural production was closely similar: 28–30 per cent of GNP (*idem*, Tables A-1 and A-6).

True, the resource cost of food consumption included some value added in food processing, transport and distribution; very small amounts of food consumed were imported, and not all farm production was of food items – there were industrial crops like cotton and flax, and seed potatoes, for example, are investment goods. But the two magnitudes were very close.

Moreover, Soviet food consumption, throughout Soviet history, was supply-constrained. Bread, potatoes and vodka were practically always plentiful. Otherwise, food items were often in short supply. Prices for most food items were not changed between the early 1950s (once the policy of price cuts was abandoned) and the late 1980s. Formal rationing schemes, always locally developed and managed, were employed from time to time; more commonly, there were just queues and shortages. Therefore, growth in food consumption, at any rate of vegetables, fruit, meat, fish and dairy products, depended strongly on growth of domestic production, until the resort to large-scale grain imports in 1963–64.

Even in the 1960s, 1970s and 1980s, the first-time foreign visitor to Moscow was apt to be puzzled by the attention given in the media to harvest preparations and harvest progress. Was this not an industrial country? Why would Muscovites care what was going on down on the farm? What might be casually attributed to an outdated Bolshevik obsession with tractors was in fact a matter of real concern to almost everyone: would there be reasonable supplies of food in the shops or not? At the time of Stalin's death, this was a very serious concern indeed.

One of the first sets of measures was sponsored by both Malenkov and Khrushchev in 1953, when they were jockeying for the leadership: compulsory deliveries from the peasants' household plots were reduced, and the prices offered by the state procurement agency for products from both the *kolkhozy* and the household plots were raised, enabling rural money incomes to rise. (Later, from January 1958, the mandatory deliveries from household plots were abolished altogether.) At the same time, rates of payment in kind for collective-farm work, based on *trudodni* (work-days; see Chapter 1) were raised. Peasants were allowed to pasture their household livestock on collective-farm land (see Filtzer 1993, chapter 5; Smith 1987; Strelianyi 2000).

The gains for the farm sector were, from an abysmal starting point, substantial. The amount officially recorded as paid by the state for deliveries from agriculture (state farms, collective farms and household plots) rose from 4.14 billion roubles in 1953 to 13.41 billion in 1958 (*Narkhoz 61*, p. 306). The official index of farm procurement prices rose almost three-fold between 1952 and 1958 (*Selkhoz 60*, p. 117). This was at a time when farm employment was almost unchanged (29.4 million people in 1953 and 30.0 million in 1958, excluding work on household plots; *Narkhoz 61*, p. 461) and when retail prices were officially unchanged.

After a generation of extreme exploitation of the countryside (1928–53), these changes went some way to reducing the extreme disparities between farm and non-farm households. The official claim was that the average 'real incomes' of peasants (*kolkhozniki*) rose 68 per cent from 1952 to 1958 (*op. cit.*, p. 601). This was greatly exaggerated, like all other Soviet official measures of 'real income' change. But the same measure for state employees (including workers on state farms, but consisting mainly of non-farm employees) was an increase of 42 per cent (*ibid.*). The figures are of interest despite the padding they contain because they present a striking improvement in peasant incomes relative to other incomes. Whatever the true overall picture might be – the CIA estimate is that per capita consumption for the whole population grew by 26.5 per cent from 1953 to 1958 (Schroeder and Denton 1982, Table A-2 – the relative improvement for farm households must have been substantial.

These common-sense measures were a big change from Stalin's practices, but uncontroversial once he was gone. A draft resolution to raise procurement prices had been prepared just before Stalin's death, but not adopted (Zubkova 2000, p. 78). After Stalin died, the ministries both of Agriculture and of Finance advised Malenkov that the countryside was over-taxed (*idem*, p. 77; on the tax burden see Nove 1953). The immediate results of the early Malenkov–Khrushchev measures were favourable. Farm output grew rapidly.

The growth in arable output was not the result solely of improved incentives. The Virgin Lands campaign was announced in late 1953, and 42 million hectares of land, mostly in northern Kazakhstan, were ploughed and sown for the first time, starting in 1954, with a net gain of 30–40 million hectares (or 20–25 per cent) to the total area sown to crops in the USSR (McCauley 1976 tells the story in detail).

The Virgin Lands programme was intended above all to boost grain output over a period of five years or so, while more investment went into both traditional grain production in Ukraine and the Russian Black Earth Zone and into fodder production. It was a gamble, on two counts.

First, of those parts of the USSR in which crops could be grown, a large proportion had an unstable moisture balance: the balance between precipitation and evaporation. Droughts were always a threat. This risk was even

Table 2.1   *Soviet net farm output per head of population and agricultural value added, 1950–53 and 1955–58 (kg, index and % shares)*

	1950–53	*1955–58*
Grain	247.9	297.6
Potatoes	172.8	163.2
Green vegetables	41.2	56.4
Milk	144.8	200.9
Meat	27.5	34.8
Eggs (units)	68.0	95.1
Value added in agriculture (1970 = 100)	49.3	67.3
Value added in agriculture as % GNP (1970 factor cost)	28.0	28.3

Sources: Product output levels from Johnson and Kahan 1959, Appendix Table 4; value added rows derived from Pitzer 1982, Tables B-7, A-1.

greater in the Virgin Lands than in traditional areas. Soil erosion was also a high risk in the newly cultivated lands unless there was also investment in counter-measures.

Second, there was massive elite resistance to increasing the share of total fixed investment going to the farm sector. Traditional Stalinist priorities had created strong coalitions of officials and managers grouped around coal, steel, electricity, civilian engineering and arms production. These restricted the growth of investment in agriculture.

Nonetheless, grain output from the Virgin Lands was substantial: about a quarter to two-fifths of the Soviet total during the Khrushchev period (McCauley 1976, p. 88). And agriculture's share of total investment did increase: in Soviet official figures, the farm sector took 11.8 per cent of gross fixed investment in 1946–50, 14.2 per cent in 1951–55, 14.3 per cent in 1956–60 and 15.5 per cent in 1961–65 (*Narkhoz 22–82*, p. 369). In fact, it seems to have been largely the Virgin Lands programme that raised the farm sector's share of the nation's capital formation. Some of Khrushchev's attempts to raise agricultural investment were blocked by the distributional coalitions surrounding other sectors (see, for example, Hahn 1972).

The return on Virgin Lands investment proved volatile. The fluctuating moisture balance in the Virgin Lands areas and the lack of anti-erosion measures saw to that. In some of the newly cultivated areas dust bowls soon developed. The whole approach was a deeply Soviet one: extensive growth of output achieved at high cost by raising inputs (new investment, new arable land, semi-compulsory mobilisation of young people to go out to Kazakhstan to plough up the virgin soil) rather than measures to raise the productivity of existing agricultural land, labour and capital. All the same, it was the kind of quick fix that the Soviet system was well adapted for. It helped boost the food supply in the years immediately following Stalin's death.

The grain harvest increased by 40 per cent between 1949–53 (when it had been below the level of 1913) and 1954–58 (official figures but comparable; *Narkhoz 61*, pp. 300–301), state procurements of grain by 33 per cent (p. 305). One reason this was particularly valuable was that grain was extensively used for animal fodder in the USSR; silage was poorly developed. State procurement of meat and poultry increased between the same two periods by 87 per cent and of dairy products by 84 per cent (*ibid.*)

Khrushchev got carried away. He had always liked, unlike the usual Soviet *apparatchik*, to get out and about, talk to people and enquire about details. Milovan Djilas describes him in 1945, when he was Party leader and prime minister of Ukraine, visiting a collective farm, inspecting the pigsty and the vegetable beds and making practical suggestions. This, Djilas observed, marked him out from other Soviet leaders, who never visited collective farms, except for some ceremonial feast (Djilas 1962, pp. 96–7). Now he developed grand ideas about agronomy: that growing maize was the answer to almost everything; that maize could be grown even in Chukotka, in the far north-east (Strelianyi 2000, p. 114); that the amount of land left fallow should be reduced; that early sowing of grain was appropriate even in the absence of the necessary fertiliser and equipment (see Smith 1987; Filtzer 1993, chapter 5). He accepted the advice of Trofim Lysenko, a quack biologist always ready to offer ill-founded guidance that would appeal to Soviet leaders. Some of Khrushchev's agricultural schemes could have made sense with additional inputs of fertiliser and new types of equipment; but these were not forthcoming. Some of the schemes were inconsistent with others. The heightened emphasis on fodder crops came at the expense of land melioration, and that led to a third of meadow land being abandoned with attendant losses in hay – another form of animal fodder. Meanwhile the introduction of more frequent ploughing, using heavy ploughs, required that more land be left fallow – which conflicted with the fallow reduction scheme (Filtzer 1993, pp. 47–8).

Lower down the chain of command farm managers often resisted: growing maize where it could be seen from the road, and other crops out of sight, for example. Still, the Khrushchevian bright ideas tended to backfire. The early surge in farm production encouraged him to talk in 1957 of overtaking American per capita meat production by 1975 (Strelianyi 2000, p. 114) – something to which the Soviet Union never came close. Reliance

on the unstable grain harvest from the Virgin Lands produced acute difficulties when the harvest failed both there and in traditional grain-growing
regions in 1963 (see Chapter 3).

Khrushchev also took organisational steps that had some sense to them,
such as the abolition of all mandatory deliveries from private plots and of
the machine-tractor stations (both in 1958), but which lacked the supporting measures that were necessary. Tractors and other farm machinery from
the machine-tractor stations (MTS) were transferred to the collective and
state farms, but at prices that constituted a heavy burden for the farms –
just when other burdens on them had been reduced. When compulsory
deliveries from the household plots were officially ended, the pressure on
the farms themselves was stepped up, and farm managers often coped by
extracting supplies from the household plots.

It is easy to make fun of what Khrushchev's successors called his 'hare-
brained schemes'. Despite the counter-productive micro-management of
choices of agricultural technology, however, Khrushchev's agricultural policies contained two lasting, positive ingredients.

First, the savage exploitation of the peasantry was reduced. To put that
more positively: Khrushchev improved incentives for farm production, mainly
by raising farm procurement prices and lowering the tax burden. His successors never reverted to the Stalinist destruction of the countryside, even
though they failed to save it from long-term decay.

Second, he increased the resource allocation priority of the farm sector.
This shows up in the medium term in the slight increase in agriculture's
share of value added (see Table 2.1 above). In the longer term it shows up
in an increase in the farm sector's share of gross fixed investment (see
above); this was something his successors in fact took further. For a generation, between 1953 and 1978, Soviet farm output grew strongly, improving
Soviet food supplies. That growth was extensive and therefore extremely
costly. But given the Soviet policymakers' aversion to any sort of 'dependence' on the outside world, that wasteful and costly route to an improved
food supply was the only route that the Soviet economic system could take;
it was not built for intensive growth.

The improvements that followed from Khrushchev's farm policies were
real. To what extent the gains should be ascribed to Khrushchev personally
is open to question. He presided over them. But the improved incentives
and priorities for farm production were, it seems, policies that all the main
rivals for the succession to Stalin would have adopted. And those were the
parts of his farm policies that endured and did not have immediate boom-
erang effects. The policies identified more specifically with Khrushchev
himself – maize in Chukotka and the like, plus perhaps the Virgin Lands
scheme – were ambiguous or downright damaging in their effects.

The *Sovnarkhoz* reform

The nearest Khrushchev came to a major organisational change was the *sovnarkhoz* reform of February 1957. *Sovnarkhoz* is an abbreviation of the Russian for council of the national economy. The term comes up earlier in Soviet history to denote a national economic management body. The Khrushchevian reform, however, was the creation of regional *sovnarkhozy*, initially 105 of them, and the transfer to them of the functions and responsibilities of most of the national branch ministries (on which see the first section of Chapter 1). The exceptions were those branch ministries that worked primarily for defence – the ministries under what later became known as the Military-Industrial Commission or, in its Russian acronym, the VPK. Those ministries never had their output targets or outcomes published, so what was switched to regional management was that part of the economy that was visible to civilian Russia-watchers in the West. The retention of central control for the VPK branches says a good deal about the stability of some Soviet priorities and methods even under Khrushchev.

The breaking-up of the civilian branch ministries was, according to most analysts, motivated by considerations of domestic political power. It shifted much economic management from the government machine to the Party. The Party was Khrushchev's power-base and, at least in late 1953 and 1954, perhaps even into 1957, it is possible to interpret the Malenkov-Khrushchev struggle for power as a struggle between the state machine and the Party machine, respectively. The 105 *sovnarkhozy* closely matched the boundaries of the regional (*oblast'*) Party administrations. The senior regional Party secretary, the *obkom* first secretary, got more control over the assets on his (it was a male profession) territory.

Even so, an economic rationale was of course advanced for the change. Branch ministries had been guilty of 'departmentalism' (*vedomstvennost'*): a narrow preoccupation with the concerns of one's own economic branch. This could mean, for example, that intermediate products were shipped great distances from one plant to another under the same ministry when supplies to the recipient could have been more cost-effectively acquired from a neighbouring plant that came under a different ministry. More generally, it meant a tendency for the objectives of the individual ministry's empire to prevail over those of the national economy as a whole.

The change to territorial management was not a decentralisation, if by the latter term one means a devolution of decision-making power to individual producers (state enterprises). Rather, it was a territorialisation of the second and third layers of the hierarchy depicted in Figure 1.1 above. This did not logically entail any change in the decision-making powers of enterprise managers. In practice, since *sovnarkhozy* were more numerous and smaller than the branch ministries and the administration was local, an individual enterprise manager may have had a better chance of influencing plans than with a Moscow-based ministry.

At all events, the economic consequences have been assessed by almost all observers as negative. The new arrangement certainly left a lot of loose ends.

First, the military-industrial sector was large, had input–output links with civilian producers, produced consumer goods (refrigerators, for instance) alongside weapon systems, and was still centrally directed.

Second, to shift branch-ministry functions out into the provinces meant moving the relevant officials out of Moscow. That was a fate, for Muscovites, only marginally preferable to incarceration in the *gulag*. 'Forty kilometers outside Moscow and you're back in the Middle Ages' was a Moscow cliché. Not even icon-collecting members of the Moscow intelligentsia were *that* fond of the Middle Ages. Many officials found ways of staying put; many who went found ways of keeping their Moscow residence permits. Even if all had gone, the average regional administration would have been short of branch expertise. As it was, they generally had to lean heavily on the industry-specific knowledge of local managers. That probably helped the managers in their constant battle for soft targets.

Moreover, in a centrally planned economy there were a number of functions, hitherto located in branch organisations, that needed to be carried out at a single national centre: the planning, for example, of the process of research, development and innovation (RDI). It is possible that a regional fragmenting of this process might allow some useful innovations to see the light of day in a sympathetic local environment, when they might not have made it through a national committee. This may have been the case for the development of group technology in the Leningrad machine-tool industry (Grayson 1982). It seems not, however, to have been the norm (Berry 1987). The planning of RDI was kept at the centre, but initially the financing of it was not – with predictable complications resulting. From 1959 state committees began to be established at the centre on a branch basis, partly to coordinate RDI (*ibid.*).

The economic drawbacks to the *sovnarkhoz* reform soon became apparent. The leadership, and therefore the media, began to complain about 'localism' (*mestnichestvo*) where earlier they had complained of 'departmentalism'. The number of *sovnarkhozy* was reduced by mergers, a process that illustrated the need for a hierarchical management system to limit its transaction costs by containing the number of reporting units to be supervised at each level.

The abolished ministries began to return to life surreptitiously in the form of branch and sector state committees, whose powers tended to increase.

Once Khrushchev was removed from power in October 1964, one of his successors' first acts was to re-establish the branch ministries.

Foreign trade, aid and technology transfer

Under Khrushchev, the Soviet Union became a more open economy. No centrally administered economy, it is true, can operate without administrative control of imports and of the supply of goods and services for export. Nor, since its currency lacks 'goods convertibility' domestically, can it have a convertible currency with exchange rates determined by supply and demand (see Holzman 1974). In these respects a centrally administered economy cannot integrate itself fully into the capitalist world economy. The old United Nations term, a 'state trading nation', conveys this. A centrally administered economy can however operate with policies that are more or less conducive to foreign transactions. Under Khrushchev the Soviet economy became more open in that sense. Once more, it was policy, not system, that altered.

Under Stalin, the Soviet Union had been, before the Second World War, a lone socialist state surrounded by capitalist states that were presumed, correctly, to be hostile. After the Second World War, Moscow acquired an empire. Even then, trade and cooperation with the new socialist states developed only slowly (see Chapter 1). Under Khrushchev, commercial engagement both with the CMEA partners and with the wider world grew substantially.

Three developments stand out: an extension of trade links to a far larger number of countries than under Stalin; the resort to foreign trade to offset a built-in systemic weakness in technological innovation; and the resort to foreign trade to offset another built-in systemic weakness in agriculture. The last of these belongs to Khrushchev's last year in office and will be described in Chapter 3. All three of these developments continued after Khrushchev's fall from power.

Between 1950 and 1958 the total turnover of Soviet foreign trade, in real terms, increased by 257 per cent (derived from *Narkhoz 22–82*, p. 580, and *VTSSSR 88*, p. 16). In the latter year almost three-quarters of that turnover was with other socialist countries (including China; *Narkhoz 61*, p. 672). But trade with CMEA partner-countries grew roughly in line with total foreign trade under Khrushchev. The segment of Soviet foreign trade that expanded fastest under Khrushchev was trade with the developing countries. This reflected one aspect of Khrushchev's foreign policy stance: his particular emphasis on cultivating relations with the non-aligned countries, as they were known at the time.

It was in this period that the USSR started to present itself as a source of aid to developing countries. The most publicised of its projects of this period was the Aswan Dam on the Nile. The failure of the Anglo-French Suez expedition in 1956 provided Moscow with an entrée (as well as cover for its own troubles in Hungary: the Hungarian uprising was crushed eleven days after the Suez expedition was launched). Khrushchev seized the opportunity to strengthen relations with Colonel Nasser's anti-imperialist regime. One result was the Aswan Dam project, finally completed in 1964 (see Khrushchev 1971, chapter 16).[1] From Khrushchev's time until the Soviet collapse, the annual statistical handbooks dutifully recorded data on the number of foreign projects constructed with Soviet technical assistance. Soviet exports of machinery rose steeply in the 1950s, but these were above all deliveries to the Third World, on soft credits, and to captive customers in the CMEA. Sales of manufactures in competitive markets remained small.

What was more characteristic of Soviet trade with the West, from Khrushchev's time, was large net Soviet imports of machinery. These began in 1958 and marked a break with the immediate Soviet past.

In the early 1930s the initial Soviet push for rapid industrialisation included comparatively large imports of Western machinery, sometimes of complete plants. These were the source of much of the new technology (new, that is, to the USSR) that was assimilated in the pre-war period (Holzman 1963; Sutton 1968). After that initial injection of foreign technology, Soviet technological development rested in part on the assimilation and diffusion of those technologies and in part on the continued absorption of foreign technology – but now by a mixture of copying ('reverse engineering') individual items purchased on a one-off basis, learning from open Western sources and industrial espionage. Lend-Lease deliveries in the Second World War constituted another large, direct injection. Then, until 1958, it was back to assimilation using only small volumes of imports.

To stress this reliance on foreign technology is not to denigrate Soviet indigenous RDI efforts. First, considerable RDI capabilities are needed to assimilate somebody else's technology. Second, catching up with the technologies already assimilated in more advanced countries is a major source of growth in all medium-developed countries.

One distinctive feature of Soviet and Central and East European assimilation of advanced technology under communism was that two major channels of technology transfer were very little used: inward foreign direct investment by transnational companies and the buying of foreign licences. (Both began to be used in later years, especially in Poland, Hungary and Romania, but only on a limited scale.) The other characteristic, particularly in the Soviet Union, was that assimilation of foreign technology was accompanied by claims that the country doing the assimilating was really technologically self-sufficient.

The surface presented by the leaders' speeches was one of technological complacency. This seemed at first sight to be justified. The Soviet economy was growing faster than the US, so Khrushchev's 'catching up and over-taking' was under way. Soviet technological confidence was boosted by the successful launching of the world's first artificial satellite, Sputnik 1, in October 1957 and later the first manned space flight, by Yurii Gagarin. At the same time, however, some Soviet scientists, engineers and economists were discussing weaknesses in the Soviet RDI process from at least 1955. Berry (1987) traces the development of this internal debate, the airing of the issue at Party Central Committee plenums each year from 1958 to 1962, and the attempts to improve things by making the planning of RDI more comprehensive. However, even after these measures and the conspicuous successes, the Soviet physicist Petr Kapitsa wrote in 1965 that the gap between Soviet and American technological levels had been widening (Kapitsa 1965, cited by Berry 1987, p. 90).

In 1958 Khrushchev started another of his pet schemes: chemicalisation of the economy. He had discovered that the Soviet chemical industry had missed out completely on about two decades of product and process devel-opment: there was almost no Soviet capability in plastics, in particular, and in the more recently developed kinds of mineral fertilisers. Characteristic-ally, he wanted the backlog eliminated fast, and with no concern for the opportunity cost of resources diverted to the chemical industry from elsewhere. Less predictably, he either encouraged or at any rate allowed the backlog to be attacked by large-scale imports of chemical plant and technology.

Western commentators were apt to see the highly visible Tolyatti (Fiat) project to produce small cars as the first major Soviet turnkey project: an investment project in which a main contractor – in this case a foreign firm – undertakes to design and install a complete plant, train workers to operate it, and finally get the plant operating at design capacity before handing it over to the customer to run for themselves. The first agreement covering the Tolyatti plant was signed in 1965, after Khrushchev's fall. In fact, the practice of assimilating foreign technology only by arm's length methods was abandoned earlier. A string of projects for Western chemical-plant contractors to design, supply, install and commission plastics, synthetic fibre, synthetic rubber and mineral fertiliser plants began in 1958. Because of the time-lags between initial negotiation and contract, and between contract and equipment delivery, the clearest jump in Soviet imports of Western machinery is seen in 1960: from $177 million the year before to $310 million in that year. In 1960–61 the chemical industry (as a destination) accounted for 35.9 per cent of all Soviet imports of Western machinery and equipment. It remained the leading branch destination of machinery imports for the following two decades, with occasional interruptions when major motor-industry projects (Tolyatti car plant and Kama River truck plant) intruded (see Hanson 1981, chapter 8).

Estimates of the effectiveness of Soviet imports of Western technology are problematic, but it is clear that large proportions of Soviet production of plastics, fibres and complex mineral fertilisers in the 1970s came directly from Western-built plants. Direct and indirect effects of such imports may have added about half a percentage point to the annual rate of industrial growth in the late 1970s. The impact on crop yields and hence food supplies of the imports of mineral fertiliser technologies was substantial. (For details see *op. cit.*, chapters 8–10.)

In the end, importing Western technology was not enough to stop Soviet growth rates deteriorating and the gap between Soviet and Western prosperity widening after the early 1970s. One reason why it did not do the trick was that the Soviet system impeded (in comparison with the capitalist system) the assimilation and diffusion of imported technology, just as it limited the effectiveness of domestic RDI. Still, it helped, and it was under Khrushchev that distrust of the outside world was suspended sufficiently to allow large injections of Western technology to be made.

At the time, it seems, what was happening looked quite different. Soviet economic growth was buoyant; the space race looked winnable (until the Americans got worried and applied themselves to it); Soviet policy-makers had neglected some particular fields, such as chemical technology, and some astute buying-in of foreign know-how would soon put matters straight.

Wages and the welfare of workers

Khrushchev's policy-making contained, it would seem, a streak of genuine idealism. The improvements in food supply were an objective Beria and Malenkov would also have pursued. Fear of the consequences of leaving both the peasants and urban food supplies in the wretched state of 1952–53 was enough to encourage them all to seek improvement – particularly when even Beria seems to have expected the powers of the secret police to be curtailed. The Soviet leadership's habitual fear of 'the people' (see Teague 1988) was clearly at work.

Khrushchev, however, also pursued other schemes for social betterment that had less obvious advantages for the Soviet elite. Some of them may even be best explained by ideology. The launching of major programmes of housing construction is more straightforward: the gross overcrowding of the

Table 2.2 *Soviet state and state-assisted housing construction 1946–65 (million square metres of total living space)*

1946–50	1951–55	1956–60	1961–66
127.1	178.1	337.8	394.4

Note: for definition, see text below. Figures from some earlier statistical handbooks are somewhat different, but the order of magnitude of changes between five-year periods is similar.
Source: derived from *Narkhoz 22–82*, p. 425.

meagre Soviet housing stock in 1953 was an apparent source of unrest, like food supplies. But the drive to reduce income inequality, to shorten the working week, to require school-leavers to experience work before going to university, to strengthen the powers of trade unions, to create 'agro-towns' – all of these schemes have a strong whiff of idealism about them. The fact that two of them were really rather batty only strengthens that impression.

The acceleration of housing construction was drastic. The figures most indicative of central policy are probably those for urban housing construction in Table 2.2. These include both direct state (municipal and enterprise) housing construction and individual (usually cooperative) housing construction by state employees, assisted by state credits. What is omitted is rural housing construction. The peasantry was left for the most part to fend for itself. In any case, housing construction on *kolkhozy* and by individual *kolkhozniki* more than doubled between 1951–55 and 1956–60, as incomes in the countryside improved.

The improvement in housing between 1953 and 1964 was very great indeed. True, a great deal still remained to be done even at the end of Khrushchev's rule. In 1964–65, in personal advertisements about the exchange of apartments, the abbreviation *malonas.*, as a description of an apartment, was still commonplace. This was short for *malonaselennaya*, or sparsely populated. From these hand-written advertisements, usually pasted to telegraph poles, it was obvious that even in Moscow people routinely expected that an apartment would be occupied by more than one household; the attractiveness of a negotiated housing swap depended among other things on how densely populated an apartment was. Still, the situation had been much worse in the late Stalin years. And Stalinist neglect of housing is apparent from the table: the period 1946–50 was after all a time of post-war reconstruction.

What the new housing programme did not achieve was much good-quality housing. The big apartment blocks that sprouted up on the outer edges of Soviet cities were usually constructed to a drab, standard pattern based on the assembly of pre-fabricated panels. Bits were apt to fall off them. The most common environment for such an apartment block, for some time after they went up, was a sea of mud, with holes and ditches for variety. They quickly became known as *khrushchoby*, a play on the word for slums, *trushchoby*. Still, the waiting lists to get into a new apartment were real enough. Most people had long been living in much worse conditions.

There were also quite substantial measures to reduce inequality and to improve real incomes and working conditions. At the end of Stalin's life, the Soviet people had seen very little increase in material welfare since the start of the five-year plans: a period of just under fifteen years if one excludes the war and the period of putative recovery in 1946–50.

McAuley (1987, p. 140) cites an estimate by the sociologist Leonid Gordon and others that in 1952 the average real wage was at about the same level as in 1928. This is less of an indictment of Stalinism than it might at first appear, though not much less. The proportion of the population participating in the workforce had risen substantially, so real income per head of population (calculated from household incomes) had probably grown. Janet Chapman (1963) puts 1950 per capita household consumption nearly 11 per cent above 1928, and her estimates imply significant further growth in 1950–53. Naum Jasny (1961, p. 447) makes the increase between 1928 and 1952 a mere 3.7 per cent – but still an increase. Whoever is nearer the truth, the improvement in prosperity was modest.

The contrast with the Khrushchev period is striking. In the CIA's 1982 recalculations of Soviet growth from 1950 to 1980, Schroeder and Denton (1982, Table A.2) put the increase in per capita consumption from 1953 to 1964 at 44.6 per cent, an annual rate of increase of 3.8 per cent. Within that period, growth is far stronger in 1953–58 than in the second half of Khrushchev's rule.

Not only did average prosperity rise; inequality also fell. Overall measures of inequality in the Soviet period are not reliable. There is a dearth of information about income distribution other than among state employees. Therefore two groups containing many poor people – the elderly and *kolkhoz* peasants – are poorly accounted for. Furthermore, the real value of a given money income varies enormously in a shortage economy. People living in Moscow had much better supplies of food and consumer goods than the rest of the population. Party officials and other members of the elite had privileged access to items in short supply.

Even so, there is no doubt that inequality was high in the late Stalin period. McAuley (1987, p. 140) cites an estimate by Rabkina and Rimashevskaya that the decile ratio amongst state employees in 1946 – the ratio of the wages and salaries of those in the top 10 per cent to those in the bottom 10 per cent – was 7.24. He compares this with an earnings decile ratio for the UK in the late 1960s of only 3.6. It is true that the UK figure takes no account of property incomes, to which the Soviet Union had almost no equivalent (interest on savings bank accounts and the inherited royalty income of children of composers and writers were the nearest the USSR came to legal property incomes). Even the inclusion of property incomes, however, would almost certainly fall far short of closing the gap. And Soviet comparative inequality in the late Stalin period is unlikely to be reduced by the inclusion of non-wage earners. In 1950 the average state pension was one-fifth of the average wage; and even in 1954 the average earnings of peasants from the *kolkhoz* were about one third of the average wage (*ibid.*). Peasants had some real income, typically, from their household plots as well. But elderly *kolkhoz* peasants received no pension at all – and indeed continued to lack pension rights until the Brezhnev era.

They also continued until 1965 to lack internal passports, and therefore to be tied to their collective farm: that is, they could not legally change jobs and move away from the village without the approval of the *kolkhoz* chairman. They were, even under Khrushchev, second-class citizens – not that first-class Soviet citizens had much in the way of civil rights. Writing of the year 1955 and of the family of a provincial KGB official, Rusanov, Solzhenitsyn portrays the snobbery with which urban dwellers viewed the peasantry: 'Look at Shendyapin's daughter,' thinks Rusanov's wife in connection with one of her husband's colleagues, 'how she'd very nearly married a student in her year at teachers' training college. He was only a boy from the country, and his mother was an ordinary collective farmer. Just imagine the Shendyapins' flat, their furniture and the influential people they had as guests, and suddenly there's this old woman in a white headscarf sitting at their table, their daughter's mother-in-law, and she didn't even have a passport' (Solzhenitsyn 1971, p. 198).

Even if we cannot monitor the change in income distribution under Khrushchev in a way that is comprehensive or reliable, there is no doubt that inequality was reduced. The decile ratio in state wages was 3.3 in 1964 (McAuley 1987, p. 145). Peasant incomes rose relative to state wages (see above).

In part, these changes were the result of a reform of wage-scales. A minimum wage was introduced in 1956. It was set at what McAuley concludes was a reasonable poverty line: 30 roubles a month. That meant that members of the household of a minimum-wage earner with dependents were still below the poverty line (p. 153). The number of different wage-scales was drastically reduced. So were skill differentials.

Much of the decision-making in the 1956 wage reform was arbitrary. It did not necessarily ensure that the demand and supply for particular kinds of labour would be in balance. And that, after all, was something that Soviet planners, with their market relationship with Soviet households, needed to take into account (see the first section of Chapter 1). But the general thrust of reduced differentials did correspond to the direction of change in the labour market. High investment in education and training throughout the Stalin period had tended to reduce the relative scarcity of skills.

Other measures such as the reduction of the working week and the government decrees of 1957–58 strengthening the role of factory trade union committees in resolving workplace disputes are harder to assess. Insofar as actual hours worked were really cut, this may have contributed to the slowdown of growth in the latter part of the Khrushchev period. And the trade unions continued to operate as part of the system of control of the workforce; even so, they perhaps became better at dealing with individual grievances.

As with agriculture and housing, Khrushchev's policies in the field of wages and labour relations were benign, if not always well designed.

Economic debate

Economic information and economic debate both opened up in the late 1950s.

The publication of the 1956 statistical handbook (*Narkhoz 56*) was an event. After years of near-total secrecy about the economy, a handbook of national economic statistics appeared. As throughout Soviet history, the presentation of data was governed by propaganda considerations. Convenient base-years were chosen so that growth looked impressive. (Later on, this was fine-tuned to show how things had improved under each successive leadership.) Information that was either acutely embarrassing (like rural real income levels and the distribution of pensioner incomes) or considered sensitive (oil reserves, gold production, gold reserves, anything to do with arms production) was simply omitted – not just in 1956 but with some minor exceptions up to 1991. Time series of major economic aggregates, such as industrial production or national income, were constructed in ways that, in comparison with standard international practice, exaggerated growth (indexes of real output weighted by the prices of a remote base year, price indexes that understated inflation, and so on).

Nonetheless, the new flow of information conveyed a great deal. Jasny (1957) promptly detected inconsistencies and tell-tale omissions in the 1956 handbook. But he and others made extensive use of Soviet primary data of physical output (tons of steel, etc.). The grounds for treating most of these as broadly usable data were set out by Bergson (1961). One compelling argument that he deployed was this: if all Soviet statistics were simply freely invented, there would be no need to suppress any embarassing data. Another was that for a number of statistics there was some, albeit rough and ready, independent confirmation: embassy compilations over many years of Moscow retail prices, for example, or the correspondence in earlier periods between captured secret documents and information that had been publicly released.

The detailed product data became a key building block in Western reconstructions of the more tendentious aggregate series. The cottage industry of Western recalculations of Soviet GNP and its end-use and sector-of-origin components developed. Before long the CIA's Office of Economic Research turned it into a high-skill, mass-production, and largely open exercise. Much of the quantitative evidence used in this book comes from CIA analyses.

So far as Soviet economic thought was concerned, there had been a prolonged freeze under Stalin. Few of the talented Soviet economists of the late 1920s had survived, though one or two who had, such as Al'bert Vainshtein, were resilient enough to engage once more in intellectual battle and to ridicule orthodoxy.

A few older survivors (L.V. Kantorovich, V.S. Nemchinov and V.V. Novozhilov, especially), together with a new generation, sometimes coming from mathematics, began to coalesce into a new school of so-called 'optimal planners'.[2]

There was also a more scholastic debate, squarely in the traditions of Marxist-Leninist political economy, on the meaning of the 'law of value'. This, too, had some practical resonance. How should Soviet product prices be set? In what sense, if any, should they reflect labour value? What role might there be for measures that captured imputed rents for natural resources and for anything resembling a return on capital? The discussions in the optimal planning school also raised these questions, but it was not only the mathematical economists who raised real issues.

Economic journalists, usually better informed than the academics about what really happened in the Soviet economy, began to say in public a great deal that was of interest: particularly about the counter-productive effects of the inherited incentive system of success indicators for industrial managers. Writers on rural themes began publicly to describe the miserable reality of Soviet village life. Vladimir Dudintsev's novel, *Not by Bread Alone*, first published in the literary journal *Noviy mir* in 1956, showed vividly how technical innovation was inhibited by Soviet arrangements (Dudintsev 1957).

Soviet economic analysis and commentary continued to develop through the remainder of Khrushchev's time in power. Most of the other hopeful developments reviewed in this chapter, however, tended to wilt in 1960–64.

Notes

1 The Aswan Dam, like other foreign projects, was not taken too seriously by many Russians. I recall in spring 1964 standing in a queue to get into a restaurant in Moscow. The man behind me called out to the doorman, 'You should let me in. I'm from the Aswan Dam.' 'Where's that?' the doorman asked. 'In the Moscow region' (*v Podmoskov'e*). Charity, it was widely felt, should begin at home.

2 They reinvented – independently, it seems – some of the ingredients of marginal analysis that was part of the Western mainstream but excluded from Marxism-Leninism. The practical significance of this was that they drew attention to the properties of an efficient allocation of resources: notably, that in order to obtain maximum output from given resources of land, labour and capital any given input (say, unskilled labour) should be allocated between alternative lines of production in quantities in such a way that the impact on output of adding one more unit of the input should be the same in all lines of production. That left open the question, by what considerations on the demand side different outputs should be valued: planners, not consumers, might, according to the optimal planners, be the final arbiters. But even with that rather large ambiguity left unclarified, the Soviet mathematical economists had developed criteria by which much of Soviet planning practice seemed grossly to neglect allocative efficiency. (This note is a very crude, abbreviated summary; the development of the Soviet mathematical school is set out with great learning and lucidity by Sutela (1984). Sutela shows among other things that the Marxist-Leninist tradition influenced and constrained even this apparently radical new school of thought.)

CHAPTER THREE

Khrushchev: Things Fall Apart, 1960–64

Khrushchev's rule was on the whole benign in its economic effects, but the last few years were a time of disappointing economic results.

Even so, when Khrushchev was ousted in the Soviet equivalent of a palace coup, in October 1964, it was not primarily for economic failures. It was perhaps as much as anything the result of his having alienated, in one way or another, most members of the Soviet elite. By trying to shift the allocation of investment towards agriculture and consumption, he had antagonised the 'steel-eaters' – the state and Party officials linked to 'heavy' industry, that is, defence production and the manufacture of industrial producer goods. The *sovnarkhoz* reform disrupted the lives of branch-ministry officials. By trying in 1962 to reorganise the Party at regional level into separate agricultural and industrial units he had extended this turbulence to regional Party officials. His cutbacks in troops and conventional arms upset the military leadership (Sergei Khrushchev 2000). And the Soviet climbdown that ended the Cuban missile crisis was a humiliation for the political class as a whole.

Still, what was happening in the economy did not help him. In his first few years as leader, he had presided over changes in priorities that brought real improvements for the Soviet people. These were changes in policy, not system. After that, the Soviet economic system, in its unforgiving way, set limits to the gains that had been made.

After the surge in food production, the successes in the space race, the launching of a major housing programme and the 1956 wage reform came setbacks: the *sovnarkhoz* reorganisation appeared increasingly to have been counter-productive; attempts to raise retail food prices produced a riot, quelled by shooting; the farms remained grossly backward and a drought in 1963 produced a severe harvest failure; Khrushchev's campaigns for particular products and processes produced disruption in industry as well as agriculture. The Soviet economy was still growing faster than that of the US, but its growth slowed in the early 1960s. Khrushchev's boasts about Soviet per capita production imminently overtaking American levels gave hostages to fortune. Just how absurd that boasting was, became clear only later.

Policies: 'catching up' and the seven-year plan

The Sixth Five-Year Plan (1956-60) was abandoned and replaced by an oddity in the history of Soviet five-year plans: a seven-year plan (1959-65 inclusive). The December 1956 CPSU Central Committee Plenum decided (in other words, the leadership decided) that the Sixth Five-Year Plan was 'too taut' (Nove 1987, p. 63).

On the face of it, this looks odd, because several major targets in the plan were in fact exceeded in 1960. Table 3.1 gives a few of the official Soviet numbers.

The two big aggregates, national income (net material product) and industrial gross output, look like a modest shortfall and a substantial over-fulfilment, respectively. However, these numbers, quite apart from having a rather precarious relationship to reality, were not what Soviet planning was about. They were numbers that could be used for propaganda purposes, but they were not operational targets. The core of the plan had to do with physical output targets, especially for supposedly 'key' products such as

Table 3.1   *The abandoned Sixth Five-Year Plan, 1956–60: some targets and outcomes*

	1960 plan	1960 actual
National income (1950 = 100)	274	265
Industrial gross output (1950 = 100)	261	304
Oil (m tons)	135	148
Electricity (bn kwh)	320	292
Steel (m tons)	68	65
Coal (m tons)	592	513

Sources: Nove 1987, pp. 61, 64; *Narkhoz 61*, pp. 174, 215.

electricity, coal and steel. Never mind that these were intermediate industrial products, and not an end in themselves. Never mind that they were wastefully used in the creation of end-products: consumer and investment goods. Intermediate industrial products of a traditional kind were for Soviet planners the symbols of modernisation; they were what grown-up countries had, so the Soviet Union must make more and more of them. It was probably the impending shortfalls in these prestigious 'heavy-industry' products that led to the Sixth Five-Year Plan being deemed too taut.

Catching up with the US, however, was still the name of the game. In fact, this target was now treated more seriously than before, with future dates attached to its achievement. In 1959 the US government analyst Hans Heymann Jr observed: 'Since about the middle of last year, and particularly coincident with the launching of the new 7-year plan, the long-held and prestige-laden objective of "catching up with America" has been rapidly transformed by Khrushchev from a mere propaganda slogan into something approaching a national obsession' (Heymann 1959, pp. 1–2).

Heymann went on to question whether a total-output contest was something that the United States should allow itself to be drawn into. The terms of such a contest would not have been too clear. At different times Khrushchev spoke of overtaking US per capita food production, total industrial production, total output, and so on; he mentioned or implied various target dates. When he spoke of attaining 'full communism' (which Marx envisaged as the ending of scarcity) by 1980, the implication was presumably that the United States would by then be lagging far behind.

One exercise in projecting hypothetical catch-up dates for total GNP was conducted by Morris Bornstein and Daniel Fusfeld. Positing alternative US growth rates of 2.5, 3 and 4 per cent per annum, and Soviet growth rates of 6, 7 and 8 per cent, they generated nine catch-up dates. The earliest was 1973, the latest 1996 (Bornstein and Fusfeld 1962, p. 2). Hypothetical though the exercise was, the fact that it was conducted at all, and the range of Soviet growth rates chosen, reveal that Khrushchev's talk of catching-up did not at the time seem entirely ridiculous.

The seven-year plan, drafted in 1957–58, incorporated some product-group targets that reflected Khrushchev's addiction to product-and-process campaigns. The chemicalisation drive was reflected in planned increases in annual output (from 1958 actual to 1965 plan) from 12 to 35 million tons for mineral fertiliser and from 166 to 666 million tons for synthetic fibres. These extraordinary targets were not met. The fact that mineral fertiliser output in 1965 was reported as 31.6 million tons and synthetic fibres at 407 million tons nonetheless shows pretty remarkable rates of growth (Nove 1987, Table 4.3; these physical output reports are more reliable than the aggregate measures such as national income).

At the same time, output of coal, machine-tools and cement fell well short of target (*ibid.*) So did output of footwear and textiles, but that was just normal Soviet practice. The fact that some (not all) traditional high-priority branches fell short of their targets was widely attributed in the Soviet press to the disruptive effects of Khrushchev's campaigns for other things. This explanation, of course, was put forward only after Khrushchev had been removed from power. His successors then made it clear that criticism of Khrushchev and his policies was not so much allowed as required.

The criticisms are plausible as far as they go. At all events, industrial growth slowed. In 1953–60 it was 8.9 per cent per annum. In 1960–64 it was 6.6 per cent per annum (sectoral value added at 1970 factor cost; derived from Pitzer 1982, Table A-5). In retrospect, we can be reasonably sure that at least part of this was the result of the long-term weakening of the Soviet trend rate of industrial growth, and not necessarily attributable to particular policy decisions of the time. But disruption due to product-and-process campaigning was also a factor.

A word should be said here in defence of these campaigns. It is easy to make fun of Khrushchev's hobby-horses. At the same time, it must be acknowledged that the routine operation of the Soviet planning system tended to produce a rigid, or at best only slowly changing, industrial output-mix (see the first section of Chapter 1). Khrushchev, however impulsive and meddlesome his pursuit of new product-and-process priorities may have been, did see the need for upgrading particularly neglected sectors – notably, the chemical industry. The planning system contained no built-in mechanisms to stimulate desirable structural change. The main stimulus that did constantly operate was American innovation in weapons systems. That affected the only part of the Soviet economy that had to respond to competition – arms production. That apart, only micro-management from the very top could effect a radical shift in the product-mix.

At all events, there was a slowdown in the early 1960s. Between 1953–60 and 1960–64, if one takes the CIA's GNP series at 1970 factor cost, the slowdown was from 6.1 to 4.7 per cent per annum (derived from Pitzer 1982). From Pitzer's series of GNP by sector of origin, with the sectoral weights (1970 factor cost) used in it, it can be deduced that the industrial slowdown accounts for about half the overall slowdown in GNP growth. Almost all the rest of the slowdown is attributable to agriculture, which had two bad years in 1962 and 1963, and a recovery in 1964 that took growth over the whole four-year period to 2.1 per cent a year, well down from the 5.1 per cent annual rate of the previous seven years (*ibid.*).

So far as Soviet elite perceptions at the time are concerned, it was the agricultural disaster of 1963 (an output fall of about a fifth in one year, on the CIA estimates) that must have seemed the most salient of the economic failures for which Khrushchev could be blamed. Together with the foreign-policy reversal over Cuba, the Novocherkassk riot (see below) and his attempt in 1962 to split local Party organisations into separate agricultural and industrial entities, this harvest failure contributed to his downfall. The fortunes of the farm sector are reviewed in the next section.

Agriculture

In January 1961, at the CPSU Central Committee plenary meeting, Khrushchev claimed that the Soviet Union would overtake the United States in the production of meat per head of population. This, he asserted, was something that the Soviet people believed (Strelianyi 2000, p. 120).

Talk of overtaking the US now looks silly. At the time, it was not obviously so. Recent past growth in farm output had been impressive (see Table 2.1 in the previous chapter). As with space travel, so, at the other end of the technology spectrum, with farming: this was a time when the Soviet economy really did seem capable of great achievements.

In fact, Soviet agricultural output was about to falter badly. It resumed its growth after Khrushchev's removal from office, and actually grew quite strongly until the late 1970s. But Khrushchev had picked a bad moment to make grandiose forecasts. Figure 3.1 shows the course of farm-sector value added over three decades from 1950. The strong growth of the early Khrushchev years helps to account for the hubris of Khrushchev's 1961 pronouncement. Even when the impact of weather changes is to some extent smoothed out by using a three-year moving average (the smooth line), it is apparent that 1962–64 was an unkind time for Khrushchev. The sharp decline of those years helps to account for his fall – even though foreign-policy failures and internal Party unrest were probably more important in his political fate.

The immediate cause of the setback was a disastrous grain harvest in 1963, which in turn was triggered by drought. Virgin Lands grain production approximately levelled off after 1958, and it fell sharply in 1963. On the official gross output figures, 1963 grain output (less net exports) was slightly less per head of population than it had been in Tsarist Russia in 1913: 462 against 483 kilograms.

One problem was the fluctuations in policies towards the private plots ('personal subsidiary holdings' in Soviet official terminology). These, producing about a third of all farm output at the time, were initially helped by Khrushchev's abolition of compulsory deliveries from them (Chapter 2). The surge in production from the Virgin Lands in 1954–58, however,

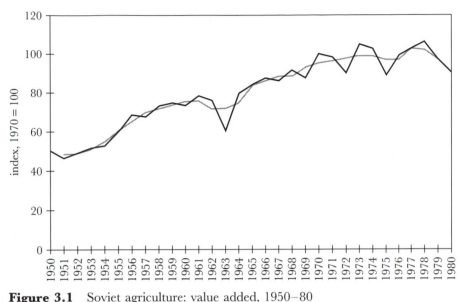

Figure 3.1 Soviet agriculture: value added, 1950–80
Note: The smooth curve plots a three-year moving average.
Source: Derived from Pitzer 1982, Table B-7.

seems to have encouraged Khrushchev to indulge his true believer's faith
in the primacy of the socialised sector of agriculture. Now the collective
farms and, ideologically best of all, the state farms would be able to feed the
nation well, overtaking American output levels in the process (Wädekin
1973, p. 272). So the use of state and collective farm land to pasture private
livestock was discouraged, with damaging effects on the latter.

After 1958, negative influences on the farm sector converged. Reduced
access to pasture for private livestock together with instructions to reduce
in-kind payments for work on the collective farm weakened the private
sector. (The payments in kind consisted in part of fodder for private-plot
livestock.) Private-plot livestock numbers fluctuated without any clear trend.
Harvests on the Virgin Lands stopped rising, and also fluctuated. A poorish
harvest year in 1962 was followed by a disastrous one in 1963.

Khrushev's initial farm policies were beneficial, but could not guarantee
sustained output growth after the first few years. Higher procurement prices
and lower taxes had boosted farm output after 1953 by the elementary
device of improving incentives. Khrushchev had raised the farm-sector
share of investment by the capital injections needed for the Virgin Lands
(see Chapter 2). But his efforts to switch more industrial capacity into the
provision of agricultural inputs ran up against the 'steel-eaters', the heavy-
industry lobby.

Meanwhile life on Soviet collective and state farms was better than before, but still harsher and more poverty-stricken than in the cities or in other rural workplaces, such as the timber mills. Fyodor Abramov's novella, *The Dodgers*, published in January 1963, describes contemporary working life on a northern Russian collective farm. Abramov, who was born in the Arkhangel region, shows a decent chairman of a collective farm trying in vain to get his workers to work. He is stuck between daft instructions from above and workers with no incentive to work on the collective farm.

The district (*raion*) Party committee instructs him to stop making hay while the sun is shining in order to meet a silage target (the trickle-down effect of one of Khrushchev's campaigns). The rain then falls, destroying the uncollected hay. Hardly any of his workers come out voluntarily to work on the silage. He combs the village, coaxing and bullying people to do some work for the collective. Some see more advantage in working on their own plots, others in going out to forage for mushrooms. Other residents again have left the *kolkhoz* to work at the local timber-mill, and cannot be tempted back.

Following the *kolkhoz* chairman's efforts to muster some labour inputs, the reader learns, along the way, the following: the farm has been unable to pay the *kolkhozniki* anything for five months; the young men of the village have got out of the *kolkhoz* (something usually facilitated by military service); the young women hope to leave by marrying out; drunkenness is pervasive; the farm is unable to provide pensions for elderly former *kolkhozniki*, and our hero is the thirteenth chairman the farm has had since the war. If the story is set, as seems likely, in 1962, that is thirteen changes of leadership in seventeen years.

The Soviet reader of the time knew much of the background: that *kolkhoz* peasants were second-class citizens who did not have internal passports and could not move from their workplace without official permission; that most did not qualify to receive a pension, and that in most farms most of the time they needed their private plots if they were to survive. The chief excitement of Abramov's story for Soviet readers was that it did not lie about the squalor of Soviet rural life or about the idiocies of the planning system and Khrushchev's agronomic campaigns. Perhaps the most instructive feature of the story for the economic history of the USSR is that it depicts the state of affairs on a collective farm *after* a period of rapid improvement in Soviet agriculture.

Another vivid picture of Soviet farm life in the 1960s is in Andrei Amalrik's memoir of his exile to a remote farm in the Tomsk region of Siberia (Amalrik 1970). This was in 1965, and far from Abramov's fictional farm in the European north. It is a record of how things looked to a Moscow intellectual whose previous experience of cattle and tractors was nil. Amalrik is a lucid, fair-minded and thoughtful observer. He notes, for example, that the police in Siberia behaved in a more civil and humane fashion than the police in Moscow – and suggests reasons for the difference. And he proposes ways in which the labour-day system of payment for *kolkhoz* could be improved. But his description of life and work on a collective farm is if anything more depressing than Abramov's.

Amalrik found that his new workmates needed their private plots to survive; that drunkenness and swearing were endemic; that anyone who found themselves in funds drank them away; that the rate of remuneration for different tasks was more or less arbitrary, and that there was no incentive to work well. At one point, Amalrik was assigned the task of putting up new poles to carry electricity cables. This turned out to be well remunerated by comparison with most other work on the farm. But when he had put up his poles, the farm ran out of wire and the cables were not put in place: the work was wasted (Amalrik 1970, p. 161). Amalrik was struck by the indifference of all concerned to this outcome; nobody expected results.

Both Abramov's fictional farm and Amalrik's real one were in remote places, and not blessed with good soil and climate. Some Soviet state and collective farms were less melancholy places. If you worked on a cotton-growing farm in Uzbekistan, life would not be quite so grim: the state paid better prices for 'technical' crops than for food crops. If you worked on a farm near a big city, you might be well placed to sell your private-plot eggs, potatoes, vegetables and milk at good prices in a big-city market – one of the so-called *kolkhoz* markets. But there was no doubt that Abramov and Amalrik – the former in a Leningrad literary journal, the latter in *samizdat* – described life as it was lived by millions of Soviet people on collective and state farms. Throughout this period, and indeed for the whole of Soviet history, agriculture remained a source of special difficulties for Soviet society. It was the victim of both policy and system.

Until 1953, its backwardness might be attributed to policy: to Stalin's ruthless exploitation of the farm sector. State procurement prices were set at levels that amounted to crippling taxation. Collective-farm work was paid from residual farm income that could be zero. There was very little net investment. Peasants (*kolkhozniki*) were deprived of the right to move, and change jobs as other Soviet (mostly) could. 'The present kolkhoz system is based, in effect, on forced labour', as Amalrik wrote (*op. cit.*, p. 168).

After 1953 much of this exploitation had ended: procurement prices were raised, peasant incomes rose, and so did investment in agriculture (though the peasants did not acquire passports until 1975). Khrushchev, in other words, presided over a general shift in policy intended to strengthen the farm sector. Later (see Chapters 4 and 5) this policy was extended until investment in the farm sector began to crowd out investment elsewhere.

But the farm sector, though its output grew quite fast for a generation (1953–78), remained especially problematic.

This was because the Soviet economic system was a massive barrier to the development of an efficient farm sector. Collectivisation had been pushed through in 1928–32 largely for purposes of political and logistic control. Stalin, like Lenin, saw peasants with their own farms, however small, as by definition enemies of socialism. To get food off the land and into the growing cities without conceding any power to the peasantry (the majority of the population at the time), those peasants had to be forced into a comparatively small number of giant collective farms from which grain and other farm products could be taken on whatever terms the Party leadership chose. To take grain, milk and animals for slaughter from millions of small farms would entail costs of monitoring and physical collection that would, in a centralised system, be enormous.

This span-of-control logic, by which a centralised economic system tends to concentrate production into relatively few, large units, was first noted and analysed for the Nazi German economy of the late 1930s (Eucken 1948). It is one of communist China's remarkable achievements that it broke out of that logic with the introduction of the 'family responsibility' system in the late 1970s (a euphemism for a restoration of independent peasant farming). The Soviet Union never broke out of it. In many activities, but perhaps most damagingly in agriculture, the span-of-control logic is incompatible with the logic of maximum efficient scale. It makes farms far too big.

Bradley and Clark (1972) set out the systemic problem for Soviet-style agriculture. The problem is to secure efficient production in a branch of the economy where work has to be done across a large territorial space by a large number of people, where the outcome (e.g. the harvest) is widely separated in time from many of the inputs (e.g. into sowing), and where unpredictably changing conditions (weather, livestock disease) require operational decisions to be made quickly and on the basis of maximum knowledge of the exact situation on the ground. Those circumstances together ensure that economies of scale in agriculture are limited, compared with, say, steel-making. In market economies, farm size is limited by dis-economies of scale (rising long-run average cost). Changing technologies (summed up by everything that is denoted by 'intensive agriculture') can over time alter optimum farm size. Economies in marketing and administration can in some circumstances favour the growth of multi-farm businesses or multi-farm marketing cooperatives. Even so, there was a gulf between the farm size dictated by the market and that mandated by the Soviet state.

The difficulty of running giant, Soviet-style farms with hundreds of employees is to do with information, incentives and supervision. In a family farm, those engaged in running the farm are motivated by the knowledge that the farm's bottom line is their personal bottom line: it is the final results that matter. A large labour force has to be paid according to its execution of the work allocated to each person by the management. This is problematic. Pay a tractor driver according to how many hectares he ploughs in a given period of time, and he will plough as shallowly as he can get away with. The final crop is not his concern.

Nor is close supervision the answer, as it might be in a factory. A territorially scattered labour force can be closely supervised only at enormous cost. In the absence of direct supervision, farm-workers need to be guided by incentives that will make it attractive for them to plough, sow, rear animals, tend fences, and so on in ways that maximise the final net output. This, given the uncertainties and the actions of others that intervene between most kinds of farm work and their effects on farm net income, is close to impossible.

At the end of 1964 the Soviet Union contained 38,300 collective farms, with an average workforce of 501 persons and an average land area of 12,582 hectares. The state farms were even larger – 10,078 of them with an average workforce of 804 (derived from *Narkhoz 64*, pp. 245, 261 and 419). This could be compared with a total of around three million farms in the US, with an average workforce of about 2 and average land-size under 200 hectares (Diamond and Davis 1979, Table 1, for 1977). The Soviet planning system could not have tolerated three million separate farms. Productive efficiency, however, was incompatible with farms of Soviet size. The combination of anti-peasant politics and a systemic bias towards farms far above maximum efficient size doomed Soviet agriculture.

The retention of a private sector, the private plots, was a tacit admission of the problem. But the personal subsidiary holdings, as they were officially called, were effectively a concession by Stalin to enable those peasants who survived the great famine of the early 1930s to continue, just about, to stay alive and to serve the state. Private-plot output was primarily subsistence production. That it was at this time about a third of all farm output reflected above all the fact that agriculture still employed a large part of the workforce – 42.1 per cent in 1960 (Whitehouse and Havelka 1973, p. 341).

The private plots were restricted to a maximum size of half a hectare and quite low maximum numbers of livestock (the exact limits varied in different parts of the USSR; in Central Asia the rules covered camels). The production units in Soviet agriculture were therefore either giants or midgets – each a long way from the size range that would have worked best, somewhere in the middle.

So far as the collective farm was concerned, this meant constant, usually frantic and unavailing, attempts at supervising the unsupervisable. As

Abramov has one of his elderly peasants say: 'No, in present conditions . . . you can't expect a decent life. There are far too many bosses around' (Abramov 1963, p. 99).

The systemic weakness of Soviet agriculture did not preclude improvement. It might never get well, but it could get better. If labour productivity is taken as one, admittedly partial, measure of productive efficiency, this could be raised by increasing and improving the stock of farm equipment. Crop yields, and therefore the productivity of the land, could be raised by better seed selection and larger applications of fertiliser and pesticides. Total factor productivity in the sector as a whole could be increased by the application of best practice within the limits set by the system.

All of this, and especially the increase in capital stock and chemical inputs, happened under Brezhnev, at any rate up to the late 1970s. Khrushchev had secured a spurt in farm output by the measures already described. He had not, as he seems to have thought in 1957–58, turned Soviet agriculture into a world-beater. His product-and-process campaigns and the tapering off of the Virgin Lands effect brought the growth in farm output almost to a halt in the early 1960s, and cruel weather conditions in 1963 made the whole exercise seem (unfairly) to have failed. The systemic handicaps remained. His successors coped by throwing resources at the farm sector, buying further output growth for a time at great cost. What was not reversed was Khrushchev's fundamental departure from Stalin's priorities, in favour of agriculture.

Foreign trade and external relations

The domestic liberalisation and the opening up of links with the outside world that followed Stalin's death had already had their fair share of unintended consequences. Signs of a thaw in Moscow created the illusion in Central and Eastern Europe that the Soviet hold on the region might be relaxed. Hence the workers' uprising in East Germany as early as June 1953, and the much larger Hungarian uprising of 1956, put down only by a Soviet invasion.

Still, the thaw had been continued. And it continued to have consequences unintended by the Soviet leaders. In 1957 an International Youth Festival was put on in Moscow. The city was flooded with young people from the West, in numbers that exceeded the security services' powers of control. Improbable as it may appear to most people now, that event seemed to some of the Muscovites who participated in it to be 'the beginning of the collapse of the Soviet system' (Kozlov 1998, p. 100). 'Now, looking back at

Table 3.2   *Soviet foreign trade volume, 1955–65 (1955 = 100)*

	Exports	Imports
1960	171	191
1965	260	253

Source: derived from Tables V and VI in *VT SSSR 22–81*.

those times from the post-perestroika present, you can see what a mistake Sof'ya Vlas'evna (as we called Soviet power)[1] made in organising that festival' (*ibid.*). What Kozlov has in mind is that anything approaching close acquaintance with the outside world undermined confidence in the Soviet system. (For an elaboration of this argument, see Zinoviev 1981.)

Stalin's actions demonstrated a firm belief that contact with the outside world was dangerous for Soviet power. Khrushchev's actions demonstrated, if not the exact opposite, then at any rate a belief that contact with the outside world could be greatly increased without danger. He was himself an 'eager tourist' (Roberts 1987, p. 218), enjoying Geneva, London, New York and Hollywood. Part of this supposedly controlled opening to the outside world was an expansion of foreign trade and Soviet aid.

As noted in the previous chapter, Khrushchev presided over a substantial growth in Soviet commercial contacts with other countries, capitalist and non-aligned as well as socialist. This secured undoubted material benefits, both in classic gains from trade and in growth-enhancing effects of technology transfers. (For some tentative measurements of the latter in the 1970s see Hanson 1981, chapters 9–11.) It also let the Soviet economy in later for some of the costs of empire (see Chapter 5 below), and politically it created some risks for Khrushchev himself.

The growth of foreign trade in the 1950s and 1960s was extremely rapid. The official Soviet estimates for the volume ('in comparable prices') of total merchandise are shown in Table 3.2.

Trade with Warsaw Pact allies remained the core of Soviet foreign trade. Table 3.3 gives the official Soviet breakdown of merchandise trade in 1960, in the trade-partner categories used in Soviet sources, but converted from roubles to dollars at the official exchange rate.

All Soviet merchandise trade was growing at that time from very low levels. It was characteristic of Soviet policy that in most years there was a surplus in the balance of merchandise trade (*Narkhoz 64*, p. 660). It was also characteristic of Soviet policy that much important detail was not reported. In the 1964 annual handbook, *Narkhoz 64*, only seven out 796 pages are devoted to foreign trade. One thing that was not readily apparent, but

Table 3.3   *The political-geographical composition of soviet merchandise trade in 1960 ($m)*

	Soviet exports	Soviet imports
CMEA partners	3,118	2,819
Other socialist countries	1,094	1,159
Developed West	1,015	1,116
Developing countries	337	534
Total	5,564	5,628

Note: Converted from foreign-trade roubles at 0.90 roubles = $1. See text.
Source: Derived from *VT SSSR 22–81*, Table II.

could be deduced with some detective work, was that in most of the Khrushchev period the Soviet Union was running a deficit in merchandise trade settled in convertible ('hard') currency.

The distinction between hard-currency trade and other (bilateral or 'barter') trade was of great practical importance. It did not correspond neatly with the trade-partner categories used in Soviet reporting, as in Table 3.3 above.

Soviet hard-currency trade was trade with the developed West except Finland and with some developing countries – chiefly the former. In its other trade, with Finland, with CMEA partners, with other socialist countries such as China, and with some major Third-World trade partners (Egypt, India and many others), the Soviet Union had bilateral settlement arrangements. That is, two-way flows of merchandise were planned to off-set one another; if one partner ended the year with a deficit vis-à-vis the other, it would normally offset that in the following year by delivering more than it received.

Bilateral balancing has all the disadvantages of barter between individuals. It is unlikely that countries will trade efficiently on that basis. Prices will typically be manipulated, or unwanted merchandise accepted, to strike an accounting balance. But a centrally administered economy cannot operate in any other way when trading with another centrally administered economy. Neither of them has a currency that is freely convertible into goods even for its own residents, let alone for non-residents. Therefore neither has a currency that the other can hold as a claim on the other country's resources: their currencies are not money in an international sense, because they are far from fulfilling all the standard functions of money even domestically. Therefore the Soviet Union could not finance a deficit with East Germany from a surplus with Hungary: it had to try to balance bilaterally with each separate 'barter-trade' partner. This practice was extended to developing countries with which the USSR had close trading links. Such close links often involved Soviet arms sales. These countries, too, often had inconvertible currencies. Bilateral trading was extended to Finland because history and geography gave the Finns very little choice in the matter. This is how Finland came to be the only state in the developed West to import Soviet nuclear reactors.

Hard-currency trade had to be planned separately from bilaterally balanced trade. The Soviet planners aimed to manage their external financial position so as either to balance their trade settled in hard currency overall (e.g. using surpluses earned in Europe to offset deficits with the US) or to keep any borrowing from the West at manageable levels that would not allow Western politicians to exert leverage on Soviet policies. The chief form that such borrowing took was the provision of official credit support (see below).

What was happening was obscured by publishing neither overall balance-of-payments nor reserves data. These were state secrets. Western efforts at elucidating the Soviet external financial position in hard currency transactions probably, however, got reasonably close to the truth. There was no inward or outward direct or portfolio investment to worry about. Services transactions (shipping, tourism, etc.) were small and amenable to estimation. Borrowing in the form of Western official credit support for capital goods exports to the Soviet Union (via the Export Credit Guarantee Department in the UK, Eximbank in the US, Hermes in West Germany, etc.) could be tracked. So, with rather more difficulty, could some borrowing on the Euro-currency markets.

Soviet sales of gold on the Swiss market were estimated with a wide margin of error. Heroic assumptions and satellite photography were used to guesstimate annual supplies of monetary gold from Soviet production. Given guesstimated gold sales, guesstimated monetary gold production and more heroic assumptions, this time about the starting level of gold reserves, levels of and changes in the gold reserves followed – as guesstimates. Much later, when the Soviet Union collapsed, rumours circulated about alleged quantities of gold that had been smuggled out of the country by Communist Party officials. Not surprisingly, it proved impossible to confirm the amounts involved.

This guesstimation of Soviet external finances gave employment to a small army of Western specialists. On the Soviet side, less than a platoon of Soviet high officials was allowed to know what the true position was.

For all the margins of error involved, there is not much doubt that the Soviet external financial position deteriorated in 1960–64. Here is a good estimate of the changing situation, made in the early 1970s.

Table 3.4   *Soviet hard-currency trade and external finances, 1960–64 ($m and %)*

	HC X	HC M	HC b/t	Gold sales	Gold reserves	Debt service	DSR (%)
1960	768	1,018	−250	200	2,555	39	6
1961	900	1,061	−161	300	2,365	76	8
1962	951	1,184	−233	215	2,250	116	12
1963	1,052	1,237	−225	550	1,800	144	14
1964	1,073	1,556	−483	450	1,495	162	15

Key: HC = hard-currency. X = merchandise exports. M = merchandise imports. b/t = balance of merchandise trade. DSR = debt-service ratio = debt service as % of merchandise exports.
Note: gold reserves are end-year figures. They are valued at the then-fixed price for monetary gold of $35 per Troy ounce.
Source: Farrell 1973, Tables 1 and 2.

If the estimates in Table 3.4 are reliable as to orders of magnitude, they suggest a mild but chronic difficulty: in its convertible-currency trade at this time, the USSR was tending to run merchandise trade deficits; this probably meant in turn that there were current-account deficits; these were financed (on the capital account) in part by gold sales, drawing down reserves, and in part by borrowing.

By the usual international standards of the day this was not particularly problematic: gold reserves at end-1964 still covered almost a year's hard-currency imports; other imports were required to be covered by exports under bilateral arrangements; the debt-service ratio was well below levels that might conventionally be considered dangerous (in that era, 25 per cent or more).

It is likely, however, that the handful of Soviet policy-makers who knew the situation and understood it, did not judge by the customary standards of capitalist international finance. If later Soviet policy is anything to go by, they were extremely risk-averse. They saw the capitalist world as hostile and very powerful. It was important not to give the West anything resembling economic leverage. Reserves should be kept high, and debts low (see Hanson 1981, chapter 7).

Why, then, did the Soviet economy at this time keep bumping up against these self-imposed prudential limits? The short answer, it may be conjectured, is as follows. The Soviet economy was particularly weak in two areas: agricultural production and the introduction and diffusion of new products and processes. Both weaknesses could be remedied in part through trade with the capitalist world, by importing food, new equipment, licences and know-how in exchange for items in which the Soviet economy had a systemic comparative advantage: non-food, non-high technology goods.

Under Stalin, the importation of food had not been on the agenda: grain was exported even when people were starving (see Chapter 1). Technological progress was achieved mainly by organised copying, boosted by two large injections of Western technology, in the early 1930s and again in the Second World War, under Lend-Lease (Sutton 1968, 1971). By the late 1950s, however, things were changing. New priorities and softer social controls made food imports an option. New injections of foreign technology to upgrade neglected sectors like the chemical industry could no longer be obtained for free. Import bills therefore increased, but Soviet export capabilities could not easily be expanded in line. Therefore the exploitation of what might be called systemic comparative advantage was constantly being constrained by the limitations on what could be found to export to the West – together with the self-imposed constraints of extreme financial prudence, rooted in fear of the West. Only the OPEC oil-price hikes of the 1970s eased these constraints for a decade or so; they strengthened the Soviet terms of trade with the West, increasing Soviet international buying power.

In the early 1960s world market conditions were less helpful. The poor Soviet harvest of 1963 (see the previous section) tested Soviet policy to the limits. In crop year 1963–64 unprecedentedly large amounts of grain were imported: 7.3 million tons, mostly from the West. This was the first occasion on which the Soviet Union became a net importer of grain – to the extent of 3.8 million tons, according to Soviet sources (derived from *Narkhoz 64*, pp. 661, 662). Total food imports in 1964 were a fifth of all imports, and somewhat over $1.5 billion (derived from pp. 660, 664). It is likely that this outcome was viewed as extremely dangerous by other members of the Soviet leadership, and contributed to Khrushchev's downfall. It would have been easy, though misleading, to say that Khrushchev's farm policies had failed, and that by recklessly approving the import of large amounts of foodstuffs he had weakened Soviet external finances and was thus jeopardising Soviet security.

The shift to larger-scale importation of Western machinery was less visible and politically less controversial. It was, however, real enough. Soviet statistics show machinery rising from a fifth of total imports in 1950 to over a third by 1963–64 (*Narkhoz 64*, p. 664). By no means all of those machinery imports were from the West. Large amounts came from the German Democratic Republic and Czechoslovakia, the most industrially advanced of the CMEA countries. But Western machinery embodied the most advanced technology and was beginning to be fairly systematically used to upgrade lagging industries: chemicals, in Khrushchev's time, and later the motor industry as well.

In particular, only Western companies could provide turnkey projects. These are projects in which a complete new plant is built under the management of a single plant contractor. The plant contractor designs, procures equipment, assembles, installs, trains local staff, tests the installed equipment and finally commissions the plant: that is, demonstrates that it will operate at design capacity, and hands it over to the customer ready to operate, usually with maintenance and service arrangements included. No communist organisation was designed to do all this. Equipment producers in CMEA countries produced equipment according to their plan targets, shipped the equipment to the centralised supply system, and had nothing more to do with it.

Turnkey projects for the Soviet chemical industry began in the late 1950s. They necessarily involved a great deal of personal contact between foreigners and Soviet citizens, both at home and abroad. The synthetic-fibre complex built at Mogilev by the Polyspinners Consortium under a contract signed in 1964, under Khrushchev, entailed the following: 52 Soviet engineers spending three months in the UK with Constructors John Brown; 20 Soviet machinery inspectors mostly spending two years in the UK; at least 110 specialist operatives being trained in the UK; 200 British technical staff spending several months at a time over a two-year period in Moscow in the detailed engineering phase, and a few hundred British construction technicians and supervisors, and their families, spending up to four years at the construction site in Mogilev (Jones 1973).

This was a remarkable change from the late Stalin era, when Muscovites would make a detour of a couple of blocks around the Metropole Hotel to minimise the risk of being accused of contacts with foreigners. Even under the more repressive regime of Leonid Brezhnev, however, such close commercial and industrial contacts continued and, indeed, increased. The need for Western technology outweighed the danger of ideological contagion.

One presentational curiosity on the foreign-trade front is worth noting. From the beginning of 1961 the Soviet rouble was 'revalued' from 25 cents (4 roubles to the dollar) to $1.11 (90 kopecks to the dollar). This looked like a sign of strength: the rouble looking the dollar in the face. That impression needed, however, to be qualified. First, the official exchange rate was of little practical importance; the rouble was inconvertible (see above), so the exchange rate had nothing to do with supply and demand for the rouble. Second, the rouble simultaneously underwent a domestic re-denomination: one new rouble was now equivalent to ten old roubles. The old rouble had been equivalent, officially, to 25 cents and the new one was equivalent to $1.11. In terms of the new rouble the dollar had risen from 40 kopecks to

90 kopecks. What had in fact taken place was a rouble devaluation – albeit of a meaningless exchange rate. It was presented as the opposite: a revaluation.

Even Soviet citizens with no experience of foreign transactions could work this out if they read the small print of the 1961 statistical handbook carefully (*Narkhoz 61*, pp. 4, 668). The overwhelming majority of Soviet citizens, no doubt, had better things to do. If anyone applauded this sleight of hand, it would have been the Western analysts.

Incomes and consumption

By 1960 the main policy changes improving the lot of Soviet people had been introduced: the shorter working week, the reform of wage-scales, the start of the housing programme and above all the improvement in incentives and investment priorities for agricultural producers. The subsequent slowdown in economic growth and the 1963 harvest failure produced a slowdown in the growth of material welfare. The best available estimate of consumption levels provides a growth rate of per capita real household consumption of 1.9 per cent a year for 1960–64 (at 1970 established prices; derived from Schroeder and Denton 1982, Tables A-1 and A-2, with the collective consumption items, health and education excluded from their total consumption index). A rate of improvement close to 2 per cent a year is of course not to be sniffed at; still, it was a slowdown.

One of the characteristics of the period was an increase in repressed inflation. Money incomes were allowed to increase by substantially more than the supplies of consumer goods and services at state-controlled prices.

In principle, this is something that central planning ought to be able to avoid. The state after all is the sole employer and universal paymaster. It is also planning and in principle determining both prices and quantities of consumer goods and services. The planners, some Western economists have suggested, should be able to achieve macro-economic balance in the market for consumer goods, since they are planning both the demand (household income) and the supply (production) sides of the consumer market. Even if they often get micro-balance wrong, overproducing some goods and underproducing others, relative to demand at fixed prices, they ought to be able to ensure that total disposable incomes, net of estimated intentional saving, should match total planned supply of goods and services at established prices.

In practice, Soviet planners regularly failed to do this. Output of food and consumer goods was particularly prone to fall short of targets, while money wages did not. And money wages, in fact, tended to overshoot

Table 3.5 *Soviet personal incomes, consumption and repressed inflation, 1960–64 (units as indicated below)*

	1960	1964	% change
1. Total disposable money incomes (R bn, p.a.)	86.25	111.94	29.79
2. Per capita money income (R p.a.)	402.47	491.61	22.15
3. Per capita consumption (1970 = 100)	69.0	74.3	7.68
4. Household savings[a] (R mn)	853	1715	101.06
5. Per capita household savings (roubles)	3.9	7.53	93.08
6. *Kolkhoz* market prices (1950 = 100)	108	138	27.78

Note: a. The increment during the year of the stock of savings in Sberbank (savings bank) accounts. Changes in the amount of notes and coins in the hands of the population should ideally be included as well, but the data are lacking.
Sources: 1. Bronson and Severin 1973, Table B-1. 2. Derived from Bronson and Severin with mid-year population figures interpolated from end-year data in *Narkhoz 64*, p. 7. 3. Derived from Schroeder and Denton 1982, Table A-2, adjusting to exclude the collective consumption items, education and health, using their weights in the total from Table A-1. 4. Derived from *Narkhoz 61*, p. 607, and *Narkhoz 64*, p. 595. 5. *Narkhoz 64*, p. 659.

targets, in part because the planners persistently underestimated the growth of the state labour force, and in part because of earnings drift, as workers were promoted to higher wage-scales and piece-rates and bonuses were above plan. Underlying the planning failure on the demand side was the fundamental character of the economy. It was a shortage economy, in which producers had little incentive to economise on inputs and constantly sought to employ more workers, overshooting the wage-bill ceilings in their individual enterprise plans. To make matters worse, the sum of approved enterprise labour-force plans could and often did exceed the national total planned employment figure (Hanson 1986).

This tended to generate excess consumer demand at established prices, and therefore queues, shortages, unintended savings and black markets. This propensity to repressed inflation seems to have been very modest in the late 1950s, as supplies of consumer goods and services expanded. In the early 1960s it emerged rather strongly, as Table 3.5 indicates.

The figures in Table 3.5 are unavoidably of lower quality than could be produced for a developed country. The picture they present, however, is clear, even if margins of error of 5 per cent are attached to all the annual totals (except the population totals used). The disposable money income data were derived by Bronson and Severin from a number of Soviet sources and should include everything: wages, pensions, other benefits, interest from savings-bank accounts, etc. The consumption series is from an authoritative, well-documented CIA study. My adjustment to exclude education and health services, in order to focus on household consumption proper, is arithmetically tiny. The official Soviet index of peasant-market prices was based on a survey of markets in 251 towns.

It is clear that money incomes rose substantially more than the supplies of goods and services available for consumption. The latter were nearly all at fixed prices. The *kolkhoz* market prices were the only prices of any general significance that were not controlled. Their steep increase over time (6.3 per cent a year) indicates increased shortages of food in the state shops, with their controlled prices. The even faster increase in the annual flow of savings per head (17.9 per cent a year) strongly suggests that at least some of that saving was 'forced' or involuntary: frustrated spending.

This environment of repressed inflation, or shortage, is not readily comprehended by Westerners or, for that matter, by young Russians with no memory of communism. Most Soviet citizens had subsidised but severely cramped accommodation – often, still, multi-household apartments. They spent little on their housing. Food supplies were increasingly becoming subsidised, as farm prices were pushed up and retail prices were held unchanged (see below). Having money in your pocket but nothing to spend it on was a common experience. People carried (in this period) string bags with them wherever they went, just in case they happened across some item in short supply.[2] Hours each week were spent queuing. Roubles were, even then, routinely referred to as 'Monopoly money'. Privileged access to scarce goods was far more important than money income in determining who got what. Simply living in Moscow was a source of material privilege; the city was far better supplied than the provinces.

The notion that a foreigner might have the opposite problem – plenty of goods in the shops but a shortage of money – was something few Soviet citizens could grasp. It was rapidly becoming well known, at any rate in Moscow, that shortages and queues were not the norm in the West. The corollary, that rationing by price meant most people lived close to or even above their incomes, was less comprehensible. Hence the apparently impudent requests to visitors for expensive items from the Western cornucopia. In the mid-1980s it was not unusual to be asked, quite casually, if you could bring someone a laptop computer on your next visit.

Consumer shortages never went away, so long as the Soviet Union lasted. Nonetheless, their existence denoted neither general poverty nor a lack of material improvement over time. Soviet citizens were consuming more, as housing, food supplies and manufactured consumer goods all became more abundant. The difficulty was that for much of the last 30 years of Soviet history the growth of money incomes tended to outrun the growth of consumer supplies, and retail prices were held mostly constant.

The reason for not raising retail prices was simple: the Soviet leaders feared it would provoke an uprising. This was not pure paranoia on their part. Nationwide increases in the retail prices of meat and dairy products in 1962 produced a wave of workers' protests (Belotserkovsky 1979). The best known of these took place in the southern Russian city of Novocherkassk in June 1962. This and similar events could be interpreted to mean that the leaders' fears were justified.

On a day when three members of the ruling Politburo (known at that time as the Presidium of the Central Committee of the Party) were in Novocherkassk, workers from the local Electric Locomotive Works marched in protest, demanding meat, milk, and wage increases. Whether they were demanding specifically that price rises should be rescinded is not clear, but the price increases had just been implemented. There was very likely no meat and dairy produce to be had in the shops in Novocherkassk at any price. But meat prices in the factory canteen had doubled overnight. 'If you can't afford to buy meat, eat liver pies instead', the factory director is reported to have said (*Daily Telegraph*, 4 June 1996).

These workers' money wages had recently been cut, and that, rather than the price increases, was perhaps the main stimulus for the protest. At all events, they marched to the local Party head office, where the visiting leaders were, in order to present their demands.

They refused to disperse. Local troops, reportedly, refused to fire on the demonstrators. Troops were brought in from elsewhere, who did fire on them, killing 22 or 23. There were protests elsewhere, though apparently with less dramatic outcomes (see Solzhenitsyn 1976, pp. 507–14 on Novocherkassk; also Filtzer 1993, p. 52; Naumov 2000, pp. 110–11).

The Novocherkassk protest was not discussed publicly in the USSR until 1990. It seems however to have had a substantial effect on the thinking of the leadership.

The regime became somewhat more repressive in general, and increases in food prices were eschewed thereafter. That produced a textbook illustration of how shortages come about. Money incomes and spending power rose. Food prices did not. Food output, including meat and dairy produce, tended in most years of the 1960s and 1970s to increase faster than population. But it did not increase rapidly enough to match demand at the controlled, and now frozen, state retail prices.

Economic debate

Khrushchev did not institute a reform of the Soviet economic system. That is to say, he did not authorise any general changes in planning criteria or in incentives for managers, and he did not preside over any attempts at devolving decision-making powers to enterprise managers. The *sovnarkhozy* (see Chapter 2) were a reshuffle rather than a reform: the intermediate level in the planning hierarchy was switched from economic branches to geographical territories. But Khrushchev did preside over a general opening up of economic discussion in the USSR. That discussion contributed to reforms – unsuccessful reforms, it must be said – that came later.

Several new economic debates got under way in the late 1950s and early 1960s. The new school of Soviet mathematical economists (see the previous chapter) raised questions about how prices should be set, by what criteria planners should allocate resources, and indeed about the extent to which decisions on what to produce and in what quantities should be devolved to the level of individual production units.

At the same time there were specialists with more mundane interests, who now were able publicly to draw attention to particular deficiencies in the Soviet economy. Solomon Kheinman and Yakov Kvasha (see Venzher *et al.* 1965) stressed a range of weaknesses in the engineering sector in comparison with the engineering industries of the developed West. V.G. Venzher proposed that collective farms should be allowed to decide for themselves what and how much to produce, responding to centrally set procurement prices – something already practised in Hungary (*ibid.*). Evsey Liberman proposed (*Pravda* 9 September 1962, p. 3) that enterprise managers be rewarded on the basis of profits – a proposal whose stress on profits and whose prominent place of publication quickly earned notoriety for it in the West. Liberman had in fact been arguing along these lines since the late 1950s, though in publications less visible than *Pravda* – the official Party newspaper. His theme was the need to make the interests of society and of the individual producer coincide. He saw the need to provide enterprise managers with better incentives for efficient use of resources, and he advocated looser, more aggregated plans 'from above'.

Liberman was, however, rather vague about how prices should be determined – a question that was obviously fundamental to the incentive effects of profits-based bonuses. Other Soviet economists, and not only the optimal planners, were aware of the problem, and showed how prices might be reformed. (See Zaleski 1967, pp. 77–83, and particularly his discussion of the 1963 and 1964 writings of L. Vaag and S. Zakharov.)

Another debate was conducted primarily among scientists and writers, not economists, though its economic significance was enormous. This was the debate on technological progress (e.g. Dudintsev 1957, Kapitsa 1966). Was the Soviet Union really catching up with US technology? Were its efforts in research, development and innovation really cost-effective?

It was in the early 1960s that a new field of studies emerged in the Soviet Union – *naukovedenie* or science studies. Developed mainly by people with a hard-science background, it encompassed citation studies and other analyses of scientific communication. The *naukovedy* showed – usually in ways that the censors could not easily unravel – that Soviet science, and not just its application, often lagged behind, and that the semi-isolation imposed on Soviet scientists hampered their work (Rabkin 1977).

The last of these debates was the one that had the greatest immediate resonance for policymakers. Worries about the Soviet Union's continuing technological lag behind the US were voiced by Prime Minister Aleksey Kosygin, though not by Khrushchev, at the XXI Party Congress in 1959; at the next Party Congress, in 1961, even Khrushchev introduced a note of concern about the dangers of 'technological conservatism' (Hanson 1981, pp. 92–3).

Practice had as usual preceded rhetoric. Khrushchev had by then already sanctioned a heavy reliance on imported technology for his chemicalisation drive (see Chapter 2). The need to make use of foreign technology, including by purchasing foreign machinery and licences, had in effect already been tacitly acknowledged. The USSR did not sign up to the Paris Convention on the Protection of Industrial Property (undertaking to acknowledge certain rights of foreign patentees) until 1965. But movement in that direction was under way before Khrushchev was ousted. In particular, a new foreign trade organisation, Litsenzintorg, was set up in 1962, to manage trade in licences (*op. cit.*, p. 111).

The public record of these economic debates is bland. All publications were of course censored. Authors therefore used Aesopian language or simply toned down what they had to say. Informal discussions were more forthright. A generation later, in 1985, the distinguished economic journalist, Vasiliy Selyunin, wrote a penetrating analysis of the shortcomings of Soviet reform experiments in general. He showed very clearly that the core problem left untouched by all these exercises was the fact that producers were always responding to output targets set from above; he explained how this created a perennial regime of shortage, with no incentives to economise on inputs. He also mentioned that he owed his insights into these fundamental problems to an economic journalist of an older generation, with whom he and others had many discussions in the editorial offices of the newspaper *Sotsialisticheskaya industriya* in the 1960s (Selyunin 1985). Before 1985 thoughts as trenchant as these about the very nature of the system could not have been published. The main writings by the Hungarian Janos Kornai on the 'shortage economy' – theoretically elaborated and more systematic than Selyunin, but with the same bottom line – were simply not published in Russian.[3]

The mathematical economists attracted the most interest in the West. Eventually they produced a mass of writings on the system of the optimally functioning economy – now essentially a curiosity in the history of economic thought (summarised in Fedorenko 1983). Amongst them there were several who later played a part, in the late 1980s, in the policy debates about truly radical reform. These included Abel Aganbegyan, Nikolai Petrakov, Stanislav Shatalin and Evgeny Yasin. Of these only one, Yasin, retained a substantial role in policy-making in post-communist Russia.

In 1963 the Central Economics-Mathematical Institute (TsEMI) was established. This provided the mathematical economists with an organisational base independent of the Institute of Economics (both institutes coming under the Soviet Academy of Scientists). Their programme of work was at first directed mainly at reforming the national system of economic information and creating the documentation for a unified national system of data-processing centres (Sutela 1984, p. 89).[4]

Behind this and similar tasks was the intellectual apparatus of linear (and also non-linear) programming which, in principle, could guide planners towards the most efficient allocation of resources for maximising a given objective function (say, total output of a given product-mix) from given resources and subject to the constraints of available technologies for transforming factor inputs into outputs and of available supplies of factors of production.

The programming approach had been developed much earlier by Kantorovich for very specific, quasi-engineering purposes: initially for improving productivity in one factory with a given product-mix. Extending this approach to the national economy as a whole generated criticisms of existing methods of planning.

To begin with, programming aimed at maximising the ratio of output to inputs. In contrast, traditional Soviet planning methods did not aim at efficiency at all; they were directed towards internal consistency (material balances showing sources and uses of major products) and increased output (national growth targets disaggregated into growth targets for all, or almost all, production units). By considering the opportunity cost of using a unit of labour (say) in one line of production in terms of what that unit might have added to output in other lines of production, the optimal planners were raising questions that the Soviet Union's real planners were not even addressing.

Second, the optimal planning approach demonstrated that prices (of factors of production, intermediate products and final products) would best guide planners towards efficient plans if they reflected marginal productivities. This conflicted with Soviet price-setting practice. Even when the mathematical economists argued only that planners should use 'shadow prices' (for planning purposes only) that would have this property, they were open to the criticism that they were departing from Marxist-Leninist orthodoxy including the labour theory of value, and importing methods from bourgeois economics. Much effort went into demonstrating the Marxist propriety of what was being proposed. The TsEMI economists, by and large, were not challenging the authority of the state to decide what final output should consist of; but they were challenging the effectiveness of existing methods of achieving desired output levels.

Third, their approach brought into focus the information problems of central planning. It cast doubt on the sustainability of existing methods of planning as the economy increased in size, in the number of final products and in the number of flows of intermediate products between separate accounting units. This in turn led many economists, not only at TsEMI, to argue that the central planners should deal only with aggregated numbers (total output of groups of products, average prices of those product groups), while individual enterprises should be free, within these aggregated plan targets, to set output levels of particular products and even particular prices. Any suggestion along those lines, in the eyes of the central planners and of their political masters, seemed to be a dilution of central control, and therefore to be feared. In this, the traditionalists were almost certainly right.

One product of the mathematical turn in Soviet economics was the re-importation of input–output analysis: 're-importation' because the origins of this technique can be traced back to early Soviet planning calculations of the early 1920s, and it was an emigré with experience in that work, the Nobel prize-winner Wassily Leontief, who developed input–output analysis in the US.

Input–output tables can be developed that show the flows of intermediate products between branches of the economy as well as flows of final products from each branch (and from imports) to final use, whether consumption, investment, exports or government purchase. A very large data-collection exercise is needed to draw up a historical picture of the inter-industry flows in a given year. Once these are known, however, they could potentially be used, along with much other information, in drawing up national production plans for a future year. The advantage – again, in principle – of using input–output in national plans is that it should provide for the indirect effects of raising the production of one product (say, tractors) on the required outputs of steel, rubber, plastic and other necessary materials, and in turn on the required inputs of coking coal, iron ore, etc. for the steel, and so on.

Input–output tables had been developed for the US economy for purposes of war mobilisation. In normal times the firms in a market economy will sort out their own supply requirements; the intervention of the central government in inter-industry flows of products would be entirely inappropriate. In the event of rapid mobilisation for war, however, some central planning might be needed to ensure that strategically vital lines of production received the material inputs they needed. For this, input–output data would be useful. At all events, those who argued, in Cold War times, for the funding of American input–output studies on these grounds, got their way. The Soviet economy, for which a case could be made for such studies for normal peacetime planning purposes, had lagged behind.

The first input–output tables for the Soviet economy were for 1959 and one (inter-industry flows in value terms between 83 sectors) was published in *Narkhoz 60*. The published versions were, for predictable reasons, incomplete. For example, sensitive industries like radio and electronics were omitted (Treml *et al.* 1973, p. 248).

Soviet input–output analysis blossomed thereafter. That is to say, it kept many Soviet economists and statisticians occupied, and it also kept a small contingent of Western specialists busy trying to fill in the gaps. But it had little if any practical consequences for the way in which Soviet economic plans were put together (*ibid.*). In this it shared the fate of Soviet mathematical economics in general.

One good reason for this is to do with the requirements of central planning. If the central authorities wish, as the Soviet central authorities did until the system collapsed, to be in control of all the detail, the planners have to set national output targets for many thousands of products and product groups (see the first section of Chapter 1). Getting base-year data for such a task entered into a computer system, even a modern computer system, is a monumental task. The Soviet planners had *ad hoc* ways of dealing with supply shortages: for instance, telling producers to get on with it anyway, and diverting some supplies in mid-plan to higher-priority users. They stuck to increasing everyone's output targets 'from the achieved levels', which tended to freeze the production structure but at least minimised the risk of major supply snarl-ups. Then continual phone-calls, telexes and telegrams during the year provided a way of muddling through. Putting all the information needed for an internally consistent plan for some 20,000 product groups on to the computer first was not a practical option.

In addition, the data were poor, and insiders knew this. Treml drew attention to the remarkable speed with which Soviet input-output tables had been compiled, and raised doubts about their quality (*ibid.*). Two economists who had been engaged in the work later recounted the many and dubious short-cuts that had been employed (Tret'yakova and Birman 1976).

Despite the ability and enthusiasm of many of the individuals concerned, the revolution in Soviet economics seems, in retrospect, remarkably unproductive. Some might question whether that distinguishes it in any way from advances in economics elsewhere. But in the Soviet case, it was not so much that economists flooded into the government machine and national economic performance stayed much the same (as in the UK around the same time), but rather that the academic economists and the practical planners remained far apart. The new ideas bounced off the planning organs and did not penetrate them. There was communication between TsEMI and like-minded economists in the Gosplan Research Institute, but very little between Gosplan and its own Research Institute.

Other ideas, like Liberman's profit-related management bonuses, did eventually have some practical consequences, in their partial implementation in the 1965 reforms (see Chapter 4), but these were often perverse in their effects. Profits in the USSR, after all, were the product of input and output prices that did not, except by chance, reflect supply and demand. With misleading prices, profits are guaranteed to be a misleading guide to efficient resource allocation.

One radical organisational experiment was undertaken in Khrushchev's time, albeit on a tiny scale. This was the freeing of two light-industry enterprises, Bol'shevichka and Mayak, from all output targets; they were then instructed to produce (from their given capacity and product range) simply according to orders received from the trade network. The results for Bol'shevichka, a clothing factory, over the year from September 1964, were monitored and reported in some detail. The percentage fulfilment of trade orders was high, but it was highest for those products for which the factory's profit margin was highest, and lowest for those products on which it stood to make a loss (for details, see Hanson 1968, pp. 196–7). This showed entirely rational economic behaviour on the part of the factory's managers, but they were responding rationally to arbitrary wholesale prices over which neither they nor their customers could exert any influence.

This was an early illustration of the pitfalls of partial reforms. There were to be many more before Russia moved on to the pitfalls of comprehensive reform.

Khrushchev and the economy in retrospect

When Khrushchev was removed from power in October 1964, it was not primarily because of economic failures. There were economic failures, and a slowdown in growth, in the early 1960s, but the leader's alienation of most other members of the Party leadership was probably the main problem.

In general, middle-level Party officials and Khrushchev's leadership colleagues had, by 1964, had their lives disrupted by frequent reorganisations and priority changes. The 'steel-eaters' – the Party and state officials based in defence and industrial-producer-goods branches – had been resisting his attempts to give agriculture and consumption a higher priority. It was easy, and not entirely unfair, to present Khrushchev as a chancer and bungler, whose re-organisations and priority changes too often made things worse. This was a characterisation that could be applied across the board – to security and foreign policy and to the management of the Party, as well as to the economy.

Nonetheless, Khrushchev's major priority changes, as distinct from his product-and-process campaigns, were not later reversed.

Notes

1   'Soviet power' is *'Sovetskaya vlast''* in Russian.

2   An economist at the Central Economics-Mathematical Institute provided (in conversation) an example. He had been in a village outside Moscow where he saw, in the village shop, a display of French camel-hair coats. He bought a dozen on the spot. The coats were there by an odd fluke of planning: there was a bilateral agreement between a French retail cooperative society and the (nominally cooperative) rural retail network of the Russian Federation. Hence these exotic garments had never made it to the urban retail system. Why buy a dozen? All he said was, 'I might never see a camel-hair coat again.' The implicit answer was that he would sell at least eleven of them at a handsome profit.

3   It seems that few people even in private conversations articulated the proposition that pervasive state ownership was incompatible with an efficient and dynamic economy. I asked the economist Viktor Belkin about this in 1990. He said that reformers like himself did not even think in the 1960s about challenging the socialist regime as such, not so much out of a belief in it but because they accepted it as a given.

4   I visited TsEMI in 1964. When I asked to see the TsEMI Trade Laboratory, I found it was not the high-tech workshop I had imagined but a room containing some chairs and tables, the excellent economist Viktor Volkonskii and a group of young women, all maths graduates, armed with copies of Samuelson's *Foundations of Economic Analysis* and English–Russian dictionaries.

CHAPTER FOUR

A New Start: Brezhnev, 1964–73

The palace coup against Khrushchev put Leonid Brezhnev in charge as Party leader. He retained that position for eighteen years, until his death in 1982. Since then his name has come to be associated with the stagnation and decay of the Soviet system. This is not entirely unfair. He really did preside over a period of economic stagnation and decaying morale. And his most famous successor, Mikhail Gorbachev, made much use of the label 'era of stagnation' (*vremya zastoya*) to denote the morass from which he, Gorbachev, wrongly supposed he was extracting his country.

Political leaders, however, are not impartial judges of their predecessors. It is not surprising, therefore, that the Gorbachev view of Brezhnev's time in office focused on the failures and neglected the successes. So far as Soviet economic performance in the Brezhnev era is concerned, three qualifications to the 'stagnation' label are needed.

First, the Brezhnev era started well, before it ended badly. In approximately the first nine years growth was reasonable: either equal to or somewhat better than in 1960–64. The slowdown became apparent from around 1973, when even the official estimates began to show Soviet per capita production no longer closing the gap with the US. Before then, there were decentralising economic reforms, drawing on the policy debates of the Khrushchev period. Until the Soviet invasion of Czechoslovakia in August 1968, it had even been possible to believe that Moscow might follow Prague and Budapest into more far-reaching reforms. (To be fair to Mr Gorbachev, insofar as he was ever clear about the dating of the *vremya zastoya*, he tended to suggest that it applied to the latter period of Brezhnev's rule.)

Second, the later, 'stagnant' part of the Brezhnev era was one not of zero growth or decline, merely of very slow growth. The figures assembled by Maddison (1995) for GDP in dollars at 1990 international prices show a rate of increase in per capita GDP from 1973 to 1982 of 0.9 per cent per annum. It was above all in relative terms that the Soviet Union was stagnating. Economic growth in the West slowed from the early 1970s as well, the break in Western growth rates being made all the more emphatic by the impact of the first OPEC oil-price hikes in 1973–74; even so, the developed Western countries suffered a slowdown that was less marked than that in the USSR and Central-Eastern Europe. What was happening was therefore bad news for the communist cause and the communist leadership of the time. It did not mean however that consumption levels were falling or even stagnating. CIA estimates for the period 1973–82 yield an average annual growth in per capita consumption of 1.9 per cent – a highly respectable outcome (derived from CIA 1990, pp. 90–93; volumes estimated at 1982 established prices).

The third qualification follows from the second. For many ordinary citizens of Russia and the other ex-Soviet states, the Brezhnev era has come to stand for a time of ease and (comparative) plenty. This surprises many Westerners, who tend to see the communist past as an undifferentiated whole. But as Vladimir Kusin (2001) has put it:

> . . . the poor classes who spent all their lives on communism's primitive outposts see it differently. They experienced three kinds of communism: the malignant (Stalin), the hopeful (Khrushchev, Dubcek, Gorbachev) and the bearable (Brezhnev). Stalin is receding from living memory, reform communism failed and has no new champions, but the Brezhnev days are remembered and compared with what followed.

The beginning of those Brezhnev days was certainly a hopeful time. There were reforms, and economic growth stabilised or slightly improved (the two events were probably unconnected). Only in the late 1960s did the political regime become more oppressive, and only in the early 1970s did the growth slowdown become apparent. (The last two phenomena are also probably unconnected.) The Brezhnev team was by past Soviet standards a coherent one, with a reasonably clear division of responsibilities. Brezhnev was the overall political leader – the enterprise director, as Muscovites put it at the time. Aleksei Kosygin, a man with long experience in industrial administration, was chairman of the USSR Council of Ministers (Prime Minister), and therefore the chief engineer. A Western analogy would be chairman of the board and chief executive officer.

Kosygin had spoken publicly of concerns about the technology lag in the Soviet Union, at a time when Khrushchev was still in triumphalist mode (see Chapter 3). In 1964 he still had to convince some of his colleagues, including Brezhnev, of the seriousness of the problem. It was a problem that was never solved. Still, in this and other matters, Kosygin's practical experience at least fostered policies that were intended to tackle real weaknesses.[1] The utopian ideas that had influenced Khrushchev's approach to the economy were readily abandoned.

Early days

At the March 1965 Plenum of the Communist Party's Central Committee the restrictions on private-plot farming that Khrushchev had introduced after 1958 were removed. This had been foreshadowed by measures taken at the republic level as early as November 1964 (Schoonover 1979, p. 99). The household subsidiary plots remained restricted in size and in livestock holdings, but some ceilings on livestock numbers were raised and usage of collective land for pasture was allowed again. A pension scheme was at last introduced for collective-farm workers. The pragmatism that had prompted Khrushchev's initial encouragement of the collective farms and the household plots was being deployed once more.

The Plenum focused on agriculture, and went well beyond this loosening of controls. Ambitious plans were announced for doubling inputs of machinery and fertiliser in 1966–70, over 1961–65 (Carey and Havelka 1979, p. 58). This was not achieved, but the raised priority for agriculture was clear and did yield some improvement (see below).

Meanwhile, many insiders considered the state of the Soviet economy to be poor. No doubt many had taken a similar view for years, and would do so for years to come, but for mid-1965 we have the text of one of the rare contemporary, unofficial and uncensored documents on the subject. This was a talk by the economist Abel Aganbegyan to a group of editors in June 1965 (Aganbegyan 1965/1982). The text (or possibly notes taken by someone in the audience) was circulated in *samizdat* (underground writings; literally, 'self-publishing'), and leaked to a Western magazine.

Aganbegyan starts with the observation that after 1958 growth in the Soviet economy had slowed markedly, and unexpectedly. He proceeds to describe Soviet economic problems, speaking in the grandiose, evidence-free mode preferred by adolescents and the Russian intelligentsia. Soviet industrial structure 'is the worst and most backward of all the industrially developed countries'. Only half the stock of machine tools is operational. The real rate of unemployment in the major cities is 8 per cent. The standard of living has been declining in 'the last few years'. The situation on the farms is so bad that '. . . if people were allowed to leave the villages, practically no one would stay there'. Many of the official statistics are 'simply absurd'. By contrast, the CIA 'gave [in 1964] an absolutely accurate assessment of the situation in our economy' (except, presumably, that the CIA had missed several years' fall in consumption levels).

The causes of this sorry state of affairs, according to Aganbegyan, were the heavy burden of defence spending (he claimed 30–40 per cent of the workforce were in defence production); losses from trade (he claimed raw material exports were sold at a loss, but did not offer the necessary calculation: how the resource-cost of what was exported compared with the resource-cost that would have been entailed in producing at home what was imported in exchange); bad policies (especially the exploitation of the farm sector); and fundamental systemic weaknesses.

Aganbegyan's speech, at any rate in the text available, is a rant. It is nonetheless of interest because it probably represents the views at the time of a great many Soviet economists. Certainly, an academic visitor to Moscow at that time was likely to hear similar views expounded, over a drink, once it was established that no known informers were around. And Aganbegyan kept a high profile in Soviet economics and in policy advice, becoming an Academician and in the time of *perestroika* acting as an adviser to Gorbachev.

Of particular interest is Aganbegyan's account of the problems stemming from the economic system. Planning methods, he says, are basically unchanged from the 1930s; prices play no role in resource allocation; the interests of the state and of the enterprise are opposed; planners have poor information; the planners' balancing of input supplies with output targets does not work. These points were familiar enough from the published economic debate of the Khrushchev period, albeit more guardedly expressed. But Aganbegyan does not even hint at an alternative vision of how the economy might be run.

He concluded the speech by saying that the *sovnarkhozy* (Khrushchev's regional economic councils, see chapter 2) would be abolished and replaced by branch ministries; but these branch ministries would not be a return to the pre-1957 order. Trusts and concerns (multi-plant management units) would be created that would be 'fully independent' and the ministries would not 'get in the way of the managers'.

How any of this would produce a planned, socialist economy that would be dynamic and efficient, Aganbegyan did not say. But that was a question that nobody managed to answer, then or later.

The 1965 reform

The September 1965 plenum of the Party Central Committee focused on reform in the sense of a decentralisation of economic decision-making. This came to be the classic sense in which the word 'reform' was used in Soviet-type economies, and the 1960s were its heyday. There had been some measures of this sort in Poland in the late 1950s and in East Germany in 1963; there were to be further decentralisation attempts in Czechoslovakia and Hungary in 1968 – the former cut short by the Soviet invasion in August of that year, the latter enduring, with both setbacks and renewals, until communism collapsed. The 'Kosygin reforms', as they came to be known, were therefore not an isolated event. The track record of such reform can now be seen to be poor. At the time, however, both policy-makers and observers had high hopes.

Behind the academic debate in Czechoslovakia, Poland, Hungary and the USSR there lurked the notion of 'market socialism'. The weight of Marxist-Leninist teaching was against the very idea that market relations (what Marxists termed 'commodity-money relations') could play a more than marginal role in a socialist economy. This was theology, however, and therefore adjustable. The Yugoslavs, who already had a nominally decentralised economy with enterprises nominally controlled by workers' councils, claimed to be more authentic in their Marxism than Moscow; in 1965 they were in the process of making their decentralisation real rather than nominal. Workers' control was for Moscow the ultimate heresy. Still, the idea of an economy in which state-owned production units contracted freely with one another, setting at least current output levels and some prices for themselves, was not taboo in Soviet public debate between about 1956 and 1968.

Like the reforms in East Germany, Poland and Hungary, the Kosygin reforms stopped well short of this. (The real decentralisation in Yugoslavia was reined back from 1973, so it lasted there for at most eight years.) Nonetheless, the Kosygin measures were important: not for their meagre practical consequences but because they were a conspicuous lesson in the limits of Soviet reform. This, I hope, justifies the space devoted to them here. So far as gains for ordinary people were concerned, Ellman (1969, p. 297) was surely right to say that the liberalising decisions of the March Plenum on agriculture, described in the previous section, were more important.

Kosygin's long speech to the Plenum on 27 September 1965 set out the measures and their rationale. He noted the recent deterioration in economic performance, and made a case for some decentralisation: 'We must give up the habit of thinking that in the relations between controlling economic authorities and enterprises, the former have nothing but rights and the latter have nothing but obligations' (Kosygin 1965, p. 4).

The new measures were listed in a Central Committee resolution published in the Soviet press on 1 October 1965. They were supplemented by many changes in detailed regulations, introduced mainly in 1966, and completed by a comprehensive revision of wholesale prices that took effect from 1 January 1967 for manufactured consumer goods (food processing, textiles, footwear and clothing) and from 1 July 1967 for other industrial goods. The speeches and leading documents concentrated on the industrial sector, but the changes also applied in construction, transport, retail and wholesale trade, other services and, in agriculture, to the state farms (the collective farms continued to operate differently, with peasant earnings determined as residual net revenue; see Chapter 1).

The main provisions of the 1965 reform were as follows. (Here and in some of the discussion of the measures I draw heavily on Ellman 1969 and Zaleski 1967.)

1. Branch ministries were re-established, replacing the regional economic councils as the second layer of the planning hierarchy. (By August 1966 there were 39 branch ministries and two sectoral state committees [Zaleski 1967, p. 18].)
2. The number of performance indicators imposed from above was reduced (in principle).
3. Bonuses for managers and other employees were to be derived from profits, calculated in relation to the enterprise wage fund (the total wage bill prescribed from above) and determined chiefly by fulfilment of targets for sales and profits. There were similar arrangements for an enterprise social-cultural and housing fund and for a production-development fund (for investment from retained profits).
4. Wholesale prices were to be revised so that a 'normally working enterprise' would make a profit. These prices were set in 1967 on the basis of branch-average cost (labour, energy, materials, depreciation) per unit of output plus a margin equivalent to a 15 per cent return on capital.
5. Enterprises would pay from gross profits (i.e. this was not treated as a cost item) a capital charge, which went to the state budget.
6. There was to be a shift from centrally planned supply of material inputs towards 'wholesale trading' among enterprises. This would be at centrally set prices but was intended to decentralise output and supply decisions.
7. Enterprises were to be given long-term as well as annual plans. This was not implemented until the 1971–75 plan.

The indicators that were to be set from above were the following.

1. Sales. This replaced gross output as the main indicator.
2. The physical quantities of main items in the product-mix.
3. The wage fund (a financial ceiling).

4. Total profits.
5. The rate of profit as a percentage of fixed plus working capital.
6. Payments due to and from the state budget.
7. Input supply allocations and the allocation by the supply organs of output.
8. The amount of centralised investment funds allotted to the enterprise.
9. Targets for the installation and introduction into use of new capacities.
10. Targets for the assimilation of new products and processes.

Of these indicators, two – the percentage increase in sales and the percentage rate of profitability – were to be 'bonus-forming indicators'. That meant that payments into the enterprise incentive fund were determined (as percentages of the wage fund) by those percentage performance measures multiplied by a coefficient set 'from above' as part of the plan. Similar rules were supposed to determine the other two enterprise funds. Previously there had been just one enterprise fund, determined chiefly by the fulfilment of the gross output target. Over-fulfilment of sales and profitability targets produced higher payments into the bonus funds than exact fulfilment, but the increase was less than proportionate (usually an increase of 0.7 per cent for every 1 per cent over-fulfilment). The same applied in reverse to under-fulfilment. However, payments into the enterprise incentive fund were not the same thing as bonuses paid out from it. Failure to fulfil the key plan targets meant that no bonuses were paid out.

In the following years there were periodic announcements about how many enterprises had transferred to the new system. These were accompanied by figures showing how the change was boosting their performance. By the end of 1968 some 26,000 industrial enterprises, about three in every four, were on the new system (Ellman 1969, p. 295). The apparent improvements were most striking early on, and tended to diminish over time. One reason for this was that the early cohorts switching to the new system received preferential treatment in supplies, almost guaranteeing improved results. In the nature of things, special treatment could not be extended to a larger and larger population of enterprises operating with the new indicators.

One result was less ephemeral. The bonuses received by managers and other white-collar workers were larger, both absolutely and in proportion to basic pay, than those received (from all sources, including the wage fund) by blue-collar workers. This, as Ellman points out (*op. cit.*, p. 293), was intended; it was meant to offset the earnings equalisation of the Khrushchev period. In the first batch of enterprises operating on the new system, blue-collar workers received bonuses that added on average 8 per cent to their basic earnings (*ibid.*). In the late 1960s and early 1970s bonuses to management were commonly as much as half their basic salaries (Berliner 1976, pp. 479–84). Many economists – and probably all managers – thought the earlier equalisation had been excessive, damaging incentives for promotion and training. The anti-egalitarian theme runs through all the reform attempts in Soviet-type economies, up to the collapse of the system.

In the next few years enthusiastic high-level sponsorship of these reforms gradually faded away. By the early 1970s they were seldom referred to. Some of the provisions of the reform were implemented in practice; others were not. The branch ministries did indeed return, but they were not the new kind of non-interfering branch authority that Aganbegyan had predicted. Bonuses and other enterprise funds continued to be derived from profits. The revision of wholesale prices on a cost-plus-profit-mark-up basis was carried out (and the next major revision came in 1982, long after costs had changed substantially). A capital charge continued to be paid to the state, though not at a uniform rate. This seems to have had some effect in inducing managers to sell off unwanted old equipment in 1966–67, shrinking the base of the capital charge. Thereafter, however, Soviet managers went back to treating capital as a free good. If investment was allocated to your enterprise in its plan, then enterprise finances would be planned accordingly. You were under no pressure to economise on this or other planned resource allocations. And you had every incentive to bargain for your plan to include as much as possible of all resources. Finally, five-year plans for enterprises were introduced in 1971, but were quickly abandoned (see the next chapter).

The provisions whose implementation was minimal were the limiting of the number of imposed indicators, the tying of bonuses to sales and profitability, the use of the production-development fund for decentralised investment, and the development of inter-enterprise trade.

Ministries often simply went on using the same indicators as before (Ellman 1969, p. 316). Moreover, the distinction between indicators imposed from above, whose number the reform sought to limit, and indicators on which the enterprise had to report to its ministry – so-called accounting indicators – was elusive. The latter were often, in practice, also imposed (Zaleski 1967, p. 154). Over time, the number of indicators imposed from above on the enterprise tended, in those industries where it really did fall, to increase again.

The sales indicator was inherently problematic. The distinction between sales and production in a shortage economy is trivial. What was produced would, with rare exceptions, be sold; more precisely, it would be sent to the wholesale supply system, who would forward it to a pre-ordained, involuntary 'customer'. At the same time, the enterprise would be receiving physical-terms (tons, metres, numbers of units) targets for the main items in its product-mix, and those targets were unequivocally production targets.

Profitability, too, was a problematic indicator, for three reasons. Prices were unit-cost-plus, not marginal-cost based; in other words, they were determined only by supply conditions and did not reflect relative scarcity. The costs, in turn, did not reflect the opportunity costs of capital and natural resources (the capital charge was low, not uniform and not counted as a cost, and the introduction of rental charges for natural resources was incomplete and based on strange calculations – it was a charge per unit output). And the costs allowed for in the 1967 price revision later changed, while the prices did not. By and large, Soviet prices were (fortunately) not allowed to have much influence on resource allocation. But in matters of fine detail (choice of exact product-mix, introduction of new products), the state-determined wholesale prices could have an effect, and it was often a misallocating effect. Thus, the introduction of new products often lowered profits. Altogether, a rate-of-profit target was not such a smart idea as it seemed.

The aims of raising decentralised investment and inter-enterprise trade were frustrated by one obstinate fact of Soviet life: the central authorities were not prepared to loosen their controls on the details of production. They continued to want their plans for production and materials supply to be comprehensive. If nearly all the output of nearly all enterprises was covered by production and allocation plans, enterprises had next to nothing in which they could trade with one another. And an enterprise that tried to spend the roubles accumulated in its production-development fund on new equipment or a building extension ran into a problem: all (or almost all) equipment and building materials were pre-empted by existing allocation plans; they already had an address to go to.

These might be called the immediate reasons why the reform came to so little. The underlying reasons are to do with the nature of a centrally administered economy. Soviet central planners were expected by their political masters to ensure that total output increased, that it contained certain specific quantities of particular items, that people worked only at tasks approved by the state, and that the general level of retail prices, as officially measured, did not increase. Experience in Hungary and in China suggests that it might have been possible to meet these requirements while leaving some labour, capital assets, natural resources, materials and energy outside the plan, for enterprise managers to decide for themselves how to use them. But this was certainly difficult, and in the Soviet Union it never happened.

What did happen was that the central planners tried to set taut plans for each industry. The branch ministries in turn tried to set taut plans for each enterprise. In this they often failed, though perhaps not by large margins. In the long-running game played between enterprise managers and the higher authorities, the former necessarily knew more about the limits of their own production. But they never had the incentive to use spare capacity productively on their own initiative. If they increased the value of their output much above their plan target for the year, they could expect only that their target for next year would be increased, making next year's bonus harder to achieve. Naturally, they weighed up the effort involved in doing better against the reward. The reward was not just this year's bonus but the present value of an expected stream of bonuses over future years. Narrowly over-fulfilling a one-year target that you had done your best to make as soft as possible – that was the choice that was normally made.

The central planners, operating with highly defective information, were reluctant to loosen their control on resources. If the tanks, aircraft, tractors and other high-priority items were to be delivered in the required numbers, it was safest to have detailed control over the allocation of all steel and aluminium products. But if almost all output was allocated by the supply system, and enterprises were rewarded for meeting output targets, not for meeting customers' wishes at least cost, the enterprises would always be clamouring for more inputs. In other words, there would always appear to be shortages of raw materials, energy, capital goods and labour. So leaving a margin of capacity for free trading amongst enterprises always seemed to be impossible.

Only if enterprise output targets were done away with altogether, and centralised supply allocation along with them, would it really have been possible to decentralise economic decision-making. This was the core of the Hungarian New Economic Mechanism, introduced in 1968. But then enterprises were still state-owned, still the responsibility of the government. They could not be allowed to fail, so they were bailed out from above when in difficulties. Profitable enterprises saw their profits siphoned off to support unprofitable enterprises. Subsidies and tax breaks were offered by the authorities in return for meeting informal targets for output and employment, so detailed central planning reappeared through the back door, and motivation to economise on input costs, to adjust to market demand and to innovate remained weak. The performance of Hungarian state enterprises was not transformed even by a degree of decentralisation that far exceeded that of the Kosygin reforms; indeed, one authoritative account concludes that improvements in the Hungarian economy came not from decentralisation of the state sector but by allowing a larger role for legal private enterprise (see Kornai 1986).

In the light of what we now know about the comparative failure of other, and bolder, halfway-house reforms in Eastern Europe, the expectations behind the Kosygin reform of 1965 seem misplaced. The conventional wisdom about them consisted for a long time of two propositions: this reform was a step in the right direction; but its implementation was impeded by officials who resisted any diminution of their own powers. Both these propositions now seem misguided.

A more persuasive interpretation is that of Vladimir Kontorovich (1988). This, crudely summarised, is that the traditional Soviet economic system was a coherent whole; modifications to it that devolved decision-making, bringing internal inconsistencies, were likely to worsen economic performance; Gosplan, Gossnab and branch-ministry officials who stymied the introduction of wholesale trade or a streamlined set of success indicators were keeping a functioning system intact, in the face of half-baked schemes that would have resulted in disarray.

Kontorovich introduces a useful categorisation of the 'success' of economic reform legislation. It may be administratively successful insofar as it is implemented in practice. If it is, the really important question then arises: are the measures economically successful? In other words, does the practical implementation of the new rules and procedures improve economic performance? Kontorovich's hypothesis is that the administrative failure of the decentralising elements of the 1965 reforms saved them from having damaging economic consequences.

Nonetheless, he suggests, some changes that were not resisted may have been the source of some economic damage. In particular, the reduction in the number of individual physical-terms product targets assigned to each enterprise probably gave enterprises more scope to alter their product-mix in favour of items that assisted (for no good efficiency reason) their sales and profits figures: in favour of nominally new products, for example, which had higher prices but did not require the additional effort that genuine product innovation would have entailed. Genuine innovation, Kontorovich argues, may have been lessened by the increased concentration of bonus payments on the sales and profit targets: he cites evidence that the proportion of innovation-related bonuses to total bonuses fell.

One effect of the reforms may indeed have been an increase in hidden inflation, showing up officially as real output growth. A consideration of both hidden and repressed inflation, which played a role in the Soviet growth slowdown, will be deferred to the next chapter. It is in the later Brezhnev period that these phenomena begin to loom large.

The improvement in growth

The most important observation about Soviet economic performance after the Second World War is that growth slowed down, so that the per capita output level in the USSR began to fall further behind the level in the

Table 4.1 *Soviet growth in the late Khrushchev and early Brezhnev periods: alternative estimates (average annual GNP growth, %)*

	1960–64	1964–73
CIA estimate in 1970 prices	4.7	5.1
CIA estimate in 1982 prices	4.6	4.7

Sources: 1970 prices: derived from Pitzer 1982; 1982 prices: derived from CIA 1990, Table A-1.

United States – the leading capitalist nation and Moscow's opposing super-power. The whole story is reviewed in the final chapter. It is encapsulated there in Figure 9.2. The striking feature of the early Brezhnev period is that it was a time when Soviet growth either did not decelerate or even slightly accelerated, in comparison with the last years of Khrushchev's rule. In other words, this period bucked the long-run trend. This is illustrated in Table 4.1.

Of these two measures, the earlier one has the merit of being in prices that fall within the period under review; the later one may have the merit of incorporating additional information not previously available. Strikingly, the later CIA measure produces a fall in output in 1959, not present in the earlier series. If one takes the view that Khrushchev's last 'good' year was 1958 (and this is not unreasonable), then even the series in 1982 prices shows an upturn: from 4.4 per cent a year in 1958–64 to 4.6 per cent a year in 1964–73.

There is also some evidence that the rate of growth of productivity increased: that is to say, the growth of the productivity of labour and capital combined. The calculations shown in Table 4.2 are for successive five-year-plan periods, not for leadership periods, but the correspondence of these with late Khrushchev and early Brezhnev is reasonably close. These estim-ates, it should be stressed, are the result of applying arguably inappropriate theory to unquestionably doubtful data. Still, they all at least point in the same direction. They suggest not merely that output growth improved, but also that this was not achieved merely by throwing larger increments of resources into the production process.

The question is: why? Why should this, admittedly modest, medium-term improvement have been superimposed on a longer-term growth slow-down? Some commentators have been tempted to ascribe it to the Kosygin reforms. This is unlikely, on two grounds.

First, these reforms might if anything have been expected to slow re-corded growth – even growth as recorded in CIA estimates – or at least to

Table 4.2   *Estimates of Soviet total factor productivity (TFP) growth,*
1960–70 (% p.a.)

	1961–65	1966–70
A. GNP		
TFP I	1.4	1.7
TFP II	−0.2	0.7
B. Industry		
TFP	0.5	1.2

Notes: All three estimates are for an output index divided by an index
of combined inputs and assume that a Cobb-Douglas aggregate
production function with constant returns to scale is appropriate. The
GNP TFP estimates are based on CIA series of output, capital stock
and labour force. TFP I is a conventional measure in which the
weighted average of growth rates of labour and capital uses what are
judged to be appropriate factor shares in national income, of 0.75
and 0.25, respectively; TFP II is based on alternative weights that
treat the contribution of increments of capital stock as more
important at the margin than conventional income-shares would
indicate: 0.55 and 0.45, respectively. The industry TFP estimates are
CIA assessments using an input measure with the following weights:
labour 0.584 and capital 0.416.
Sources: GNP: Hanson 1990; Industry: Greenslade and Robertson
1973.

have no effect on measured growth. Ellman (1969, p. 296) observes that
the intention was to move the economic system away from an excessive
dependence on output targets in the direction of greater responsiveness to
customer requirements. If that had produced the desired effect of widening
product ranges and improving quality, those gains would probably not have
been captured in measures of output growth – rather, on the contrary, any
diversion of resources away from quantity to quality would probably have
slowed measured growth. This happens in even the most sophisticated statistical reporting systems.

Second, the reforms largely failed, as we have seen, to achieve their
intended effects on producer behaviour. That failure might explain why
there was no deterioration in measured growth, but it can hardly account
for an improvement.

Which parts of the economy performed better in the early Brezhnev
period? According to the CIA estimates of GNP by sector of origin in 1970
prices, the growth of industry slowed from an average of 6.7 per cent a year
to 6.1 per cent, and the growth of the service sector slowed marginally:

from 4.3 to 4.1 per cent a year. Arithmetically, the improvement in growth between the two periods, in this set of measurements, comes from agriculture, which accelerated from 2.1 to 3.1 per cent a year, and the rest of the economy (construction, transport, communications, trade, military personnel and 'other branches'), whose combined growth rate increased slightly less (by 0.8 per cent a year). The weight of agriculture in the series (its factor-cost weight in 1970) is about a fifth of GNP, while the rest of the economy, in the above sense, has a weight of about a quarter. So both contributed about equally to the improvement. Between them, in other words, they more than offset the more modest deceleration in industry and services. (Derived from Pitzer 1982, Table A-1.) The later CIA estimates in 1982 prices shows a very broadly similar pattern, albeit with all growth rates lowered by the use of later-year prices and only a mild acceleration in the growth of farm output (CIA 1990, Table A-1).

It appears therefore that part of the story is that improvements in the farm sector helped to boost the growth rate. The fortunes of that sector are considered in the next section.

Changes in the performance of different broad sectors convey something about the supply side of the economy. Changes on the demand side can also provide clues: was investment growing particularly fast in the early Brezhnev period, or consumption, or defence? The CIA's calculations are no help here, because they studiously avoided identifying defence explicitly in their national income accounts for the USSR (see Maddison 1998, p. 315).

The immediate reason for this was that estimates of Soviet defence spending were built up from information about physical data: numbers of servicemen, changes in the stocks of weapon systems, and so on, which were then priced in dollars for comparisons with the US. When converted to roubles, these numbers were not (I believe) compatible with the GNP numbers that the CIA calculated with greater reliance on Soviet economic data. Whether, as Maddison speculates, security considerations ultimately lay behind the CIA's failure to integrate defence spending estimates explicitly into its national accounts estimates, is at present an open question. Some other Western estimates, however, are available.

Ofer (1988, p. 30) and Cohn (1973, pp. 151–2) concur in showing the defence share of final expenditure rising in the 1960s. (Cohn shows a strongly fluctuating rise, with sharp increases in the late Khrushchev period.) Cohn provides some statistical evidence that, at the margin, increases in defence spending tended to be at the expense of fixed investment. A defence constraint on investment could reasonably be expected to have a dampening effect on growth, but only in the longer run. The gestation periods for Soviet investment projects were notoriously long: some took more than a decade to bear fruit. Therefore negative effects on capacity and output would show up only several years after a curbing of the flow of investment spending.

It is possible therefore that a proportionally larger resource allocation to the military in the 1960s contributed to a deceleration of output growth in the 1970s – the classic 'era of stagnation'. One should however be careful of attributing too much importance to modest changes in the military burden. Large econometric models of the Soviet economy, assembled at a later date but probably capturing long-standing relationships, showed such low returns to capital investment that the opportunity cost in output forgone at a later date was very small (see Ofer 1988, p. 69).

At all events, the CIA's estimates in 1970 prices show consumption accelerating from 3.2 per cent a year in 1960–64 to 4.6 per cent a year in 1964–73, while investment growth slowed from 7.1 to 6.4 per cent a year. Given their weights in the total GNP series (54 and 28 per cent, respectively), it appears that the acceleration in consumption more than offset the deceleration in investment, and in addition accounted for all the acceleration of total output (derived from Pitzer 1982, Table A-6). These numbers, to repeat, take no explicit account of defence spending – which was probably growing faster in the later period.

The first half of Brezhnev's time in office, then, displayed a return to early Khrushchevian values: the growth of consumption and of the farm sector received a boost. There was not, however, any repeat of the large military manpower cuts of the late 1950s; rather, the defence effort continued to grow strongly.

How much of this was the result of deliberate choice by the leadership is not clear. Soviet leaders and planners did not operate with a system of national accounts that showed clearly the resource allocations between consumption, investment and defence. What does seem to be the case, however, is that there was no attempt to reverse the enhanced priority that Khrushchev had given to consumption and to agriculture.

Agriculture

The new regime seems to have made two explicit choices in favour of agriculture. First, they ended some of Khrushchev's excesses in agricultural meddling, and improved incentives by raising procurement prices in 1965 and introducing in 1966 a guaranteed minimum income for *kolkhoz* work. The latter was recommended rather than ordered but was in fact introduced in nearly all farms by 1968 (Wädekin 1989, p. 27). These measures helped farm-sector growth to resume.

Table 4.3   *Soviet agricultural output, inputs and factor productivity (1950 = 100)*

	Output	Inputs	TFP	Memorandum item: US farm TFP
1953	106.8	105.7	101.0	105.3
1960	159.2	130.0	122.5	121.3
1964	164.7	141.9	116.1	127.9
1973	230.5	169.6	135.9	143.3

Notes: The output series is a three-year moving average of net farm output in 1970 prices. The input series is a weighted average of inputs of land, labour, capital assets, livestock herds and current material purchases. TFP stands for total factor productivity and is an index of the ratio of output to inputs. The estimates of US farm TFP use the same method of calculation, except that the output series is not a three-year moving average.
Source: Diamond and Davis 1979, Table B-1.

In addition, the Brezhnev leadership allocated a substantially larger share of fixed investment to the farm sector. This, like the incentive measures, was probably prompted by a desire to avoid a repetition of the large grain imports of 1963–64 (see Chapter 3). Such imports were no doubt seen as a humiliating admission of failure and as entailing a dangerous 'dependence' on the West, particularly the USA. It could well be argued (and later was, in Washington) that large grain sales in fact gave the US no leverage: the international grain trade involves many traders and a product whose origin is not readily detectable; the US government could not in fact control it – and in the face of the US farm lobby would be only too happy not to try. But clever arguments of that sort seem never to have cut much ice in the Kremlin. In international economic relations, the Kremlin motto was: if in doubt, don't trade.

The shift in investment priorities was striking: between 1961–65 and the Eighth Five-Year Plan period of 1966–70, fixed 'productive' investment in agriculture rose 62 per cent, while total investment in the whole economy rose only 43 per cent. Consequently the farm sector's share of investment grew from 16 to 18 per cent. This was still slightly less than agriculture's share of national output, but it was a reassertion of priorities over which Khrushchev had tangled with the 'steel-eaters'. This new priority was then maintained. The farm sector's share of investment was planned to rise to 21.6 per cent (albeit measured in different prices) in the Ninth Five-Year Plan for 1971–75 (Bush 1973).

The pattern of farm-sector growth is shown in Table 4.3. In this case, a sector almost destroyed under Stalin shows slow growth and very little productivity growth in the last three years of Stalin's life. Then output growth is very rapid: 3.9 per cent per annum over the next 20 years, but accompanied by rapid growth of inputs. Output growth slows and productivity growth turns negative in the late Khrushchev years, as policy errors and micro-meddling hamper the sector's performance. Then policy corrections and a further heightening of the farm sector's priority bring a renewal of strong growth, including a highly respectable increase in the productivity of inputs.

Over the period as a whole American agriculture exhibits faster productivity growth, though the difference is not large. The Soviet farm sector is in catch-up mode: according to Diamond and Davis's calculations, total Soviet net farm output was 61 per cent of that of the US in 1950, and 86 per cent in 1973 (p. 48; the ratios are the geometric means of calculations in dollar prices and in rouble prices). But this is done with a comparatively large increment of inputs. The Soviet farm sector's growth, in other words, is more extensive (despite the respectable productivity increase) than that of US agriculture.

The early Brezhnev period was the time when agriculture was established as a major claimant on Soviet resources. Khrushchev had already moved in that direction. Under Brezhnev the farm sector (in the narrow sense of agriculture, not including agri-chemicals, farm machinery and food processing and distribution) settled down to claiming a fifth or more of gross fixed investment. When, later in the 1970s, farm production ceased to grow – or at any rate, to grow more than sluggishly – this came to seem more and more a drag on Soviet economic performance.

Soviet citizens as consumers

For the time being, the new priority was paying off: the Soviet population saw a real improvement in their everyday life. The consumption of food (not counting beverages and tobacco), as estimated by the CIA at 1970 established prices, grew at an average annual rate of 4.4 per cent between 1964 and 1973. That was a far more significant development than increased food consumption would be in a rich country. Indeed food supply was central to Soviet consumption levels. It is one indication of the comparative poverty of the Soviet population that, as late as 1970, food accounted for about two-fifths of the average household budget (derived from Schroeder and Denton 1982, Table A-1, excluding collective consumption items). Net imports of food contributed to the Soviet diet, it is true, but the strong growth of farm output (3.8 per cent a year at 1970 factor cost) must

Table 4.4 *Some indicators of Soviet consumption, 1965-73 (physical units)*

	1965	1970	1973
Per cap. food cons. (kg p.a.)			
Meat	41	48	52
Dairy products	251	307	307
Fish	12.6	15.4	16.2
Potatoes	142	130	142
Green vegetables	72	82	85
Fruit	28	36	40
Per cap. cons. of soft goods			
Cloth (m^2)	26.5	30.4	32.7
Knitwear (units)	4.2	5.3	5.7
Footwear (pairs)	2.4	3.0	3.0
Stocks of durables (per 1,000 pop.)			
Radios	165	199	216
TVs	68	143	195
Cameras	67	77	77
Motor-cycles	17	21	23
Refrigerators	29	89	142
Washing-machines	59	141	173

Source: Schroeder 1975, Table 1.

have largely accounted for the strong growth in food consumption (4.4 per cent a year at 1970 established prices).

Overall, consumption as estimated by Schroeder and Denton increased at 5.2 per cent a year between 1964 and 1973, or 3.9 per cent per annum per head of population (*op. cit.*, Tables A-1 and A-2). It was not, by West European or North American standards, a time of plenty, but it was unquestionably a time of real improvement. Schroeder (1975) provides per capita indicators as shown in Table 4.4.

These improvements left the average Soviet household well ahead of people in really poor countries but still substantially behind people in the rich world. Soviet consumers were also consuming less than their own planners officially considered to be required by the 'rational consumption norms' they had devised.

The comparatively low quality of the Soviet diet, with its heavy reliance on bread and potatoes, is clear from Table 4.5. The exception is the comparatively high figure for milk (in fact, milk and dairy products), but this is

Table 4.5 *Soviet consumption levels: selected comparative indicators, 1968–73 (food items in kg per head per year; consumer durable stocks in units per 1,000 population)*

	USSR 1973	US 1971	UK 1970	USSR Rational cons. norms 1968
Food consumption				
Bread	145	65	73	120.4
Potatoes	124	66	102	96.8
Meat	52	110	76	81.8
Eggs (number)	195	321	283	292
Milk	307	254	216	433.6
Stocks of durables		US 1972	UK 1972	
Radios	216	1695	340	
TVs	195	474	305	
Phones	53	627	314	

Sources: Schroeder 1975, *loc.cit.*; Bush 1975, Tables 1 and 2; rational norms: Artemova 1969.

slightly misleading. Fresh milk remained scarce in the cities, and a very large proportion of milk output was turned into the ubiquitous, and not unpleasant, Soviet cheese: almost certainly a larger proportion than people would have freely chosen had processing, refrigeration and distribution been more advanced. The lag in consumer durables, despite the recent rapid increase in their rate of supply, is very clear. Telephones for ordinary citizens had, understandably, a particularly low priority. This was still, and would remain into the late 1980s, a country in which copying machines were kept under lock and key and all means of uncontrolled communication were hampered.

The rational consumption norms were one of the quainter Soviet planning tools. Norms for food were prepared by the Institute of Nutrition of the USSR Academy of Medical Sciences. How recommended nutritional requirements were converted into 'rational norms' for particular food items is not clear. It does not appear to have been done as a programming exercise: least-cost diet delivering a prescribed amount of various nutrients. It was probably done either by the famous Soviet planning formula, 2P4S,[2] or by taking a reasonably deserving Western country and targeting its current levels. If the latter method was employed, the resemblance to contemporary British levels (bread and cheese apart) suggests that a rather mediocre West European economy represented the height of Soviet ambition. At all events, the rational norms provide another standard by which to assess the progress being made by the Soviet consumer: the Soviet planners' own avowed targets.

(There was also a 'rational wardrobe', but it is hard to believe that the planners responsible for that were entirely serious.) These norms, it should be added, seem to have faded from view around this time. As a tool for medium-term planning, they were a *dirigiste*, prescriptive alternative to projecting changes in demand arising from changes in real income levels. In practice, it is doubtful whether either approach was ever systematically used.

It was during the Brezhnev era that cars began to become available to private citizens. In 1960, the total stock of passenger cars was about 500,000: mostly state-owned cars for official use and including taxis (Welihozkiy 1979). This was in a country with a population of 214 million. By 1970 there were an estimated 1.7 million cars, just under half privately owned (*ibid.*) among 243 million people. By 1975 the estimated stock was 4.7 million cars, but by then almost three-quarters were privately owned. The growth in car production came mainly from the Fiat-built VAZ complex at Tolyatti, on the Volga (see the next section), so it was above all something achieved by importing the technological capability for large-scale production of small cars.

This was a remarkable change. On the one hand, it was part of the softening of Soviet society. As Alexander Zinoviev observed, if you want to promote dissidence, you should provide more housing, more phones and more cars – all things that give individuals more room to manoeuvre, and all of them things that Soviet leaders after Stalin tried to provide. (There were some differences amongst these leaders, however. Khrushchev, having seen a traffic jam in America, had reservations about mass car ownership. Brezhnev was softer on cars. In the mid-70s he owned a Rolls-Royce Silver Cloud, a Maserati, a Lincoln, a Mercedes and a Cadillac [Smith 1976, p. 66], so it was rather democratic of him to preside over an expansion of car ownership for the people.) On the other hand, it still left the Soviet Union decades behind the developed West in car ownership. By 1975 there were 54 people per passenger car in the Soviet Union, compared with two in the US and four in the UK.

Soviet citizens, despite the general improvement in consumption levels, had to cope with pervasive inefficiency in the production and distribution of food and manufactured consumer goods. There was at this time quite extensive discussion in the Soviet press of the problem of accumulating inventories of poor-quality or simply unwanted items (Schroeder 1975). This problem co-existed with shortages of many items: in other words, demand for those items exceeded supply at the controlled retail prices. Queues and black market deals were everyday experiences for Soviet citizens in the early 1970s, just as they had been ten or twenty years earlier. Food other than bread and potatoes tended to be *defitsitnyi* (deficit, or in short supply). The very vocabulary, *defitsitnyi*, with its opposite, *nedefitsitnyi* (not in short supply), suggests the scale of the problem.

Table 4.6   *Partially repressed inflation: state and* Kolkhoz *market food trade, 1965, 1970, 1975*

	1965	1970	1975
Peasant market sales as %			
Total at actual prices	5.3	4.4	4.3
Peasant market sales as %			
Total at state prices	3.8	2.8	2.3
Hence, peasant-market prices as	139.5	157.1	187.0
% state prices			

Sources: first two rows: *Narkhoz 22–82*, pp. 466–7; third row: author's calculation.

The state retail price index for food showed no inflation in 1965–70, and a tiny increase of 0.9 per cent over the following five years (*Narkhoz 22–82*, pp. 480, 481). But while state retail prices for food (or at any rate for standard items like one-kilo loaves of white bread) were indeed kept unchanged, excess demand tended to grow as money incomes rose. Demand for meat, green vegetables and fruit, in particular, tended to outrun state supply at state-set prices. Distribution was geographically highly uneven, with the best supply situation maintained in Moscow, and so on down the pecking order until one got to stores in small towns and villages, with a few miserable items in stock, plus bottles of vodka to alleviate the misery.

The inflationary pressure, however, was not fully repressed. In the urban peasant (so-called collective-farm, or *kolkhoz*) markets, food was sold at prices that were only fitfully and indirectly controlled. The difference between peasant-market and state-shop prices for food reflected in part quality differences and in part the repressed inflation so far as state food supplies were concerned. Soviet official figures that indirectly revealed this are shown in Table 4.6.

The implication of these numbers is intriguing: food supply per head of population was improving rapidly, but food shortages in state trade were if anything getting worse; or, to put it another way, repressed inflation in the consumer market for food was intensifying. The policy of freezing state retail prices while encouraging the farm sector to produce more (in part by higher procurement prices) and allowing money incomes to rise comparatively fast was producing a growing disequilibrium in consumer markets, at any rate for food.

The problem of chronic shortages was to worsen sharply towards the end of the Soviet era, contributing to a widespread feeling that the Soviet way of life was breaking down. In the early Brezhnev period, however, it was merely an inconvenience that accompanied real and sustained improvements.

Foreign trade and payments

Foreign trade contributed to the general improvement in this period, but perhaps to only a modest extent.

For a developed market economy, increasing integration into the world economy can plausibly be treated as a source of economic growth. If the role of foreign trade in a nation's economy increases, this is likely to mean that opportunities to specialise in production are also increasing, bringing classic gains from trade and perhaps also economies of scale; in addition, a higher rate of importation of foreign machinery and know-how should accelerate the diffusion of advanced technology, raising factor productivity. Maddison (1995, Table 2.6) provides calculations for six advanced countries, indicating that in the post-war 'Golden Age', 1950–73, a rising share of trade in GDP may have made substantial contributions to output growth, whereas in 1913–50 and 1973–92 any such contribution was much more modest.

It is tempting to see the continued expansion of Soviet foreign trade both under Khrushchev and in the early Brezhnev period as producing similar benefits. Official Soviet data certainly show high and accelerating rates of growth of merchandise trade at this time: export volume increasing at 8.8 per cent a year in 1961–65 and 9.9 per cent a year in 1966–70, and imports growing correspondingly at rates of 5.8 and 6.4 per cent a year (*VT SSSR 22–81*, Table VI). It is highly likely, in fact, that there were real benefits (see Chapter 3). These were, however, more limited than the rapid increase in total trade might suggest.

First, the Soviet Union, with its large population and very large territory, was less open to benefits from trade increases than a smaller country would have been. Maddison's estimates of merchandise exports as a percentage of GDP in 1990 prices, for the year 1973, yield a share of 3.8 per cent for the USSR. That is in the range for very large countries: the equivalent figure for China was 1.1, India 2.0 and the US 5.0 (Maddison1995, Table 2-4). For medium-sized countries like the UK (14.0 per cent) or West Germany (23.8 per cent) or small countries like the Netherlands (41.7 per cent), the influence of trade was much stronger (*ibid.*).

Second, about half Soviet merchandise trade at this period was with fellow members of CMEA. In 1970 the figure was 50.1 per cent (*VT SSSR 22–81*, Table IV; current prices; trade with Cuba and Vietnam subtracted, since they joined the CMEA only later). Trade with the developed West was at the time about a fifth of the total (21.3 per cent) and with less developed countries (LDCs) around one seventh (13.5 per cent). Intra-CMEA trade and part of Soviet-LDC trade were conducted on a bilateral basis and were full of inefficiencies (see Chapter 3; the possibility of Soviet losses from CMEA trade in the 1970s are considered in Chapter 5). Indeed, we cannot be at all sure what proportion of Soviet trade CMEA and LDC transactions would have constituted at this time if they had been straightforward commercial deals; if they had been, the prices would have been different and therefore the 50 per cent share of CMEA trade may be somewhat misleading.

At all events, the share in GDP of that component of foreign trade that could be expected to bring efficiency gains was certainly less than the 3.8 per cent share of total trade. A plausible guess might be about 1.5–2 per cent for the mid-Brezhnev year of 1973. This 'efficient' trade had apparently been growing fast: the volume of imports from the developed West is shown as increasing at 11.2 per cent a year, 1966–70 (*VT SSSR 22–81*, Table VI). Even so, the absolute size of the increment of trade with the West, if compared with GDP, was very small.

This assessment may seem unduly West-centred, as though little good could come from trading with anyone else. Unfortunately for the economic fortunes of the USSR, that is not an unreasonable conclusion. Intra-CMEA trade came to be pilloried within the CMEA region as an 'exchange of inefficiencies'. The reasons for this require a brief, extremely summary, excursion into the workings of the Soviet-dominated trading bloc.

First, all CMEA countries had systemically built-in protection against competition from imports, and indeed from competition of any kind, so their manufacturing sectors were likely to lag behind Western and East Asian firms in quality and technical level of production. This conjecture is supported by their declining share from 1965 on in OECD imports of manufactures (Poznanski 1987).

Second, the fixed, non-scarcity prices, inconvertible currencies and administrative allocation characterising all CMEA member-states left them at a great disadvantage when they traded with one another. What should be exported? What should be imported? This was a difficult question even in their trade with market economies; it was even trickier where trade among themselves was concerned. If the price of a Czechoslovak milling-machine, converted at the meaningless official exchange rate from its meaningless domestic price to a notional price in roubles, was less than that of a similar Soviet milling-machine, did that necessarily mean that it was better to import such machines than to produce them at home? And if the same applied in reverse to a Soviet lathe when its price was converted to korunas, did it necessarily follow that the Soviet Union should be specialising in lathes, exporting them to Czechoslovakia and importing milling machines?

All concerned knew that no such conclusion followed. It might simultaneously be true that this trade would bring losses, not gains. In other words, the resources used in the USSR to produce enough lathes to pay for 100 milling machines might in fact be greater than the resources that the Soviet Union would have used to produce those 100 milling machines for itself. In short, following established prices and exchange rates could produce losses, not gains, from trade. Consequently, there was a minor CMEA academic industry of calculating foreign trade criteria, in part by 'cleansing' and adjusting established prices, in the hope of providing guidance to efficient trade decisions. But practice, as usual, had little to do with the academics' formulae.

What was used was Western trade prices. When socialism conquers the world, East European economists used to say, we will have to keep one capitalist country, so that we know what prices to trade at. In other words, 'world market prices' for 'comparable' goods were supposed to be the ultimate source of guidance. Until the 1973–74 oil-price hike, CMEA practice was to agree prices on the basis of the previous five years' capitalist world prices and use those, unchanged for five years, as the basis for intra-CMEA trade.

More precisely, this was CMEA practice in principle. CMEA practice in practice was unavoidably more arbitrary than that. For many products, and particularly for manufactures, it is very hard to say what is a comparable item, and what constitutes 'the world market price'. In practice, as the Hungarian economist Sandor Ausch showed from hitherto unpublished CMEA data, there were huge variations in the nominal prices at which given items were traded amongst different countries within CMEA.

Two categories of goods evolved in intra-CMEA negotiations: so-called 'hard' goods and 'soft' goods. The former could be sold at acceptable prices on world markets, the latter could not. Very loosely speaking, food, energy and raw materials tended to be hard goods and manufactures tended to be soft goods. There was real intra-CMEA bargaining to get hard goods from trade partners, and a willingness to take a certain nominal value of soft goods – whose prices could be adjusted to make the bilateral flows balance – was often the key to concluding a deal (see Ausch 1972; Hewett 1979; Lavigne 1985).

This is not to say that commonsense vetting of import requirements did not yield some benefits from intra-CMEA trade in manufactures. But the practitioners (of whom Ausch was one) knew that a great deal of dross was exchanged as well.

Therefore the rapid growth of Soviet foreign trade in the 1960s and early 1970s was not the unalloyed blessing it might have seemed likely to be. After the dramatic rise in world oil prices in the early 1970s, the question was raised, indeed, whether the USSR was on balance losing from its transactions with its CMEA partners. But that question belongs in the next chapter.

In trade with the West, the Soviet gains continued to take the form already described in the last chapter: the core of the trade was an exchange of

Soviet hydrocarbons, minerals, metals, furs, timbers and the like for Western farm produce and machinery. Systemic comparative advantage prevailed.

The year 1972 provided a vivid example. Soviet hard-currency merchandise exports in that year were about $2.9 billion; orders were placed for Western machinery and equipment to the value of just under $2 billion, and $2 billion-worth of grain was ordered. Orders at this level were possible partly because there were Western credits on offer (official credit support from national governments for capital goods exports, and for grain US Commodity Credit Corporation loans and the like), partly because deliveries would be staggered over several years, and partly because Moscow could sell some of its gold reserves (Farrell 1973, pp. 692–6). Even so, the tendency to run into hard-currency deficits, constraining trade with the West, seemed at the time to be immutable.

Nonetheless Soviet imports of machinery and equipment rose strongly, from $489 million in 1964 to $1,574 million in 1973. Allowing for inflation in international machinery prices, this was a real increase of 108 per cent, or 8.5 per cent a year (Hanson 1981, Table 8.1). This was almost certainly a growing share of Soviet equipment investment (the understatement of inflation in available figures for the latter makes it impossible to be precise).

This was the time of the giant Fiat car-making project at Tolyatti, in what is now Samara province. A new city was built to support the new car-making complex. (The standard transliteration from Cyrillic of the city's name, Tolyatti, slightly blurs its provenance: the new city was named for the former Italian Communist Party leader, Togliatti.) A cooperation agreement between Fiat and the Soviet State Committee for Science and Technology was signed in 1965; the main plant contract, for $320–360 million, was signed in 1966. Large cross-border flows of people were involved: about 2,500 Western specialists and skilled workers to the construction project and to design bureaux in Moscow and elsewhere, and a similar number of Soviet citizens to Italy, mainly for training in operating the equipment that was being installed. Production began in the early 1970s, with capacity operation reached in 1974. The city's population now is over 700,000, and the car-making complex, the Volga Automobile Works (VAZ), though now in disarray, remains the largest in the former Soviet Union.

The general development of such turnkey projects, initially for the modernisation of the chemical industry, began under Khrushchev, and was touched on in the last chapter. The motor industry was the next major sector to receive this treatment: first at VAZ and then at the Kama River truck works, KamAZ.

Fiat acted as general contractor for the VAZ complex. That meant that they had overall responsibility for designing, equipping, installing and commissioning the production facilities, including the training of Soviet workers and a great deal of subcontracting to specialist suppliers, by no means all of them Italian. When the even larger Kama River complex was planned, no single Western company was prepared to take on the financial risk of being general contractor, so the project was parcelled out to a number of Western contractors.

It was in the early 1970s that so-called 'technology transfer' from the West to the USSR became an issue – primarily in the West, but also to some extent in the Soviet Union itself. In earlier chapters it has been pointed out that such transfer was a continuing process that can be traced back to the Second World War, and indeed before. It is hardly surprising that such transfers should have occurred. They are a normal part of commercial life throughout the world, and a major source of economic growth (through productivity increases) in any country that is trailing behind the North American-West European-Japanese leading-edge developments. Such transfers, though more important for countries catching up the most advanced nations, flow in all directions, from Brazilian subsidiaries back to American parent firms in the motor industry, and indeed from the Soviet Union to the West: some Soviet steel-making technology, for example, has been used in Japan and the US.

What focused attention on technology transfer in the early 1970s was the scale of the Fiat-Tolyatti and Kama River projects, and the concurrent pursuit of *détente* with Moscow by President Richard Nixon. The strategy of Nixon and his national security adviser, Henry Kissinger, was to improve relations between the two superpowers in part by offering improved trading relations: most-favoured nation treatment of imports from the Soviet Union and eligibility for Eximbank credits (official credit support for US capital goods exports to the USSR). In 1972 Soviet–US trade agreements made these benefits available. In early 1975 the agreements were abrogated by the USSR. This was something effectively forced upon Moscow by demands in the US (led by Senator Henry Jackson) that Moscow make an explicit commitment to issue specified numbers of exit visas for Soviet Jews, as a condition of congressional ratification of the agreements. The emigration was already occurring, but on the basis of informal or at least unpublished understandings between Moscow and Washington; the public commitment now asked of the USSR was humiliating and not acceptable, so Moscow-Washington *détente* ended. *Détente* in this commercial sense had long been in place between Moscow and West European capitals, and that continued.

In the American debates surrounding this foreign-policy development, critics of the Nixon–Kissinger strategy made much of the gains made available to the Soviet Union from easier access to Western machinery and know-how. There was controversy about the scale of the resulting economic benefits for the Soviet Union. There was also controversy about a narrower issue of direct security concern: an alleged weakening of Western strategic export controls designed to impede Soviet gains in military capability derived from the acquisition of Western know-how.

Meanwhile a number of Central-East European countries – most notably Poland and Hungary – had embarked on a strategy of import-led growth, in which increased imports of capital goods and technology were expected to enhance domestic production and export capabilities in the future. Their strategy involved running current-account deficits now, and therefore borrowing, on the calculation that these debts could be paid off later by a modernised and more internationally competitive export sector.

The Soviet leadership never committed Moscow to this strategy; they were too cautious. And in any case, the steep rise in oil prices from 1973 gave their foreign purchasing power an enormous, and entirely fortuitous, boost. That lessened the need to borrow in order to import substantially more machinery. Even before then, however, the Soviets were coming to rely on comparatively large imports of Western machinery and know-how to upgrade particular sectors of the economy: first chemicals, then motor vehicles as well, but also several other branches and sub-branches. This subject is taken up again in the next chapter.

The more worldly-wise Soviet citizens saw nothing remarkable in all this. They knew the Soviet Union had been 'borrowing' Western technology for decades. The most profound thinker about Brezhnevism, in a passage about Ibanskian (Soviet) science, put it like this (Zinoviev 1976, p. 350):

> On top of all that, there's abroad. If only it didn't exist! Then we'd be home and dry. But they're eternally dreaming up something new over there. And we have to compete with them. To show our superiority. No sooner have you pinched one little machine from them than it's time to pinch the next one. By the time we've got it into production, the bastard's obsolete!

That passage was not published in the Soviet Union. What was said in public there on the subject was more decorously put, and less dismissive of Soviet capabilities. But there was a growing acceptance that the world capitalist economy was a going concern after all, and that the Soviet Union could benefit from trading more actively with it.

Economic debate

The public discussion of economic reform grew more muted in this period. The Kosygin reforms were being implemented, with progressively less public attention paid to them after about 1968. The more extensive reforms launched in Czechoslovakia were squashed by the armies of the Warsaw Pact in the summer of 1968; that event seems to have strengthened a backlash against ambitious reform ideas being aired in public. The notion of market socialism was by 1969 something one was allowed to attack but not to promulgate. This was part of a general crackdown on dissent (Sutela 1984, pp. 121–2).

At the same time, the crushing of the Prague Spring not only dealt a blow to the world communist movement from which it never recovered, it prompted a whole generation of young Soviet intellectuals and Party officials to query the bases on which the Soviet system was built. They included many people who were, in the early 1980s, to rise to prominence in the Party hierarchy around former KGB chief Yurii Andropov. Specialists at the Institute of the World Economy and International Relations (IMEMO) were studying Western economies and producing arguments for trading more extensively with them, in particular because of the opportunities for absorbing new technology. This was typically expressed in the – entirely reasonable – formulation that no one country could be technologically self-sufficient, and all stood to gain from specialisation and exchange of technology, whether embodied in machines or in disembodied form (licences, know-how, training) (see, for example, Maksimova 1974).

One particularly interesting commentator was a high official, Nikolai Smelyakov, a deputy minister of foreign trade, with a steel-industry background. He wrote admiringly of the high technical standard of production in Japan and Germany, and of some American business practices. He also pointed out that Soviet producers typically regarded the assignment to them of an export order as a form of punishment. He did not spell out all the reasons for this, but implied that the problem was that export production required a concern for quality and timely completion that even a large mark-up on the domestic wholesale price did not compensate for (Smelyakov 1973).

This was, therefore, a period in which Soviet public discussion went cool on the market in theory but provided reasons for cosying up to market economies in practice.

Conclusion

In the early-to-middle 1970s the Soviet Union was probably ceasing to catch up the United States in per capita GDP. The whole question of catch-up and slowdown is considered more fully in the next chapter, and

Table 4.7   *Soviet measures of Soviet net material product as a percentage of US, selected years, 1963–85*

1963	63
1969	65
1970	>65
1974	67
1980	67
1982	67
1985	66
1986	

Sources: from or derived from *Narkhoz 67*, p. 138; *Narkhoz 69*, p. 94; *Narkhoz 74*, p. 103; *Narkhoz 22–82*, p. 91; *Narkhoz 82*, p. 56; *Narkhoz 85*, p. 581.

there is a retrospective summary in the final chapter. One intriguing question, meanwhile, is what Soviet political leaders and advisers thought was happening, in the middle of Brezhnev's time in office, to the great Marxist-Leninist project of catching up and overtaking.

Growth had picked up slightly from a stutter in the early 1960s (see above); the material prosperity of the Soviet people had been improving quite rapidly. But a time of economic turmoil was impending in both East and West, out of which the Soviet Union would emerge trailing further behind the West: ceasing to 'catch up and overtake'.

There is one indication of the officially sanctioned, contemporary picture of Soviet relative economic achievement. The Soviet annual statistical handbooks regularly published comparisons of the dollar value, as estimated by Soviet statisticians, of Soviet national income (net material product), either alongside an equivalent figure for the US or simply as a percentage of the US figure. These were not Western-definition national income figures: most of the service sector was omitted. The dollar valuation was at a purchasing power parity, not at the exchange rate. What is interesting is not the absolute level of the figures in any one year, but how they moved over time. Table 4.7 provides a compilation for selected years.

Quite possibly nobody in the Politburo was aware of these figures. Certainly, Soviet economists (off the record) did not trust any Soviet official figures. Little regarded or mistrusted as they may have been at the time, however, they now offer us something for the historical record: the official, internal assessment was that, from somewhere around 1973–74, the great

Soviet economic project of catching up the United States was beginning to fail.

Notes

1 Kosygin had more knowledge of the outside world than most of his peers. In 1971 a Labour MP with a Manchester constituency described him to me as 'knowing Manchester like the back of his hand'. This may have been overstating things a little, but Kosygin had quite extensive experience of trade deals.

2 *Pol, potolok i chetyre steny* (floor, ceiling and four walls – that is, out of thin air).

CHAPTER FIVE

The 'Era of Stagnation': 1973–82

When Mikhail Gorbachev, in the late 1980s, referred back to the 'era of stagnation' his Soviet audience was not shocked. Soviet citizens had by the mid-1970s become pessimistic about their own material prospects. The view that the economy as a whole had slowed down, if not actually gone backwards, was widespread. The belief that private consumption levels were stagnant or falling was even more common. Insofar as we can reconstruct what really was happening in the economy at the time, we can say that this deepening economic pessimism was well-founded. Even if it had not been well-founded, the loss of confidence in the system would still have been an important development.

A survey of about 2000 Soviet emigrés who had left the USSR in the late 1970s found that three out of four believed labour productivity had been falling around the time they emigrated. The prime cause, in the view of these informants, was poor incentives. They tended to believe, contrary to Soviet official figures, that real wages were falling and that poverty was quite extensive (Gregory 1987).

Emigrants, one might think, are more likely to see faults in the country they have chosen to leave than are the great majority who stay behind. In the case of Soviet emigration, however, this is not such a safe prediction as it might be with many other emigrations.

To begin with, not all who wished to emigrate were able to do so. Those who left were able to leave by virtue (in the case of the study just cited) of being Jewish: more precisely, of belonging to households that contained at least one Jewish person. As the saying went in Moscow at the time, 'A Jewish wife is not a luxury but a means of transportation'. There were probably many discontented people who did not have a chance of emigrating.

Second, emigrants from the USSR were not always especially critical of the country they had left. Surveys of the earlier wave of Soviet emigrants, just after the war, found that they took a favourable view of the Soviet system in general; it was the leadership, i.e. Stalin, that they resented (Bushnell 1980).

Most directly to the point, the evidence that the Soviet population as a whole took a dim view of its material situation and prospects is strong, even though it is not, and cannot be, derived from systematic surveys. John Bushnell (1980) presented good grounds for believing that the Soviet managerial and professional middle class had shifted from economic optimism in the 1950s and 1960s to economic pessimism in the 1970s. He drew on his personal experience of living and working in the Soviet Union in 1972–76; he also drew on a variety of small, informal polls and on a range of circumstantial evidence. Other visitors, Soviet informants, uncensored Soviet writings and indeed much openly published Soviet fiction support his assessment.

'Civic cynicism and alienation are so pervasive,' wrote Bushnell, 'that by comparison post-Watergate America seems a hotbed of utopian optimism: few members of the Soviet middle class will admit that they do more than go through the motions of their professional and civic duties' (p. 186).

Bushnell argued that the growth of economic pessimism was attributable in part to the real economic-growth slowdown that occurred in the USSR in the 1970s. This slowdown will be considered below in this chapter, with a retrospective view of the Soviet slowdown over the whole post-war period deferred to the final chapter. Bushnell considered, however, that the shift from optimism to pessimism about the economy did not match at all precisely the sequence of economic developments. The harvest failures of 1963 and 1965, he observed, seem not to have dented Soviet middle-class optimism, whereas that of 1975 apparently deepened the pessimistic mood considerably. He suggests two other factors: a general increase in materialism in the outlook of the Soviet middle class, and greater opportunities to make comparisons with other countries.

These points will also be taken up below. Here it is worth noting that Bushnell judged the influential comparisons to be, not with the West, but with Eastern Europe. He estimates that between 1960 and the end of 1976 some 12 to 15 million Soviet citizens had visited Eastern Europe, some more than once, whether as tourists, official visitors (trade delegations, sports teams and so on) or as soldiers stationed there. The last of these categories he puts at 2.5 million (Bushnell 1980, p. 192). Eastern Europe was for many Russians their accessible West. (So, too, were the Baltic states: '*nash malenkii zapad*' – 'our little West'. I recall in 1971 a Moscow artist saying to me: 'Imagine! In Estonia even the chairman of the Union of Artists is an abstract painter!') The pessimism, if Bushnell was right, was not so much about the economic system – shared, after all, by Eastern Europe – as about the Soviet economy in particular.

The perception of deteriorating performance grew at a time when the Soviet Union was achieving, or was believed to be achieving, approximate strategic parity with the West. 'The 1970s,' wrote Condoleezza Rice in 1987, 'will probably go down as the "Golden Age" for the Soviet Union in international politics' (Rice 1987, p. 193). Yet it is doubtful whether the build-up of military resources under Brezhnev had much to do with the slowdown in the economy (see the previous chapter, and below in this chapter).

The Anti-Ballistic Missile Treaty of 1972 was one indication of strategic parity. It was based on an understanding between Washington and Moscow that enough overkill was enough; mutual assured destruction was available, and it was therefore in the interests of both sides not to waste resources on additional warheads or on anti-missile shields that would disturb the strategic balance.

Oddly enough, this was also a time of continuing, almost routine, Soviet usage of imported Western food and technology (see the previous two chapters). To say that the USSR had become 'dependent' on the West would be to beg too many questions: for example, could the regime cut these imports if it chose to with no risk to its control of the country? Did the extent of these imports, given the dispersed and competitive nature of their supply, really confer any leverage on Washington or on NATO? At all events, the perception that the USSR did not feed itself or independently propel its own technological progress probably contributed to the population's sense of failure.

The equivalent observation in a small, open economy with a tradition of trade – the Netherlands or Sweden, for example – would dismay nobody. But this was the land of Socialism in One Country. The capitalist world was there to be overtaken, not to be trusted.

Two other international concomitants of the late Brezhnevian stagnation are at first sight puzzling. First, the Soviet Union was a beneficiary, not a victim, of the oil-price hikes of the 1970s. As a net exporter of oil and gas it derived very large terms-of-trade gains from the actions of the Organisation of Petroleum Exporting Countries (OPEC). The increased revenues allowed Moscow to import more from the West than it would otherwise have done. This should have enabled – and probably did enable – total domestic final spending on consumption, investment and government purchases of goods and services to be higher in real terms through the 1970s and into the early 1980s than they would otherwise have been.

Yet the 1970s were precisely the time when it became clear that Soviet economic growth was slowing down. If the rate of progress is measured by the growth of per capita GDP in 1990 dollars, this slowed from 2.7 per cent a year in 1964–73 to 1.5 per cent a year in 1973–85 (derived from Maddison 1995, Table D-1; see also the final chapter below). Those who read the more esoteric Soviet scholarly publications could even find alternative measurements of performance that differed sharply from those sanctioned by the State Statistics Committee. The remarkable Grigorii Khanin, who had been beavering away for years on the fringes of the Soviet academic establishment, making his own estimates of Soviet growth, published some of them, in a heavily disguised form, in 1981 (Khanin 1981). One conclusion that can be inferred from that paper is that Khanin estimated Soviet industrial growth from 1970 to 1980 at only 1.7 per cent a year. The official figure was 5.9 per cent (derived from *Narkhoz 22–82*, p. 150).

One conjecture is that the windfall gains may have helped to prop up the rate of growth of Soviet production in the medium term (among other things, by increasing the capacity for productivity-enhancing technology imports), but not by enough to stop the deceleration.

Another conjecture might be that the USSR was a victim of the so-called Dutch disease, in which natural-resource export gains have effects that hamper the development of other sectors. The Dutch disease in its standard form, admittedly, cannot have affected Soviet production. The standard Dutch-disease diagnosis is that new natural-resource discoveries, generating natural-resource exports, or higher world prices for those exports, increase income and therefore demand, drawing in more imports of other tradable goods and pulling resources from the manufacturing sector into the non-tradables sector. This comes about partly because the natural resource export growth strengthens the exchange rate, and that in turn makes the rest of the economy (more precisely, the production of other tradable goods and services) less competitive than it otherwise would be. In the Soviet Union, however, the exchange rate had almost no practical significance, and domestic demand had no automatic effect on domestic production. Dollar, sterling or Deutschmark prices for exports could be freely chosen, without reference to domestic costs and prices or to the exchange rate. Possibly, however, the Soviet Union suffered from some other form of 'resource curse'; the question will be taken up below.

The second paradox about the 'stagnating' USSR and the wider world was that this was a period when, unusually, the Soviet leaders sanctioned military adventures of some substance. In December 1979 Soviet troops invaded Afghanistan. Moscow also provided military assistance, without overt participation, in civil wars in Ethiopia and Angola.

So this increasingly creaky economy, led by increasingly creaky old men, was enjoying its strategic golden age, throwing its military weight around, alarming NATO countries and its close neighbours, while trading more intensively than ever with the traditional enemy and benefiting from wind-fall gains in energy prices. Neither the muscle-flexing nor the petro-dollars, apparently, did much to alleviate the country's deep-seated economic problems. Oddly enough, they probably did little, as I shall try to show, to exacerbate them, either.

The next section of this chapter is a review of the evidence for a slowdown from the early 1970s, and of the main elements in it. Then there is a review of policies, followed by sections on agriculture and on foreign economic relations – both of which loom large in the developments of this period.

The growth slowdown

The deceleration of Soviet growth was of a general kind. Table 5.1 shows that, on the supply side, both industry and agriculture experienced a slowdown; and on the demand side, both consumption growth and investment growth also slowed.

The slowdown cannot, in other words, be identified with a particular sector or a particular end-use. In this context, it makes very little difference arithmetically whether one contrasts the first nine years of Brezhnev's rule with the last nine (he died in November 1982) or with a twelve-year period to the end of 1985, which includes the brief interregnums of Andropov and Chernenko and the first few months of Gorbachev's rule (Gorbachev became leader in the spring of 1985). The latter part of the table, Table 5.1B, therefore treats 1973–85 as the period of stagnation, for illustrative purposes.

On the supply side, the estimated growth rates of industry and agriculture slowed down, as it happens, by the same amount as GNP as a whole. Between them they accounted for only a little over half of GNP, but clearly the sum of transport, construction and services experienced a closely similar slowdown.

One supply-side factor attracted particular controversy: energy production, and the output of crude oil in particular. In April 1977 the CIA published what became one of its more widely cited reports (CIA *Oil*, 1977, followed in July by CIA *Oil Supplementary*, 1977), arguing that the Tenth Five-Year Plan target of 640 million tons annual output (12.8 million barrels a day) in 1980 would not be reached, and that the country's total oil output would fall at some point between 1979 and 1983. At a time when oil was increasing its share in the Soviet energy balance (the shift from coal, like other technological shifts, came late in the USSR), and was contributing substantially to export earnings, this was a sensitive topic.

Table 5.1A *'Stagnation': the slowdown in Soviet growth in the 1970s and early 1980s (selected measures and years, % p.a. rates of change)*

	1964–73	*1973–82*	*1973–85*
GNP	4.7	1.8	1.8
By sector of origin			
Industry	5.8	3.0	2.9
Agriculture[a]	3.0	−0.3	0.1
By end-use			
Consumption	4.5	2.5	2.5
Investment	5.8	2.3	2.4

Table 5.1B *Components in the slowdown between 1964–73 and 1973–85*

Component	*Change in growth rate (% p.a.)*	*Weight of component in GNP (%)*	*Effect (% p.a.)*
Industry	−2.9	32.4	−0.9
Agriculture[a]	−2.9	20.6	−0.6
Consumption	−2.0	55.3	−1.1
Investment	−3.4	30.4	−1.0

Notes: a. Growth rates of agricultural output derived from changes between three-year averages centred on the end-point year of each sub-period. Therefore the arithmetical measure of contribution to the slowdown in Table 5.1B is only approximate.
General: Based on CIA estimates in 1982 roubles, factor cost. Sector and end-use weights are for 1982.
Source: derived from CIA 1990, Tables A-3 and A-6.

In reaching their conclusions, the Agency's analysts proceeded as usual from careful study of a mass of Soviet published information. Therefore part of what they were saying was in line with official assessments by Soviet specialists. The accessible reserves west of the Urals were being depleted, and a major shift was under way to developing massive fields in West Siberia, chiefly in Tyumen' region. There was at the same time a declining ratio of new reserves proved to current output. All of that was common ground. And nobody disputed that West Siberia floated on a sea of oil and gas. The Agency's specialists advanced arguments for a projection in which the decline in output west of the Urals proceeded faster than Soviet plans allowed, while the build-up of production east of the Urals developed more slowly. (See also Lee and Lecky 1979.)

Up to a point, everybody was right. Output in 1980 was indeed below target, at 603.2 million tons (*Narkhoz 22–82*, p. 182). West Siberian production exceeded its 300 million tons target for 1980 but ran into trouble later. Production west of the Urals did indeed fall more steeply than the planners envisaged. But total output kept on increasing through 1983, to just over 616 million tons. Then, exhausted by the effort of discrediting the CIA's predictions, Soviet riggers, well-head operatives and pen-pushers took a breather; output declined a little, to just under 613 million tons in 1984, and then slipped badly, to 595 million tons, in 1985, a year for which the Eleventh Five-Year Plan target had been 630 million tons. But 1985 was also the year for which CIA analysts had predicted in 1979 an output of only 500 million tons. (The figures quoted here are from *Pravda*, 28 October 1976, pp. 2–3, and 18 November 1981, pp. 2–3; Lee and Lecky 1979, p. 598; *Narkhoz 22–82*, p. 182, and Stern 1987, p. 503.)

It is entirely possible that there were geopolitical considerations behind the release of the original CIA report. It is also possible that it had the effect, presumably unintended, of galvanising Soviet efforts. At the Central Committee plenum of December 1977, eight months after the original CIA report, a new programme was announced of rapidly concentrating labour and capital in West Siberia. And indeed it was West Siberia that saved the day – or rather the year, 1980. Still, the CIA analysts had a point. The top of the range of oil production targets in the abortive Twelfth Five-Year Plan was 640 million tons in 1990 – the same as the Tenth Five-Year Plan target for 1980. Actual output got to 624 million tons in 1988 and then, in the general collapse of the Soviet economy, fell to 571 million tons in 1990 (*Narkhoz 90*, p. 397).

In an economy in which energy was so wastefully used, it may seem strange to describe energy supplies as a constraint on output. In an engineering sense they were not. But the wasteful usage of energy, prompted by soft budget constraints on producers and below-cost pricing to households (as well as to producers), as well as the reliance on oil and gas for hard-currency earnings, led Soviet policymakers to pour resources into the oil and gas industries, as they also did into agriculture. These two sectors, farming and hydrocarbon extraction, were highly inefficient and swallowed up resources to the detriment of the rest of the economy.

On the demand side investment growth slowed much more markedly than consumption. This was at least in part the result of a deliberate policy decision to plan for slower investment growth in the 1976–80 and 1981–85 five-year plans (see the next section). In these CIA estimates, investment and consumption together account for 85 per cent of the total GNP, and their slowdowns together account for 2.1 per cent out of the 2.9 per cent overall slowdown.

This raises a question: what else was happening on the demand side of the economy? Or, perhaps one should ask, what else did the CIA think was happening on the demand side of the economy? In particular, what was happening to the Soviet defence burden? The Agency's statistical fudge over defence spending – not to mention the Soviet authorities' even fudgier fudge – does not help (see the previous chapter). By not explicitly identifying defence expenditure in their reconstruction of Soviet national income accounts, CIA analysts left this question open.

In separate assessments, however, CIA analysts concluded in the early 1980s that Soviet defence spending had also, in real terms, experienced a slowdown in growth. Up to 1976 it had been growing, they reckoned, at 4–5 per cent a year; their estimates for 1976–82 produced a figure of 2 per cent a year. For the specific defence spending category of military hardware procurement they could find no growth at all in the latter period (Kaufman 1983; CIA 1983). With a time-lag, and with due allowance for arms exports, military hardware procurement must reflect the production of weapons systems and other military kit. It is possible, therefore, that the growth of military production slowed right down at some point in the 1970s.

There is no question that by the early 1980s the Soviet economy was in severe difficulties. There had been serious grain-harvest failures in 1972, 1975 and 1981. Farm output as a whole virtually ceased to grow in the late 1970s (see below). Household consumption of goods, as estimated by the CIA, fell by 0.3 per cent in 1982, which meant a per capita decline of just over 1 per cent (derived from CIA 1990, Table A-6; population from *Narkhoz 82*). Total household consumption (goods and services) increased, on the CIA's estimates, but by marginally less than population. In a number of provincial cities food rationing was introduced (Tenson 1982).

In 1981–82 the Brezhnev leadership seems to have been alarmed by the possibility of consumer grumbles turning into active discontent. They may indeed have already been haunted by this fear in the mid-1970s, if one can judge from some of the policy decisions of the time. This topic is taken up in the next section.

Why did this slowdown occur? Some of the broader interpretations of the whole post-war trajectory of the Soviet economy are considered in the final chapter. In Table 5.2 an effort is made to identify some of the key symptoms that showed up in the late Brezhnev period.

The table presents sources of growth in the six-year period 1976–82. The underlying assumption is that it can make sense to account for growth using an aggregate production function, in this case a Cobb-Douglas production function with constant returns to scale. Changes in the quantities of

Table 5.2   *The Soviet economy in 1976–82: a growth accounting exercise (GNP growth in this period 2.5% p.a.)*

	Growth (% p.a.)	Weight	Effect (% p.a.)
Primary Inputs			
Capital	6.8	0.33	2.24
Labour	1.2	0.62	0.74
Land	0	0.05	0
Other sources of output	−0.5		
change of which			
Natural resource depletion	−0.6		
Resource shifts between sectors	0.3 (?)		
Change in average weather	−0.7		
Organisational change	0		
Other, incl. morale/effort; bottlenecks; technological innovation and diffusion; skill change	0.5		

Source: adapted from Hanson 1992, Table 1–4. Input and output series used were CIA estimates from *HES 1982*. Detailed explanation in present text.

labour, capital and land used in the economy are estimated to affect the level of output, other things being equal, in ways that might be expected in theory and that have been shown to fit fairly well in growth accounting exercises for several Western countries. (For an extended discussion of methodological and data issues relating to the Soviet Union, see Ofer 1988.)

In practical terms, with the simple Cobb-Douglas approach used here, this means taking a weighted average of the growth rates of these inputs, and treating the difference between that overall input growth rate and the growth rate of output as a measure of total factor productivity change or, less presumptuously, simply as the 'residual' (unexplained change in output). This is what the first four rows of figures in Table 5.2 do.

In most developed economies in most periods of five years or more the residual comes out as a positive amount, part of which can be expected to be the result of technological progress: the introduction and diffusion of new products and processes in the economy. But other growth sources can also play a part: major natural resource discoveries, improved skills in the workforce, shifts in resource allocation from lower-productivity to higher-productivity sectors, and so on.

The illustrative calculations in Table 5.2 suggest the following. The growth of combined inputs of labour and capital might have been expected, other things being equal, to raise output at about 3 per cent a year. However, actual growth of output was half a percentage point less than this. It appears at first glance, therefore, that some factors were operating in ways that, on balance, tended to drag output down. The last five figures in column 1 of the table are tentative guesstimates of the effects of the various influences that could have produced this net negative effect. (For more detail see Hanson 1992; for another – broadly compatible – review of these issues see Levine 1982.)

Some of these factors were beyond the influence of the Soviet authorities. The depletion of oil, gas, coal and mineral resources in the European part of the USSR was forcing new natural-resource extraction to move east of the Urals – mainly to West Siberia. Extraction costs per unit of output were not necessarily higher in these new locations (though in some of them, in the far north, they were). However, these new regional developments required investment in transport, communications, housing and other infrastructure and the transport westwards of most of the energy and materials extracted, since the great bulk of manufacturing and urban settlement remained west of the Urals. Soviet studies of associated total cost increases, cited in Hanson 1992, provide a basis, admittedly highly conjectural, for the guesstimate in Table 5.2 of the effect of this geographic shift.

The rate of population shift from country to town and of labour from agriculture, meanwhile, was slowing down as the economy matured. 'Resource shifts between sectors' refers to the movement of labour from agriculture to industry alone, as the most salient inter-sectoral shift that was going on. Given the differences between labour productivity in agriculture and in industry, and given the rate of movement of labour from the former to the latter, the modest positive effect shown in the table, 0.3 per cent per annum, is plausible (and it is less than in earlier periods).

The incidence of poor harvests was somewhat higher than in earlier periods. For reasons touched on in Chapter 2, grain harvests had broader economic consequences in the Soviet Union than they had in other industrial countries. Here, too, is a negative influence, in comparison with the recent past.

Other influences could be thought of as being, at least potentially and in the medium term, open to influence by policy-makers. These were systemic change or reform, treated in Table 5.2 as zero (see the next section); changes in morale and effort; the emergence of input–output bottlenecks affecting the supply of key inputs (much discussed in the Soviet literature at the time), and technological progress in the closely related senses of (a) the introduction and diffusion of new products and processes and (b) the growth of skill and know-how in the workforce.

The three exogenous factors plus organisational change, as guesstimated here, more than account for the original 'residual' of −0.5 per cent per annum. Logically, then, the net effect of the remaining influences would be precisely enough to offset that −0.5 per cent per annum; it is therefore put at +0.5 per cent per annum.

These calculations are, to repeat, illustrative only. They do at least support the commonsense view that technological progress was continuing, at however unsatisfactory a rate, probably with output-enhancing effects that were partly offset by morale effects (see the introduction to this chapter) and some worsening bottlenecks.

The notion of declining morale and effort affecting output levels may seem a bit too touchy-feely to be taken seriously. We need however to take notice of the extensive Soviet discussion at the time of a decline in 'plan discipline'. In any centrally administered production system, it is reasonable to assume that rewards and coercion (carrots and sticks) can both be used to elicit effort from managers and workers, and that each has, from the centre's point of view, its associated costs of monitoring and implementing, as well as its associated yields in higher total output. Harrison (2001a) has argued that monitoring costs rose over time in the USSR, inducing the central authorities to relax the role of coercion in the running of the economy.

Harrison sees the real effect coming only at the very end (from 1988) when the central authorities 'gave up' on attempts to coerce and control. Some other economists, however, envisage the loss of coercive power having observable adverse economic consequences from at least the early 1970s.

Certainly, Brezhnev's policy of stability of cadres – that is, keeping senior managers and officials in post for long periods of time, in reaction to the instability inflicted on the elite by Khrushchev (not to mention Stalin) – must by itself have made enterprise managers feel less vulnerable to disciplinary measures.

In addition, it was widely believed in the 1970s and early 1980s that *korrektirovki* ('corrections') to an enterprise's annual-plan targets in the course of the year were to an increasing extent downwards adjustments to output targets without corresponding cuts in planned inputs, and that enterprises were commonly reported to have met their output targets at the end of the year even though all they had done was to meet a target adjusted downwards to suit them. Levine (1982, pp. 164–5) cites a (rare) Soviet quantitative study of plan adjustment and fulfilment reports at 175 production units during 1970–78 inclusive: the study does indeed find this practice to be common: only a very small minority of enterprises failed to collect their plan-fulfilment bonuses, even though a much larger number did not in fact meet their original targets.

This evidence is not conclusive. Comparable information from earlier periods would be needed to determine whether this evidence on *korrektirovki* represented a relaxation of plan discipline. What can be said is that Soviet economists and commentators, some of them involved directly in industrial management, believed that plan discipline was going soft. In this they concurred with the emigrés cited at the beginning of this chapter.

Bottlenecks in supplies of steel, non-ferrous metals and building materials were widely cited as hindering the growth of investment. In 1975 a decision was taken to slow the growth rate of investment – both total investment in general and gross fixed investment in particular. The latter in fact grew by only 3.4 per cent a year in 1976–80, compared with close to 7 per cent a year in the previous five years (Leggett 1982; later CIA recalculations in 1982 roubles produce appreciably slower rates for both periods, but still a marked slowdown between them. See CIA *Measures* 1990). The slow investment growth strategy was continued in the 1981–85 plan. (See Leggett 1982 and Levine 1982, as well as the next section, for discussion.)

Policies relating to the slowdown are considered in the next section. What appeared to be happening to the Soviet economy in the late 1970s and early 1980s was that growth had slowed, affecting all three main uses of output: consumption, investment and defence. The reasons for the slowdown were to be found at least partly in factors beyond the policymakers' control. However, only an improvement in productivity growth could have offset the growth-dampening influences, an overall deterioration in the weather, natural-resource depletion, the decelerating resource shift out of agriculture and (probably) a softening of plan discipline. That improvement in productivity growth was being sought by policymakers. Hence the burgeoning literature and speechifying about a shift to more intensive growth. But it was probably unattainable under the system.

From about 1980, the policymakers had another growth-dampening effect to worry about. The growth rate of the labour force was slowing drastically, for demographic reasons. The ratio of new entrants to the working-age population to departures from that population was falling. This, again, was something beyond the reach of policy, at any rate over anything less than an eighteen-year period.

Meanwhile, there was considerable doubt about what was really happening in investment. The Novosibirsk economist Val'tukh presented evidence that reported growth in the volume of fixed investment was misleading: if compared with increments of capacity, sector by sector, measured in physical terms (additional steel capacity in tons per year, additional mineral fertiliser capacity in tons per year, and so on), reported increases in investment in constant prices were greatly overstating the growth in capital stock (Val'tukh 1982). Others produced evidence that the time-lags in the Soviet investment process were so large that increments in capacity stemmed from much earlier investment outlays than the planners calculated, and that this contributed to grave imbalances between sectoral capacities (Baryshnikov and Lavrovskii 1982). This, according to these analysts, made the slowdown in investment more dangerous to future growth prospects than it seemed.

Policies and reforms

The extent to which the slowdown in both investment growth and the growth of the defence effort was intended by the leadership remains unclear. It is possible that at least into the mid-1970s they were trying to extract more investment and more defence from their economy than they were able to, and in the case of investment simply made the best of a bad job by publicly lowering their sights. It is also possible, however, that there was such anxiety about possible discontent among Soviet citizens that defence and investment priorities were deliberately reduced. The early 1970s *détente* with the US, including the ABM treaty, might have been deployed as grounds for curbing the military effort.

Certainly there were high officials who were concerned about the slowdown and sought to promote policies that might reverse it. In 1975 Gosplan sent a report to the Party Central Committee describing the country's economic problems and proposing measures to tackle them. This was rejected by Brezhnev (Baibakov 1993b). It may nonetheless have influenced policy-makers to slow investment growth. Ten years later, when Gorbachev sought to re-accelerate the growth of investment, he found Gosplan opposing him. (See Chapter 7.)

Some of the thinking behind the investment slowdown was revealed at the XXV Party Congress of February–March 1976, when the main plan targets were unveiled, two months into the period they referred to: the Tenth Five-Year Plan for 1976–80. This was also an occasion for making some personal points. There had for some time been rumours that Leonid Brezhnev was in poor health. In October 1975 he had said to French journalists, 'There is too much talk about my health. It is better to talk about something else' (*EIU QER* 1975, no. 4, p. 2). At the Party Congress four months later he talked for five hours about the plan. If the Soviet leader was on his last legs, they could still support him for long periods of time.

Speeches at the Congress indicate that the leadership really was trying to respond to changed circumstances. It also looks as though they were very nervous about consumption levels. Strikingly, Brezhnev remarked that 'we have not yet learnt how to combine rapid growth of industry with rapid development of consumer goods and services'. He also noted the demographic hindrances to continued rapid output growth, observing that increases in the labour force would slow down in the 1980s (as they did). The new five-year plan, he announced, would be the plan of effectiveness and quality (*Sotsialisticheskaya industriya*, 25 February 1976; subsequently repeated in the Soviet press *passim* and *ad nauseam*).

Kosygin, ever the nuts-and-bolts man, explained in his speech (*Pravda*, 2 March 1976, p. 5) that capital stock growth would not slow down anywhere near as much as new fixed investment, because the gestation period of capital investment was long enough to ensure that past investment was still being completed at a high rate. Lest anyone should conclude that the slowdown in capacity growth would merely be deferred (which it was), Kosygin also explained that the share of machinery and equipment in investment would rise at the expense of building work; more priority was to be given to re-equipping existing plants and less to building new ones. This latter shift in priority was announced again by Gorbachev ten years later. The Stalinist industrialisation emphasis on new-plant construction, appropriate enough in the 1930s and in post-war reconstruction, had proved to be extremely persistent, long after it should have ended. Producers with soft budget constraints always found it in their interest to 'book' as much investment spending into the plan as they could get away with.

At all events, the Tenth Five-Year Plan (1976–80 inclusive) contained the lowest-ever five-year-plan targets for the growth of investment (lowest, that is, in percentage terms). Total fixed investment was planned to grow at only about 4.5 per cent a year between the 1971–75 and 1976–80 plan totals (Brezhnev's speech at the XXV Party Congress, *Sotsialisticheskaya industriya*, 25 February 1976). More precise figures, announced when the plan law was finally published in *Pravda* eight months later (30 October), set state-funded investment to grow between 1975 and 1980 at only 2.8 per cent a year. The difference between these two figures was purely presentational. There was some officially non-state-funded investment – by the collective farms – but the main reason for the difference between the two figures is that the plan 'front-loaded' investment, tapering year-on-year growth in it to almost zero in 1980.

The downgrading of investment in aggregate was combined with a heightened emphasis on investment in agriculture. Brezhnev's Party Congress speech quoted figures for investment in farming that implied that it would amount to just over 27 per cent of the total; though actual figures for the previous five years were not exactly comparable, this appeared to entail a small further increase (by 1 per cent) in the sector's share. Yet again, the worry about food production is evident. So, too, is the enhancement of the priority change initiated by Khrushchev. In the first half of the 1960s agriculture's share of investment had been pushed up (against opposition) to 16 per cent. In the second half of the 1960s it had edged up to 18 per cent (see Chapter 4). Now it was over a quarter and still rising. There are some definitional changes that slightly blur these comparisons; see the section on Agriculture, below. The comparisons are also muddied by changes in the base-year prices on which these figures are based, but there is no reason to doubt the direction of change and its order of magnitude.

At the same time as emphasising agriculture and trying to cut back on wasteful new building, the investment programme contained an extravagant 'project of the century' in the worst traditions of Stalinist gigantomania. This was the Baikal-Amur Mainline (BAM) project to add a second rail route between Lake Baikal in Siberia and Komsomolsk-na-Amure in the Russian Far East, duplicating the existing Trans-Siberian but further north: a new railway 2,200 miles long (details are set out and discussed in a symposium in the Novosibirsk journal, *EKO*, 1976 no. 2). It had been started in 1974, was scheduled for completion in 1983, actually took longer, and in 1975 employed 40,000 workers.

Constructed partly in an earthquake zone and entirely in a wilderness, with swamps, and including six miles of bridges and ten miles of tunnels, the BAM project was visionary in the worst sense. It was claimed that the rationale was to develop a timber- and minerals-rich zone either side of the new railway, but very little of this ever happened. Bottlenecks on the Trans-Siberian were west of Baikal, so the BAM did nothing to expedite trans-Siberian cargoes. Some foreign commentators suggested that the real motive was strategic: to develop a route further from the Chinese border than the Trans-Siberian and thus less vulnerable to forcible interruption or threats of interruption. This would be consistent with a long tradition of developing remote regions for geo-strategic rather than economic reasons, extending from pre-Soviet to post-Soviet Russia (President Putin's address to the Federal Assembly on 3 April 2001 lists regions to be assigned special development funds for strategic reasons; www.strana.ru, 3 April 2001).

Overall, however, the priority changes in the mid-1970s were intended to favour the consumer. They reflected alarm about the slowing growth of the economy and the prospect of a further slowdown in the growth of labour supplies: an alarm focused especially on the need to improve living standards.

In 1980–81 the same broad strategy was repeated for the Eleventh Five-Year Plan (1981–85 inclusive). The official measure of national income favoured at the time, 'national income utilised', had shown in 1976–80 an average annual rate of increase of 3.9 per cent (*Pravda*, 24 January 1981), the lowest recorded in any peacetime Soviet five-year-plan period. The target for 1981–85, when it was finally set in the law on the five-year plan, was lower again: 3.4 per cent per annum (*Pravda*, 20 November 1981). The growth rate of fixed investment (always measured as the average rate between the totals for each five-year period, rather than between the start and the finish of a plan period) had worked out at 5.2 per cent a year in the Tenth Five-Year Plan, and was set to average only 2.0 per cent for the next plan (these two numbers come from the same sources as the previous two figures).

Any pathologically alert reader will have noticed that the reported outcome for investment growth in the 1976–80 plan was in fact rather higher than the plan target. In this, it differed from the outcomes for all the other large aggregates targeted: national income (Soviet-definition, or net material product; on the definition, see Chapter 1), industrial gross output and agricultural gross output. Many Soviet economists assessed the official investment figures as containing an above-average amount of concealed inflation; 'real' increments of capital stock (in effect, the consequences for capacity of spending on fixed investment, visible after a time-lag) seemed to be diminishing over time (Val'tukh 1982; Baryshnikov and Lavrovskii 1982). A similar view was held by some analysts in the West, but economists in the CIA's Office of Economic Research believed at the time that they lacked data to adjust their own recalculations for the concealed inflation in equipment investment, (JEC *Growth*, 1982, pp. 44 and 117). Quite apart from the question of the reliability of the data on reported outcomes, the plan and the outcome figures were known to be calculated in ways that made precise comparison between them impossible.

To cut a long story short, we can say that the Soviet planners almost certainly knew that real investment growth had slowed considerably, and they chose to slow that growth further in the late 1970s and early 1980s. Behind the decisions in 1975–76 and 1980–81 was an acknowledgement that delays in investment projects were massive, that most projects were under-staffed most of the time, and that completed new capacity often could not be manned (see Hanson 1986). Against a background of slowing overall growth of output, worries about stagnating consumption levels and possible unrest, and the knowledge that in the 1980s labour-force growth would slow substantially, the change of strategy was not self-evidently foolish.

Reform, meanwhile, remained in abeyance. Or rather, the economy was, in Gertrude Schroeder's phrase, 'on a treadmill of "reforms"' (the quotation marks are hers; Schroeder 1979, 1982): no radical devolution of decision-making but constant tinkering with incentive schemes and other organisational details, in a manner familiar in the British public sector since the 1970s, but without privatisation.

A decree of 1973 called for the formation of large groupings of enterprises into 'industrial associations' that would be responsible for much of the detail of planning for their constituent enterprises and for some of the internal financing of investment. These would be in fact a third tier in a new hierarchy that would go: enterprise – production association – industrial association – branch ministry. Some production associations had been formed, in a very rare example of Soviet bottom-up organisational innovation, in some regions during the *sovnarkhoz* (regional economic council) period of 1957–65. Later their formation was promoted from above and became something for which targets were set.

Both production and industrial associations had potential advantages. The production association might succeed in re-allocating product lines amongst its constituent enterprises, of which there were usually between three and five, so that production runs were lengthened and economies of scale obtained. It might seem unlikely that the existing giant-sized, single-plant enterprises, producing a rather narrow range of final products, could reap economies of scale. In fact, the vagaries of the supply system were so bad that the typical enterprise tried as far as possible to make its own components, sub-assemblies and other material inputs, often doing so on less than minimum efficient scale. Internally, many Soviet enterprises were highly diversified even when their planned output that went to the supply system was quite restricted in product-mix. Over and above any such gains through increased plant specialisation, the production association held out the possibility of some of the detail of enterprise plans being handled by the association, not the branch ministry or Gosplan.

Another variant of the production association, the science-production association, was thought capable of tackling another deficiency: the poor record of product and process innovation. A science-production association was one headed by a research institute or design bureau. It might succeed in bridging the much-discussed gap between research and development on the one hand, and production on the other. (See Cooper 1982.)

The industrial association was, in some respects and rather faintly, reminiscent of a large Western corporation. This was probably no accident. Greater experience of doing business with Western firms (nearly always with large firms, since few small firms could commit the large resources needed to break into the Soviet market) had familiarised some senior officials with large corporations. And this was a time when the notion of a managerial corps wielding power without ownership was fashionable. J.K. Galbraith's *The New Industrial State* had an elite readership in the USSR, where it was taken seriously. Moscow, like Paris, had a taste for grand theory. A grand theory that proclaimed East–West economic convergence was particularly chic. That the Russian translation was initially available [only] 'for official use' probably increased its appeal.

One difficulty with all these organisational innovations was that they were, in the soft, Brezhnevian style, negotiated not imposed. Those whose decision-making powers were threatened by them – enterprise directors and branch-ministry officials – by and large made sure that the threats came to nothing. Enterprises within production associations kept their juridical identities, their separate bank accounts and pay-scales, and their separate room to manoeuvre in negotiating over plan targets. Branch ministries made sure that the industrial associations, when they eventually took shape, remained for practical purposes the same as the sub-branch main administrations they were meant to replace. The aim of branch-level financial self-sufficiency was pursued only by the handful of branch ministries, such as Minpribor, a civilian ministry responsible for industrial control instruments, that could benefit every year and across their product range from the higher prices they could negotiate for nominally new products: that is, from concealed inflation in the name of new-product pricing. (See Schroeder 1979, 1982; Hanson 1983.)

Another organisational device, first introduced in 1971, was counter-planning. The planners knew very well that the games hitherto played between central planners and producers generated hidden reserves and ratchet effects (see the Annex to the Introduction). The enterprise director had every incentive to seek a soft plan, with a high input allocation for his output target, and typically had the advantage over the planners in that he knew with greater confidence and precision than they did what his enterprise's production capabilities were. So long as his target in each annual plan was derived by extrapolating from his actual output in the last plan period, he would exaggerate his input needs and underplay his output potential.

The idea of counter-planning was that each enterprise would be set a target for each year in a five-year-plan period or, better still, over rolling five-year plans extended five years ahead each year. Certain bonuses could be earned from meeting those targets. But if you (the enterprise director) volunteered a higher target, you would get a higher bonus (without prejudice to your basic plan-fulfilment bonus or future years' targets, and higher than was obtainable simply by over-fulfilling the initial target). Thus enterprises were to be encouraged to reveal their hidden reserves, secure in the knowledge (it was hoped) that next year's basic target would not be revised in the light of this year's out-turn. They would therefore make better use of their available resources, raising output: input ratios, that is, productivity.

What was aimed at was an improvement in the operating efficiency with which a given, plan-determined product-mix was produced, not an increase in allocative efficiency. This was nonetheless well worthwhile, if it could be done. It required among other things that planned allocations of labour, capital and current material inputs be unaffected by whether an enterprise offered a counter-plan or not.

This might have worked had planners had far better detailed information than they did (the root of the original problem) or if they had been content to set very soft, undemanding five-year targets, stick to these over five years and not reward enterprises that offered counter-plans by allocating more inputs to them. From the outset, however, the initial targets were not set deliberately low, the few, naïve enterprise directors who volunteered counter-plans had their basic plan for the next year altered accordingly, and the offering of a counter-plan was rewarded with additional input supplies, undermining the intention of raising productivity.

Articles in the October 1979 issues of the weekly *Ekonomicheskaya gazeta* gave illustrations of virtuous managements who had adopted counter-plans for 1980. In three of the five examples, the counter-plan increase (over the 'basic' targets) was greater for output than it was for labour productivity. This implied that enterprises adopting counter-plans for output might be allocated more labour inputs – negating the whole purpose of the exercise. By then, in any case, it had become an insignificant side-show. From figures given by a senior Gosplan official, it could be deduced that in 1978 the 17 per cent of industrial enterprises that had offered counter-plans were in so doing adding only 0.043 per cent to total gross industrial output that year (Hanson 1983, p. 8). In other words, this innovation had dwindled to a show-and-tell ritual of almost no practical importance.

In July 1979 the Party Central Committee and the USSR Council of Ministers issued a joint decree 'On the Improvement of Planning and the Strengthening of the Action of the Economic Mechanism on the Raising of Effectiveness of Production and the Quality of Work' (*Ekonomicheskaya gazeta* 1979, no. 32, pp. 9–17). The text of the decree, even excluding its title, exceeds 10,000 words. Its practical results appear to have been negligible. It is nonetheless worth some attention because it illustrates the dead end that Soviet policy-makers had reached.

The decree is in part an assembly of already-proclaimed organisational adjustments: counter-planning, for example, is included. It also lays down that the success indicators on which enterprise bonuses are based will be modified. Henceforth, the main bonus-forming indicators are to be labour productivity, quality-mix (of output reported in three quality grades) and fulfilment of delivery plans (of output to users assigned by the plan). Output is to be planned and reported not as gross output (approximately, turnover, in Western terms) but as 'normative net output' (NNO). NNO, in this decree, was related to value added. It was the wage and social insurance costs plus profit reckoned to be appropriate to the enterprise's level of output: not actual labour costs and profits but 'normative' labour costs and profits, as calculated for price-setting purposes per unit of output, times the number of units of output (per year, per quarter, etc.). Labour productivity, according to the decree, would be measured as NNO per worker, not gross output per worker.

As usual with Soviet organisational innovations, there were obvious merits in this change. Product-mix decisions would not (in principle) be distorted any more in favour of product lines with high unit costs for current material inputs. On the other hand, there were obvious limitations: Soviet cost measures for pricing purposes did not closely approximate opportunity costs (relative scarcities) in general, and they were inflexible, not being altered for long periods. This problem was alleviated by a major revision of industrial wholesale prices, involving 2,020 new price lists, with effect from 1 January 1982 (Hanson 1983, p. 2). Even so, NNO measures complicated an already highly complicated planning system. Deliveries of output were recorded, reasonably enough, in terms of gross output, not NNO. It was gross output that the supply planning system dealt in. Many officials appear to have continued to set labour productivity targets in terms of gross output, not NNO. (Details in Schroeder 1982; Hanson 1983.)

Well after the decree was published, the setting of key targets in terms of tons of output – not the 'sales' figure that should have been used since 1965, never mind the new-fangled NNO – was still common. A steel-mill manager who was eccentric enough to make lighter castings because that was what his (centrally assigned) user factories wanted, was penalised by his ministry for not meeting tonnage targets (*Pravda*, 10 August 1981, p. 2). The same paper reported (28 September 1981, p. 2) that the practical planners in Gosplan were happy to confirm – notwithstanding reform decrees and the writings of their own boffins in the Gosplan Research Institute – that it was tonnage figures that they wanted. This was not mere cussedness or stupidity. The supply plan for shipments of many (not all) goods was couched in tons of steel or metres of cloth. Producers had to be instructed to produce what the supply plan required.

The economist Abel Aganbegyan summed up the problem thus: the 1979 decree would work if there was 'a good, well-founded, balanced plan for resource use. . . . [But] in several respects we do not know how to make a good plan' (in a round-table discussion in *EKO* 1982, no. 1, p. 65).

This inability to make a good plan was not a failure to do clever things but a failure to do what might appear to be simple things. There was not the remotest possibility of drawing up a plan that would allocate resources efficiently; but then there is not the remotest possibility either that a market economy will in practice produce an efficient allocation of resources, in the textbook sense of Pareto efficiency. The most immediate Soviet plan problem was simpler: a lot of plan numbers did not add up.

Many examples could be quoted from the Soviet press of the period, for the late Brezhnev years were the heyday of Soviet investigative journalism about the economy – centrally approved, of course, or at any rate centrally tolerated, but often revealing more about mistakes and failures than could easily be discovered and written up about private firms in the West. Here is one example. In 1978 the Gosplan target for the growth of labour productivity in the industrial sector was 3.8 per cent. The sum of the targets approved by ministries for industrial enterprises was 2.5 per cent (*Sotsialisticheskaya industriya*, 27 April 1979).

The political leadership probably was not expecting too much from all their decree-mongering. There is a remarkable passage in Brezhnev's speech to a Party Central Committee plenary meeting in November 1978. Major campaigns on fuel conservation, he says, are having no effect; the same is true of campaigns to accelerate construction projects by improving labour productivity. Decrees are issued but ministries do not respond to them (*Pravda*, 28 November 1978, pp. 1–2). The implication of these remarks is: we have tried everything, and nothing works; the economy just slows down and down. Poor Leonid, the reader thinks, at least he's got his collection of high-performance cars and expensive shotguns to console him.

Others – probably thousands of others: a large part of the economic elite – did not think everything had been tried. In the same round-table discussion from which Aganbegyan has just been quoted, a foreign trade official said, 'The customer must have the right of choice of production [to purchase], it cannot be distributed and allocated as it is in our system of material-technical supply' (*EKO* 1982, no. 1, p. 66). An enterprise director, writing in *Pravda* (1 September 1981, p. 2), said supply problems could be resolved only when enterprises could choose for themselves their sources of supply. The Moscow University economist Gavriil Popov, later to become mayor of Moscow, proposed in *Pravda* (24 May 1980) that the construction of a new car plant should be financed by funds provided by people on the (years' long) waiting list for cars, who would then be compensated in cars. This proposal for the introduction of capitalism did not cause the sky to fall. It was not, however, implemented.

There is nothing the least bit surprising about managers and officials entertaining such thoughts, as the defects of the Soviet economy came ever more visibly to the surface. What is surprising is that they were published. It was almost as if the Soviet elite had declared open season on its own economy.

Agriculture

Throughout this period the Soviet leadership was preoccupied with the farm sector. They might order the invasion of Afghanistan (Christmas 1979) and extend military assistance to Angola, but they showed every sign of worrying much more about meat and milk supplies.

The Tenth Five-Year Plan (1976–80 inclusive) revealed, as was noted above, a priority for agriculture that was remarkable in the light of earlier Soviet history. Brezhnev's subsequent pronouncements on the subject were striking. At yet another Party Central Committee plenum devoted to agriculture (3–4 July 1978), the Soviet leader declared that the farm sector's share of investment must stay at least as high in the Eleventh Five-Year Plan as it was in the current plan: 27 per cent (*EIU QER* 1978, no. 3, pp. 6–8).

This figure is not precisely comparable with some cited earlier for the share of agriculture in total investment; it is slightly higher. In this period three different definitions of 'agriculture' came into use. First there was the traditional usage to refer to agricultural production of all farms and private plots. Second, there was 'agriculture according to the whole complex of works'. This included agricultural research, land improvement and the non-agricultural sidelines of state and collective farms. Third was the 'agro-industrial complex'. This was the second definition plus agricultural machinery and mineral fertiliser production, food processing and 'downstream' transportation. Brezhnev's pronouncement applied to the second definition, which at the time entailed about 5–8 per cent more investment than was going to the narrowest definition of the farm sector. The investment share implied for the farm sector in the narrowest sense was, therefore, 25–26 per cent.

Brezhnev's pledge was an unusual public move to pre-empt strategic investment decisions ahead of any formal five-year plan announcements. Agricultural procurement prices (the prices paid by the state to the farms) were raised again on 1 January 1979 (*ibid.*). Retail food prices remained unchanged, so the food subsidy grew. At the XXVI Party Congress in February 1981 Brezhnev again emphasised the importance of agriculture (*Pravda*, 24 February 1981, p. 6). Then at the Party Central Committee plenum of November 1981 he said, 'The food problem is the central problem of the five-year plan [referring to 1981–85], on the political plane as well as on the economic plane' (*Pravda*, 17 November 1981, pp. 1–2).

At the next Central Committee plenum, in May 1982, the new 'Food Programme' was unveiled (*Pravda*, 25 May 1982, pp 1–2, and 27 May 1982, pp. 1–4). Again, Brezhnev projected a 27 per cent share of investment for agriculture into the next plan period (1986–90). He set a long-run target of one metric ton of grain per inhabitant, explicitly to reduce dependence on foreign grain supplies; announced another rise in procurement prices from the start of 1983; and introduced a new organisational animal: an agro-industrial commission at both republic and all-Union levels, with a sub-structure of agro-industrial associations at rural district level, combining in their remit the supervision not only of agriculture proper but also of related infrastructure, procurement, and processing.

The Polish workers, it seems, had a lot to do with all this. As early as 1970 there were rumours in Moscow that a planned, but unannounced, rise in Soviet retail food prices had been cancelled when workers in Poland went on strike and protested about food-price rises there. 'We owe a debt of gratitude to our Polish comrades,' people said at the time, 'for keeping down our cost of living.' Whether the rumour reflected reality or not, the perception was that the men in the Kremlin were casting worried glances westwards. And if the KGB was doing its job (a big if), the Kremlin should have been aware of the popular interest in what the uppity Poles were getting away with. Then, as Soviet farm production began to stall, with bad harvest failures in 1975, 1979, 1980 and 1981, the Polish workers kept disturbing the Soviet Politburo's sleep with further illustrations of a worst-case scenario for the USSR: renewed protests in 1976, and then the rise of Solidarity at the end of the 1970s. (For an extended account of the relation-ship between Polish unrest and Soviet policies, see Teague 1988.)

If John Bushnell was right, it was comparison with Central-Eastern Europe that contributed strongly to the growing economic pessimism of Soviet citizens. It seems also to be the case that growing unrest in Central Europe had its effects on the Soviet leadership.

The Russian food-supply problems were real. Even in Moscow, which received top priority in food supplies, restaurants and cafeterias were or-ganising 'meatless days' in 1976 (*EIU QER* 1976, no. 2, p. 4). This was not because they had been taken over by evangelical vegetarians. Elsewhere, supplies were even worse, and provoked scattered protests. The *Figaro* cor-respondent reported strikes and disturbances over food supplies in Rostov-on-Don, Kiev and Riga (*ibid.*). Dock-workers in Riga were jailed for their part in such strikes (*EIU QER* 1976, no. 4, p. 5). Later, workers in Tula protested about food shortages by refusing to accept their pay-packets (Soviet workers were normally paid in cash), on the grounds that there was nothing to spend the money on. The Soviet authorities (probably after jailing a few ringleaders) responded in this case by declaring Tula a Hero-City. This was not a homage to the people who had refused to accept their wages, but an adjustment to history: Tula was declared to be a city whose people had fought heroically in the Great Fatherland War (1941–45). It was therefore to be honoured with the title of Hero-City. That had the effect of promoting the city by one grade in the pecking order for food distribution (*EIU QER* 1980, no. 3, p. 10).

Late Brezhnev policy on agriculture, and indeed on broad economic priorities in general, seems to have been driven by a profound fear of a popular uprising. This is a conjecture supported by a good deal of circumstantial evidence, rather than a testable and well-tested hypothesis. The slowdown in overall investment growth after 1975 was deliberate (see the previous section). So was the increase in the farm sector's share in that more slowly growing total. The investment slowdown was thought at first by some analysts to be designed to make space for a faster growth of defence spending. But early 1980s US intelligence assessments found almost no growth in military hardware procurement over the period (see, again, the previous section).

Either the worsening of bottlenecks in steel and other key supplies thwarted a growth of military production that had been planned, or there was a deliberate slowdown in the growth of military hardware production as well as in that of investment. Either way, Soviet policy-makers were in great difficulties and, either way, they were sufficiently worried about farm production to give it an enhanced priority at a difficult time. And when domestic food production stalled, the importance attached to food supplies was attested by the large amounts of convertible ('hard') currency spent on grain and other food imports, supported by gold sales and international borrowing (see the next section).

Great importance was also attached to not upsetting people by raising food prices. An attempt was made to soak up some of the excess purchasing power in the hands of the population by raising retail prices of a few luxury items (in June 1977, March 1978 and July 1979; *EIU QER* 1979, no. 3, p. 9). But these were timid, and always accompanied by what were said to be 'offsetting' price cuts on other things, such as small black and white TVs. Meanwhile the annual subsidy to retail prices of meat and dairy produce in 1976 or 1977 was said by the Chairman of the State Prices Committee to be 19 billion roubles; the full cost of producing and distributing top-quality beef, he said, was 3 roubles 50 kopecks a kilo, and the retail price was 2 roubles (*EIU QER* 1977, no. 1, p. 8). The total livestock-product subsidy was equivalent to 3.9 per cent of 1976 GNP as calculated by the CIA at 1970 factor cost (*JEC Growth* 1982, Table A-1). The most appropriate comparison would be with 1976 GNP at current prices but, if such a comparison were possible, the order of magnitude should still come out at 3 per cent plus – a very substantial call on resources for one particular subsidy. The total subsidy to farm products would be larger. When further procurement-price increases were announced for 1 January 1983, the *additional* cost in subsidy (for all farm products) was put at 16 billion roubles a year (*Pravda*, 25 May 1982, p. 1).

The most systematic estimates of Soviet farm subsidies in this period were made by Vladimir Treml (Treml, 1982b). He concluded that the annual subsidy on all farm products, net of a surcharge on milk, rose from 20.9 billion roubles in 1976 to 31.4 billion in 1980, while net subsidies on manufactured goods sold to agriculture (machinery, mineral fertilisers, electricity, etc.) rose from 1.5 to 3.6 billion roubles a year over the same period. Thus the total subsidy in 1980 was of the order of 6 per cent of GNP.

The meaning of the agricultural output stagnation of this period can be seen in Table 5.3 below. There is high variability from year to year, particularly for grain, and in several years a fall in the domestic output per head of population. The period is too short to reveal trends, but there was clearly every reason for the authorities to worry, so long as they were not happy to take advantage of international trade and 'rely on the West' on anything but an emergency, short-term basis. If the Food Programme

Table 5.3 *Soviet output and output per head of population, selected farm products, 1977–82*

	Grain	Sugar beet	Potatoes	Green vegetables	Meat (live weight)	Milk	Eggs
A. *Officially reported output (including private plots; millions of tons, except eggs in billions of units)*							
1977	195.7	93.1	83.7	24.1	14.7	94.9	61.2
1978	237.4	93.5	86.1	27.9	15.5	94.7	64.5
1979	179.2	76.2	91.0	27.2	15.3	93.3	65.6
1980	189.1	81.0	67.0	27.3	15.1	90.9	67.9
1981	149	60.8	72.0	25.6	15.2	88.1	70.9
1982	176	71	78	29	15.2	90.1	72.1
B. *Output per head of year-end population (kg, except eggs in units)*							
1977	752	358	322	93	57	365	235
1978	905	356	328	106	59	361	246
1979	678	288	344	103	58	353	248
1980	709	304	342	102	57	341	255
1981	554	226	268	95	57	328	264
1982	649	262	288	107	56	332	266

Note: The 1981 and 1982 grain harvest figures are semi-official figures communicated by the Soviet Minister of Agriculture to his Canadian counterpart, and not officially reported in the normal way.

Source: Hanson 1992, Table 1–2, where original Soviet and other sources are given.

long-run target was a metric ton of grain per head of population, the Soviet farm sector was further from that objective in 1981–82 than in 1977–78.

Fluctuations in harvests were large by international standards. This was sometimes ascribed to the highly unstable moisture balance (between precipitation and evaporation) and the susceptibility to extreme cold to which most Soviet farmland was geographically doomed. It has been pointed out, however, that variability in Canadian harvests, under very similar climatic conditions, was much less. The difference has been ascribed to the much greater use of summer fallow for grain in Canada (Johnson 1982, p. 12). If Soviet farms extended summer fallow, Johnson argued, they would slightly reduce average output levels but greatly reduce variability. Since they threw nearly three times as much seed on their fields (240 kg per hectare against 85 in the US), the saving in seed would offset much of the output loss.

This was no doubt sound advice, but there was no reason for any manager of a Soviet farm to take it. The running of Soviet state and collective farms was, with perhaps a handful of exceptions involving remarkable individuals, not concerned with good husbandry. It was all about coping with orders from above that were ill-informed and internally inconsistent, in an environment where there was no incentive to economise on inputs, skill shortages were desperate, the supervision of huge numbers of farm employees was unavoidably patchy, and most of the peasants found work on their private plots a prime necessity.

Soviet investigative journalism is a help in understanding the real operating conditions. An article in *Pravda* of 11 May 1981 described conditions on the Bolshaya Volga collective farm in the Uglich district of Yaroslavl' region, north of Moscow. The farm was in an area of 'roadlessness' (*bezdorozh'e*: as with *defitsit*, the existence of the word tells a great deal; the entire Soviet Union still had well under a million kilometres of hard-surface roads), and was said to be difficult to reach even by tractor for much of the year. Nikolai Averov had been persuaded by the Party to take on the chairmanship of the farm, that is, to be the boss, with a promise that he could retire after five years. Before him, the farm had had six chairmen in ten years. Averov in fact stayed eight years, worked very hard and greatly improved the farm. He then fell ill, took a holiday on medical advice and was sacked and expelled from the Party for doing so. (His being a member of the Party was probably what made the 'invitation' to take on the chairmanship impossible to refuse in the first place: he was subject to Party discipline. He appealed against the Party decision, got nowhere and fell back on writing to *Pravda*, who investigated.)

The situation was said by the *Pravda* journalists to be not uncommon. They would have been licensed to go ahead and write it up only if high-level Party officials deemed such public exposure to be necessary, in the face of a general problem. The farm's predicament, of lurching from crisis to crisis in a failing institution, resembles that of many schools and hospitals in the British public sector, but with more mud.

Even in the period of stagnation, under the supposedly unenlightened, sleepwalking leadership of Leonid Brezhnev and his elderly Politburo colleagues, there was an effort to employ private initiative. Legislation was passed to allow upper limits on private-plot livestock holdings to be removed at local initiative; the Russian Republic Ministry of Agriculture called on collective and state farms to help the private plots with feed, seed and young animals to rear (*Ekonomicheskaya gazeta* 1980, no. 41). There was a move to encourage farms to organise their workers into small brigades that would have overall, year-round responsibility for particular crops or livestock products, and would be assigned the necessary resources and incentives to get on with the job as they thought best (*Pravda*, 25 May 1981).

Identifying the consequences of such initiatives is difficult. Perhaps here and there they made a difference. But every effort to devolve decision-making to the level of the firm or farm ran into the fundamental resistance of everyone higher up the system, whether in Gosplan or in the branch ministry or in the regional Party committee. They were being held responsible for outcomes by their masters; any reduction in their power to micro-manage – however ineffective their micro-management might be – would happen only over their dead bodies.

Meanwhile the failings of the 'agro-industrial complex' were made less damaging by a large-scale resort to imports, even though that, as Brezhnev made clear in 1981, was held by the leadership to be undesirable. As temporary expedients so often do, however, it was becoming an established routine.

Could anything be done to revive Soviet agriculture? One sign of the leadership's deep concern about the farm sector was that in October 1980 the septuagenarian Politburo promoted to its own ranks an agricultural specialist who was disgracefully young: forty-nine. He was Mikhail Sergeevich Gorbachev. He already had the Party leadership's agriculture portfolio (he was promoted from candidate member of the Politburo). Perhaps that was reckoned to be enough to keep him out of mischief.

Foreign economic relations

In the late Brezhnev period Soviet economic entanglement with the West increased. One variable had a huge influence: the world market price of oil. There was a tenfold increase in world oil prices during the 1970s. This radically improved Soviet terms of trade (net barter terms of trade, to be precise: in effect, the purchasing power on world markets of a physical unit of Soviet exports). On Joan Parpart Zoeter's calculations, the Soviet terms of trade in hard currency transactions improved by 134 per cent between the end of 1972 and the end of 1981 (derived from Zoeter 1982, p. 486).

The oil-price rises also triggered massive disturbance in the world economy. The advanced Western countries experienced both short-term output falls and increased inflation as they adjusted to new energy prices. The major Middle Eastern oil exporting nations built up huge dollar reserves, and these flowed into international markets, making for cheap and abundant lending.

All of this followed a change in policy by OPEC after the 1973 Yom Kippur War and, later, the Iranian revolution. Though not an OPEC member, the USSR, as a net oil exporter, benefited. Since all energy prices are linked, Soviet exports of natural gas also benefited. (Gas, being delivered mostly on long-term contracts through fixed pipelines, is less flexibly priced than crude oil. But gas contracts usually include a pricing formula in which the price of the main alternative fuel looms large.)

This should have been, on the face of it, a great opportunity for the Soviet Union; all the more so as it came after the Nixon–Kissinger–Brezhnev *détente* of 1972, and the improved commercial relations between the US and the USSR (see Chapter 4).

That Moscow benefited on balance, in the short to medium term, cannot be doubted. In other words, Soviet economic difficulties in the 1970s and early 1980s would have been a great deal worse with oil at $3 a barrel on world markets. But the improvement in Moscow's international purchasing power was soon followed by a string of harvest failures that, in the tradition established by Khrushchev in 1963–64, were remedied by large grain imports; by the breakdown in the Soviet–US commercial *détente* that was mentioned briefly in the last chapter; by the adverse secondary effects of oil-price rises, in the form of accelerated inflation in Western prices and a slackening of Western import demand in real terms; and by Western sanctions following the Christmas 1979 invasion of Afghanistan.

One consequence of all this was that the USSR tended to run deficits in its hard-currency trade. These were financed by selling gold, by hard-currency arms sales and by borrowing, in part from banks awash with petro-dollars. (Neither gold nor arms were included in the Soviet export figures, even though the Soviet Union was a gold producer and could therefore be considered to be selling gold as a product, not purely as a form of international monetary settlement from reserves.) However, the USSR's imports were larger than they could have been with a lower oil price, given Soviet caution in external finance. The Kremlin never went for an import-led growth strategy as Poland and Hungary did (see Chapter 4); when grain imports were high, Soviet policymakers cut back on purchasing of Western machinery and technology. In 1981 hard-currency imports of farm products (not just grain) totalled $11.3 billion and machinery imports around $4.5 billion. In real terms, machinery imports declined slowly after 1976 (Zoeter 1982, p. 501). The debt was not allowed to get out of hand. On Zoeter's calculations, the debt-service ratio in the hard-currency accounts, if measured as debt service as a percentage of all hard-currency revenue, remained under one-fifth (p. 494). This was an eminently sustainable level so long as oil prices did not collapse. Indeed, Zoeter estimated a Soviet current account surplus in hard-currency transactions in 1977 through 1980 (p. 483) and treated gold sales as a capital account item.

Another consequence was that Moscow's relations with its CMEA partners came under strain. The intra-CMEA prices of Soviet energy supplies (see Chapter 4) were especially favourable when the world oil price shot up. From Moscow's point of view, the opportunity cost of supplying oil and gas to Central-Eastern Europe increased dramatically. The conflict of interest was softened in two ways. First, from the beginning of 1975 intra-CMEA prices were set every year on the basis of the average of world prices in the previous five years (a rolling five-year average) rather than being adjusted to reflect past world prices only once every five years. Second, the Soviet Union began to limit the physical quantities of oil (especially) that it delivered to its CMEA partners, and moved its allocations of oil exports between the West and the CMEA gradually in favour of the former. It also organised a new form of CMEA cooperation: the other European CMEA countries, except Romania, provided labour, rising to 30,000 workers, to help build a gas pipeline from Orenburg to the western border, for which they were to be reimbursed in gas deliveries (*Izvestiya*, 26 April 1975). The severe limits to CMEA integration were indicated by the fact that there was very little precedent for such cross-border movements of labour. In general Moscow behaved towards its CMEA partners like a benign landlord at a time of rapid inflation: putting the rent up in stages and with a time-lag.

Indeed, it was believed by Western specialists that in this period the Soviet Union was 'subsidising' Central-Eastern Europe. There was certainly some justification for this. The scale and rationale of such subsidies, however, were extremely hard to assess. The underlying notion – entertained both by Soviet specialists and by Western analysts – was that Moscow's CMEA partners tended to get away with relatively high prices (compared with the world market) for machinery and other manufactures delivered to the USSR, while they were also getting away, for much of the 1970s and early 1980s, with paying less than world prices for oil, gas and raw materials from the USSR. Therefore analysts concentrated on quantifying these price differences, with widely varying conclusions.

Interpretations of the results also varied. One view was that they were basically the outcome to be expected in a customs union, albeit in this case a rather unusual customs-union equivalent developed among centrally planned economies. Another was that they were finely calibrated Soviet 'payments' for political services rendered in the wider world.

One persuasive account (Poznanski 1988) produced relatively modest figures for Soviet implicit 'transfers' to Central-Eastern Europe. Poznanski found evidence that the Soviet Union tended to pay significantly more than average world prices for its machinery imports from the West; this meant that the opportunity cost of buying machinery from CMEA partners was much less than it appeared if comparison was simply with 'world prices'. The transfers, or opportunity costs, associated with oil and gas sales to CMEA partners were the core of any apparent transfers, and they fluctuated over time in a predictable way that followed from the intra-CMEA pricing rules. Indeed, in the late 1980s a point was reached where Central-Eastern Europe was paying (on paper, at least) more than world market prices for its Soviet oil. This was again a mechanical result of the CMEA pricing rules, once world oil prices began to fall.

To many citizens in Central Europe, to whom it was axiomatic that Moscow exploited them, all this seemed so much academic hot air. Their gut feeling on the subject should not be condescendingly dismissed. First, whatever message can be derived from the prices needs to be modified by a consideration about quantities: in most instances, it was Moscow that dominated in decisions on how much would be delivered in each direction. Soviet policymakers did indeed soften the impact of oil-price rises considerably for their CMEA partners; but they also began to cut back the amounts of oil they provided. Second, an important long-term consequence of being locked into the Soviet bloc was that their producers missed out on both the competitive pressure towards greater efficiency and the pervasive transfer of technology from which they would have benefited had they been part of Western Europe. The latter consequence could hardly be called exploitation by Moscow, since Soviet producers lost out in the same way. But it was part of the visibly worsening lag behind the West, for which the citizens of at least the more developed Central-Eastern European countries could reasonably blame Moscow. All in all, intra-CMEA arrangements had a great many unintended consequences.

At the same time, and more particularly towards the end of this period, the question began to be asked by Western bankers and governments whether Moscow was holding a financial umbrella over its CMEA partners. Would Soviet policymakers stand by and let, say, Poland slide into default – as began to look increasingly likely? There was a classic moral-hazard problem here. If the Soviet government had confirmed officially that there was a 'Soviet umbrella', the Polish and Hungarian governments would have continued on their spending spree and Western bankers would have continued on their equally ill-advised lending spree.

On 24 April 1981 Soviet officials said publicly that no such bail-out arrangement existed (*Financial Times*, 25 April 1981). They could hardly have said anything else. There was in fact some Soviet hard-currency lending to Poland, but it was small. At all events, Moscow managed to convey to all concerned that, with or without a prior bail-out arrangement, it might be risky to count on a Soviet rescue.

Soviet gold production, reserves and the official balance of payments accounts remained state secrets, which helped. (Foreign analysts adopted exotic methodologies, including the estimation of rates of gold extraction from photos of people standing beside spoil-heaps at gold mines; the people provided a clue to the height of the spoil-heaps, and then there were quite a few more steps in the calculations after that. Had the Soviets, guided by Norse mythology, employed dwarves to mine gold, the errors would have been even larger than they [probably] were.) From 1981 the grain harvest also became a state secret. This probably helped Soviet policymakers by creating a useful degree of uncertainty about the scale of their intended grain-buying on world markets in each crop year. Certainly the 1983 Soviet–US grain agreement was judged to be rather favourable to the USSR (Butler 1983).

There were various ways of limiting Moscow's cash-flow problems. Foreign ownership of assets on Soviet soil was not allowed (the law was changed only under Gorbachev, in 1986). Therefore Western direct investment was not available. However, various forms of industrial cooperation were developed. These had two things in common: the Western business partner had a medium-to-long-term interest in the success of a capital project on Soviet territory; and the Soviet side did not have to pay cash, or borrow, up front.

There were, first, plant contracts such as those described earlier for chemical plants, VAZ and KamAZ. In these the Western contractor might be on-site for several years, and would collect their payments only when the plant was shown to be up and running. In their simplest form, these deals were concluded with the final payment when the plant was commissioned. A second variant allowed for payment in part (rarely in full) by delivery of the output produced by the new plant. These product-pay-back arrangements became common in the 1970s for chemical plants, but were not confined to chemicals. A third variant entailed the signing of a formal 'industrial cooperation' agreement between a Western company and a Soviet partner – often the State Committee for Science and Technology, covering a variety of long-term flows of products and technology.

Kosygin's son-in-law, Dzherman Gvishiani, flourished at this time. Sharp-suited and dark, he could have passed, language apart, for an Italian businessman; he was in fact Georgian. As chairman of the State Committee for Science and Technology (SCST), he travelled widely, signing up Western companies to cooperation agreements that were expected to yield solid commercial advantages. Often they did not, but Western executives developing business with the Soviet Union came to believe that an SCST agreement was necessary, if not sufficient, to land a major contract. On the domestic scene Gvishiani proselytised for modern management methods. It was a period when the latest management fashion from the West, or at any rate the fashion before last, could be advocated but serious economic reform could not.

How 'dependent', if at all, was the Soviet Union on the West at this time? Exports to or imports from the West as shares of GDP or GNP were only about 4 per cent if the trade figures are converted at the official exchange rate; if the trade flows are estimated in Soviet domestic prices, however, the export share remains small but the import share looks more like 20 per cent (Treml 1983). The total separation of domestic from world-market prices made such discrepancies possible. But what do Soviet domestic prices tell us about relative scarcities? Very little.

Disaggregation helps. Vladimir Treml, in an ingenious but convincing exercise, concluded that in 1981 Soviet net imports of food and fodder (including grain for livestock feed) provided, directly and indirectly, between 17.4 and 23.4 per cent of the calorie intake of the Soviet population. That refers to imports (less exports) from all trade partners in a year of particularly high food imports. Following Treml's approach, I calculated that in 1983 net food and fodder imports from the West accounted for 9.8–12.6 per cent of the population's calorie intake (Hanson 1988, p. 23).

The other product group of strategic importance was machinery and equipment. Estimates of their direct and indirect contribution to Soviet economic growth were mentioned in the previous chapter: they were modest, but not negligible. The Soviet economist Fal'tsman (1985) put imported equipment at about a third of Soviet equipment investment in the early 1980s. A large part of that, as measured in the trade returns, was from Central-Eastern Europe. My estimate of the share of Western imports in Soviet producer durables investment, including large-diameter pipe for gas pipelines, was, for the same period, about 10 per cent (Hanson 1988, p. 24).

There was a good reason for all this interest in calculations about 'dependence' in the 1970s and 1980s. It was a time of unstable relations between the two superpowers. The West, led by the United States – and often the United States without any followers – experimented with sanctions, embargoes and so-called 'linkage' policies. The *détente* of the early

1970s was itself a form of linkage policy, based on US trade concessions designed to develop smoother East-West relations.

On 14 January 1975, Soviet citizens who listened to foreign broadcasts learnt that their country had rejected the US–Soviet trade agreements of 1972. US Secretary of State Henry Kissinger announced this before the Kremlin did (*EIU QER* 1975, no. 1, pp. 8–9). Those agreements had been on trade, credits, shipping and the waiving of Soviet Lend-Lease repayments. They gave the USSR Most Favoured Nation (MFN) status in the US, lowering some US tariffs on Soviet goods and making the USSR eligible to receive official credit support (for US capital-goods exports to it) from the US Eximbank. The original agreement between Nixon and Brezhnev had to be ratified by both parliaments – a matter of rubber-stamping in Moscow but not in Washington. The US Congress voted to require that Eximbank credits for the USSR should not exceed $300 million over four years and must be conditional on explicit Soviet guarantees of 60,000 exit visas a year (for Soviet Jews to emigrate).

This worked out, over the four years, at $1,250 per exit visa, in credit that was subsidised but still due to be repaid with interest. It would also have been a public humiliation for the Kremlin to accept it. Soviet rejection of a deal on those terms was entirely understandable.

Exit visas continued to be issued for Soviet Jews, but at modest rates that went up a bit when Soviet leaders thought there might be some return on their generosity, and down a bit when they were in a huff.

America's allies were interested bystanders. They maintained their long-established MFN status and official export credit support vis-à-vis the Soviet Union. In 1975, the British government of Prime Minister Harold Wilson, an old Russia-trade hand, sought to repair an earlier breach of diplomatic relations with Moscow with a £950 million line of credit at 7.1–7.5 per cent, at a time when inflation in Western Europe was ranging between 10 and 20 per cent a year (*EIU QER*, 1975, no. 2, p. 10). US-based multinationals channelled Soviet business through European affiliates.

After the collapse of Soviet–US commercial *détente*, in other words, life continued much as before. True, Western politicians and analysts, not to mention farmers and grain traders, got quite excited about the series of poor Soviet grain harvests that brought Soviet buyers into the world grain markets on a large scale. But this turned out to provide little or no leverage for Washington.

Some grain could be bought from Western Europe, Canada, Australia and South America; some came from the US. More precisely: international grain-trading firms could sell to Soviet foreign trade organisations and the grain would come from somewhere: its provenance was moot. If it was Canadian grain, then American grain might replace that Canadian grain in another market. The exact physical origin of a particular ton of grain reaching the USSR was optional.

That, at least, was the view taken by American grain-trading companies and the US farm lobby. On the whole, US Administrations were prepared to be persuaded. A 1975 Soviet–US grain agreement survived.

When the Soviet Army marched into Afghanistan, however, Western politicians deployed a range of economic sanctions. The European Economic Community (as it then was), Australia and Canada agreed not to increase their sales of grain to the US, while Washington aimed to limit deliveries of US grain to 8 million tons per crop year. Argentina refused to cooperate. Restrictions were placed on Soviet fishing in some Western countries' economic-resource zones; some EEC export subsidies on butter were suspended; anti-dumping restrictions were enforced on some Soviet exports that might otherwise have been spared; EEC member-states agreed to abide by the OECD consensus on minimum export credit conditions (a cartel arrangement to avoid a price war, and one that they should have been observing anyway); and the US tried to set a good example by renouncing any exceptions for its own producers on strategic export control guidelines for deliveries to the Soviet Union (*EIU QER* 1980, no. 1, pp. 7–10).

A year later, these measures seemed to have had little effect, partly because many of the Western states involved quietly forgot about them. In crop year 1979/80 the Soviet Union managed to import 34.5 million tons of grain, possibly including less than before of US origin (*EIU QER* 1981, no. 1, pp. 18–19). The original US intention had been to restrict Moscow to about half that amount.

Throughout this period, and particularly while Ronald Reagan was President of the US, the efficacy and design of sanctions was much discussed. So was the separate issue of strategic export controls. Sanctions are meant to send signals, preferably accompanied by some economic harm to the recipient. They are intended to influence the recipient government's behaviour, whether in its treatment of dissidents or in its relations with other countries (invading them, for example). Strategic embargoes are meant to hamper – at least to slow down – the target nation's development of military capabilities. The Western strategic embargo, coordinated by CoCom (a coordinating committee representing mainly NATO governments), was directed at Warsaw Pact countries. It either ruled out or required prior screening for deliveries of weapons and, much more controversially, of a range of 'dual use' (civilian and military) technologies that might directly or indirectly enhance Warsaw Pact capabilities. These were on the 'CoCom list'. For example, Italian-made machine-tools delivered to make Zhiguli/Lada (Fiat 125) cars at VAZ were reviewed to see if they could be diverted to making tanks (it was decided they could not). In this case, as in many others, the

American hand was strengthened by the fact that many of these machine-tools were made under US licence. Computer systems delivered, after such screening, for the management of reservations by Aeroflot and Intourist, were another (controversial) example.

President Reagan presided over a general tightening of sanctions and of the strategic embargo, directed against the Soviet Union. There was also talk, within his administration, of economic warfare as a feasible and desirable policy. It is not clear, however, what – short of a ban on all trade – 'economic warfare' can sensibly mean. The phrase never graduated into formal policy pronouncements. In general, the European allies were reluctant to follow the US lead in these matters. Even so, the sanctions, however soon they were diluted, probably did deliver a message. It appears that Soviet policy-makers were taken by surprise by the vehemence of the Western reaction to their invasion of Afghanistan. (They were to be even more shocked, as time wore on, by the growing domestic opposition to this unwinnable war.) The strategic embargo, too, probably did have some retarding effect on the development of Soviet military capabilities (see Hanson 1988).

The late Brezhnev era in retrospect

After 1973 or so, the humane shifts of policy initiated by Khrushchev seemed to become impediments to sustained economic growth at anything above a crawl. The softening of totalitarian social control had extended to a softening of plan targets and plan monitoring. The enhanced priority for agriculture had gone so far as, finally, to include the issuing of internal passports for *kolkhoz* peasants (from 1975); they were no longer, in official documentation, second-class citizens. At the same time a fear of popular discontent led policymakers to subsidise farm products on a scale (relative to GDP) beyond the farm subsidies of other countries, and to allocate more than a quarter of investment to the farm sector. It probably also contributed to the decision to slow the growth of investment and therefore, with a time-lag, of capital stock, in the economy at large. The farm sector had responded for a generation to better treatment. But by the late 1970s those improvements in productivity were dwindling. The profoundly inefficient character of state and collective farming under central planning seemed to be setting a ceiling on performance.

The same fear of unrest drove Soviet policymakers, I believe, to sustained food imports on a large scale. These, though always intended to be temporary expedients, became entrenched. They limited technology transfer from the West by squeezing imports of machinery and equipment, and ate up much of the terms-of-trade gains that OPEC had obtained for all oil-exporting countries.

Nikolai Baibakov, who headed Gosplan in 1955–57 and again from 1965 to 1985, later summed up in five-year-plan terms 'what we got for [our] oil and gas': $5 billions worth of food, mostly gained in 1971–75, $15 billion in 1976–80 and $35 billion in 1981–85 (Baibakov 1993a). These figures match fairly closely US government estimates of Soviet hard-currency spending on grain alone: $5.2 billion, $14.0 billion and $26.3 billion, respectively (Ericson and Miller 1979; Zoeter 1982; McIntyre 1987). Baibakov goes on to observe that this process of 'repairing' the Soviet livestock sector (by importing feed grain) could not be sustained when oil output and prices fell.

In turn, the oil and gas sector, partly because it generated around a half of hard-currency earnings, became another major investment priority, squeezing the shares of other sectors.

It could be argued that expanding oil and gas production was the most cost-effective way of increasing grain supplies. More thorough, and sustained, use of the gains from trade would probably have been economically rational. Jan Vanous, using 1981 price and cost data, produced the following calculation: by trading on world markets the Soviet Union could get 1.6 tons of wheat for the proceeds from the sale of 1 ton of crude oil; at the margin, in the domestic economy, the resources needed to produce an extra ton of oil would produce only a fifth to a quarter of a ton of additional wheat (*International Herald Tribune*, 19 October 1982, p. 6). One might quibble about his oil cost estimates: marginal domestic resource costs in Soviet oil production were probably higher than Vanous allowed, although this depiction of Soviet options would probably hold, broadly speaking, for gas if not for oil. But there was no way the Soviet leadership would deliberately choose long-run reliance on foreign trade to feed its population.

Underlying the slowdown, across all sectors, was the slowing growth of labour and capital inputs and the diminishing scale of resource shifts from agriculture to industry. Growth of inputs can raise output. Shifts from higher to lower productivity sectors can raise the aggregate productivity of given inputs. With both these growth sources dwindling, perhaps accompanied by negative effects from the decline of plan discipline, the Soviet economy could maintain reasonable growth rates only by generating a more rapid growth of factor productivity in most sectors. That in the long run would have to come chiefly from a higher rate of introduction of new products and processes. This was something the system simply was not able to provide.

CHAPTER SIX

Three Funerals and a Coronation:
November 1982 to March 1985

Leonid Brezhnev died on 10 November 1982. He was succeeded by a member of his own generation, Yurii Andropov, who had been head of the KGB from 1967 to May 1982. Andropov's assumption of the leadership was a victory for Western kremlinologists. They had all said that Brezhnev would be succeeded either by Andropov or by somebody else. Andropov, in turn, died on 9 February 1984. He was succeeded by another elderly Politburo member, Konstantin Chernenko, who died on 10 March 1985. At this point the remaining septuagenarians in the Politburo must have concluded that resistance was useless. Mikhail Gorbachev, still in his early fifties, became the next Party leader.

The period of 28 months from the death of Brezhnev to Gorbachev's arrival in power does not lend itself to an extended treatment of economic developments and economic policies. The period is nonetheless an interesting interlude in Soviet economic history. Public debate, and apparently internal policy discussion as well, loosened up. Policies were all over the place. There were some moves to tighten social discipline. There were also very tentative reform moves, and certainly far more discussion of economic decentralisation. The Brezhnevian deliberate slowing of investment was questioned, and for a time reversed.

In the rest of this chapter the sequence of topics is rather different from that in previous chapters. It will be: economic discussion, then policies, then outcomes.

Economic discussion

Many Soviet economists and managers believed by now that centralised economic administration was part of the problem. Leonard Silk described in the *New York Times* a series of interviews he had conducted in several Soviet cities in early 1983 (Silk 1983). His interviewees were characteristically derisive about the economic order they worked under and, seemingly, unafraid to say things that went well beyond the censored public debate. 'Do you know what I think is the fundamental thing wrong with this country?' one senior manager asked, 'The absence of competition.' Another of Silk's respondents blamed job security.

Less surprisingly, most economists in the Academy of Sciences' prestigious Central Economics-Mathematical Institute believed that supply planning should be dismantled and enterprises should be able to choose their own sources of supply – a recipe for competition (interview with Professor Viktor Volkonskii at the Institute, 7 September 1983).

The word *perestroika* (restructuring) began to be heard more often. It was later made internationally famous by Gorbachev. He adopted it as one of the catchwords to denote what he was trying to achieve in the economy. Like other political slogans it had the advantage of opacity. The word had been used for decades to denote reorganisation. In the Andropov-Chernenko interlude, however, it began to be used, often with a qualifying adjective, in what became the Gorbachevian sense of a radical reform. The title of a symposium in the most go-ahead Soviet economic journal, *EKO*, in the August 1983 issue was 'Nuzhna reshitel'naya perestroika': 'Decisive Re-structuring Needed'.

The economic commentator Otto Latsis, reviewing readers' letters about the difficulties in the economy, in the weekly *Literaturnaya gazeta* (Latsis 1983), made a particularly striking point. Twenty years ago, he said, many letter-writers saw the solution to any economic problems in decision-making by a single [national] centre. Now, hardly anyone believes that the centre can solve the significant problems.

One piece of new thinking about the economy became a major news story in the West, at any rate in the more highbrow sections of the media. Dusko Doder of the *Washington Post* obtained a copy of a reportedly confidential paper, evidently written by the leading economic sociologist, Academician Tatyana Zaslavskaya (Zaslavskaya 1983). This was probably a paper for a meeting of policy analysts, arranged by and including members of the secretariat of the Party's Central Committee; its exact provenance was later fudged. It became known in the Western press as the 'Novosibirsk memorandum' or the 'Novosibirsk report', since Zaslavskaya was at that time based in the Academy of Sciences' Siberian division.

The title of Zaslavskaya's report was circumspect. Literally translated, it was 'Report on the need for deeper study in the USSR of the social mechanism of development of the economy'. Its contents were not circumspect. One of its themes was that the present economic system tended to produce 'a main type of worker' who worked badly, and was prone to laziness and corruption. It did not advance any particular reform recipe. Being written by an academic, it concluded with a call for more research to be funded. But it portrayed quite bluntly a social and economic system that was wasteful, riddled with corruption and averse to innovation. Zaslavskaya did not claim that things were ever thus in the USSR. What she said, in effect, was that the current top-down system may have worked quite well for a largely peasant society being dragooned into the building of an industrial base, but it was no longer appropriate; in fact, it was now holding back progress.

This last point was also made in censored publications. In a round-table discussion in the Novosibirsk journal *EKO* ('Samostoyatel'nost',' 1984), Professor R.G. Karagedov described the existing 'economic mechanism' as having once been 'historically justified', but as now no longer appropriate; the statute governing the powers and functions of the state enterprise should be revised, and enterprise decision-making powers enhanced. One of the few Soviet economists familiar with the work of the Hungarian economist Janos Kornai, Karagedov had followed Kornai's example by carrying out survey work on the decision-making of enterprises. Such empirical research into enterprise behaviour was rare in the USSR. Karagedov concluded, amongst other things, that the production associations were not in fact playing any part in determining plans; that enterprises were not in fact receiving stable five-year or even two-year plans, as they were supposed to under the 1979 decree (see the previous chapter); and indeed that enterprise plans were mostly changed during the course of a single year, so there were not even stable one-year plans (*ibid.*).

In 1983, especially, nobody knew which way the wind was supposed to blow. Andropov, though not a career secret policeman, had been in charge of the KGB for 15 years. He had been largely responsible for crushing the dissident movement, mixing foreign exile, internal exile, imprisonment and incarceration in mental hospitals to make it clear where Soviet citizens' duties lay. He had begun his short time as leader with a discipline campaign. So surely it was now right to come out in favour of old-fashioned plan discipline in the economy? On the other hand, he also had a reputation as an intellectual. He talked of the need for changes in the economic system. So perhaps he was a closet liberal? The new leader was, in general, a mystery.[1] At all events, some old-fashioned advocates of Stalinist planning also decided they could safely raise their voices.

Ignatovskii, the chief editor of the Gosplan journal, wrote an article in the top Party theoretical journal, *Kommunist*, in which he called for a wholesale return to plan targets exclusively in tons, metres and other physical units and deplored the increased use of value indicators (sales, profits, etc.) (Ignatovskii 1983). Adopting the market mechanism was incompatible with socialism; what was really needed was proper political checking and selection of cadres.

In a somewhat similar vein, the wartime People's Commissar of the Tank Industry, together with his then assistant, described the successes of the Second World War tank production in Chelyabinsk (Zal'tsman and Edel'gauz 1984). This experience could, they argued, still be learnt from. The message that comes out of their account, however, seems to be above all about a wartime spirit of voluntary cooperation which ensured that plans were both taut and fulfilled.

Priorities, as well as organisational change, were being debated at quite a fundamental level. Many Soviet economists had their reservations about the deliberate slowdown in investment growth for which the Brezhnev leadership had opted in the mid-1970s. One of the most vigorous critics of the investment slowdown was Val'tukh (1982); another was V.K.Fal'tsman (interviewed 7 September 1983; see also Fal'tsman and Kornev 1984). Their view, crudely summarised, was that the real growth of investment, proxied by increments of capacity in physical units of annual output, had for long been well below the reported growth rate. That, plus long but sectorally variable delays in investment projects, had produced serious imbalances between available capacities in different industries. There was, for example, a bottleneck in steel supplies for this reason. This situation had been made worse by the deliberate slowing of investment growth (as officially measured). What was needed was a re-acceleration of that growth, to widen bottlenecks that were hampering the growth of total output.

The opposing view was succinctly put by Buzhinskii and Kheinman (1983): yes, all of the above was true, but it was the outcome of a pervasively wasteful system. The real need was to increase efficiency in production and investment. Simply committing a larger share of resources to a bloated and inefficient investment programme was an admission of defeat.

In short, a great many options were being canvassed: democratise and devolve economic decision-making; go back to tougher, direct control from above; raise the investment share of national income again; seek reforms that would raise the rate of factor productivity growth, allowing growth to become more 'intensive'. Market socialism was not being advocated explicitly, but some sort of combination of market mechanisms and state ownership was quite frequently hinted at.[2] Ignatovskii's robust assertion that the two were incompatible was still regarded by right-thinking people as quaint and reactionary.

Andropov himself enunciated the general sense that some sort of momentous change was needed. At the June 1983 Central Committee plenum he said, 'We are now approaching a historic dividing line; . . . it is inevitable that there will be profound qualitative changes in the forces of production, and a corresponding change in the relations of production' (*Pravda*, 16 June 1983, p. 1). This was Marxist-Leninist mumbo-jumbo, but it was not *only* Marxist-Leninist mumbo-jumbo. In some unspecified way, the economic system would have to change, because the circumstances in which the economy operated had changed. This could mean that Andropov had accepted the arguments of Zaslavskaya, Karagedov and others about the need for a radical devolution of decision-making. He did not live long enough, however, for anyone to find out how far he was prepared to go.

One rather unobtrusive theme in public discussion at this time merits more attention than it has received. Academician Oleg Bogomolov's Institute of the Economy of the World Socialist System (IEMSS) was engaged in a study of the experience of other socialist economies (its core activity), but now with a brief to draw useful lessons from it for the Soviet Union. The first articles published about this work, in 1983, tended to say little or nothing about Poland. The reason, no doubt, was that the recent Solidarity upheaval was politically highly sensitive. By 1984, however, the articles became less coy. One by Lushina is of particular interest (Lushina 1984). It draws attention to the advantages of small-scale non-state production of goods and services. A distinction is made between individual (*individual'noe*) enterprise and private (*chastnoe*): only the latter entails employment of others (exploitation). However, the article mentions without disapproval recent Polish legislation allowing private firms to employ up to 15 people.

This sort of public discussion was a precursor of further discussions and legislation under Gorbachev, which began to undermine socialist orthodoxy in Soviet practice. People from Bogomolov's institute, including Bogomolov himself, were to play a leading role in debates in the late 1980s. Once again, John Bushnell's stress on the importance of Central-Eastern Europe in changing Soviet minds is reinforced. The most radical thinking in the 1980s did not come from the 'mainstream' economic institutes like TsEMI or from the institutes that specialised in studying the West, such as the Institute for the World Economy and International Relations (IMEMO) or the Institute of the USA and Canada (ISShAK). All of these were institutes of the prestigious USSR Academy of Sciences. Informally, IMEMO and the USA Institute were more prestigious than the others. The most radical thinking, however, came not from them, but from people familiar with both practice and intellectual debate in Central Europe. This was

168

partly (I suggest) because Bogomolov provided a haven for unorthodox intellectuals and partly because the academic study of the West was a route to the good life for well-connected people.

Policies

Andropov began with a crackdown on labour discipline. The police were deployed as truancy officers, demanding identification from people shopping during the working day, for example, to establish whether they should have been at work. In the soft atmosphere of the Brezhnev regime it was common practice to take unofficial time off from work. The chronic shortages of everything meant, however, that many did not take time off to enjoy themselves but to shop (the two really were alternatives; only a masochist could enjoy shopping in the USSR). Another purpose of such checking was to identify people who simply were not employed – and therefore guilty of parasitism if they were able-bodied, of working age and not in full-time study.

Nobody could possibly know how far this campaign might go. Even though Stalin had died thirty years before, people knew either from direct experience or from their elders just how harsh that regime had been; they feared a return to terror. For a time, at least, workplace discipline really was strengthened

Andropov himself put his discipline campaign in perspective. In January 1983 he visited the Sergo Ordzhonikidze machine-tool plant in Moscow, talked to workers there and made a speech that was, naturally, on the front two pages of every Soviet newspaper. 'Although it is impossible to reduce everything to discipline,' he said, 'That is what we have to start with' (*Pravda*, 1 February 1983, pp. 1–2). Start he certainly did. According to one report, the number of people found to be guilty of unemployment (i.e. parasitism) in three towns was greater than the reported labour 'shortage' in the entire region (*Pravda*, 4 August 1983, p. 3).

There were two snags in this sort of operation, even if we leave to one side any question about civil rights. First, the labour 'shortage' was itself a product of an inefficient system – a shortage economy – in which labour was wastefully used. Second, there was a practical difficulty in checking on people's employment status. The same press report announced with horror something that most Soviet readers knew already: in these degenerate days, Soviet able-bodied adults could lose their work books with impunity, making their employment status hard to document. (Your work book officially had to be kept by your employer; if you were not employed, you had in

theory to be able to produce your work book and account for yourself.[3])
Either the authorities had to turn the clock back and credibly threaten
execution or imprisonment for the most minor infractions of the law – or
for nothing at all, just to make sure; or they had to try something completely different, such as capitalism.

In practice, they chose neither of these options. Consequently, 'idlers'
may have adopted a lower profile in the face of the discipline campaign, but
they did not cease to idle. The bourgeois souls of the Soviet proletariat, or
at any rate of those who wrote letters to *Pravda*, continued to be shocked to
the core. 'Why are the gangs of thrill-seekers and flagrant idlers increasing?'
was a characteristic enquiry (*Pravda*, 3 December 1983, p. 2).

There was no unemployment benefit, Therefore these people were not,
in the terminology of the British press, welfare scroungers. Anyone who
deliberately chose to be unemployed was presumably making a living in the
black, shadow or informal economy. Perhaps more characteristic of the
times were people who had a notional, official job somewhere, but spent
most of their time in unofficial activities.[4] A survey of late 1970s emigrants
found that in their last normal year of life in the USSR (before applying for
an exit visa) urban dwellers from 'northern' USSR (Russian Federation,
Baltic states, Belorussia, Moldavia and Ukraine) were getting on average
about a third of their household income from private activity against two-
thirds from 'legitimate socialist income' (Grossman 1987; the data relate to
households containing at least one person in full-time, legitimate employment; for pensioner households the share was smaller; for non-pensioner
households in Armenia, much higher). Income from the shadow economy
carried certain risks. If you engaged in private enterprise on a substantial
scale, you might be executed for 'economic crime'. But at least you would
not be taxed.

Did the discipline campaign, then, achieve anything? Joseph Berliner,
commenting on Andropov's policies, pointed out that a labour discipline
campaign, even if it could achieve the immediate objective of keeping tru-
ants off the streets, had its limitations. Given official working hours, it could
increase the number of hours that people were in fact present at their
workplace rather than absent without leave. It could not ensure that, when
present, they applied more effort than they had previously done (Berliner
1984).

This may not, however, be the whole story. If the tightened discipline
applies not just to rank-and-file workers but to supervisors, managers and
branch-ministry officials as well, it may mean that they, too, become more
nervous about engaging in any sort of back-sliding; if this happens, it may
reduce the incidence of downwards 'corrections' of enterprise plan-targets
and thus elicit more managerial effort in the pursuit of bonuses. Something

of this sort is strongly suggested by research carried out on developments in particular branches of the economy (Kontorovich 1985). At all events, there was an improvement in economic performance in 1983, as the next section shows.

Three organisational measures introduced under Andropov were of some interest: the Law on Workers' Collectives (*Pravda*, 19 June 1983, pp. 1, 3); a joint Party-state decree on some experiments in enterprise guidance (*Pravda*, 26 July 1983, p. 1), and a government resolution on accelerating technical progress (*Pravda*, 5 August 1983, pp. 1–2).

The Law on Workers' Collectives was seen by some as a vehicle for tightening labour discipline, by others as a gesture towards worker participation, in response to the rise (and subsequent suppression) of Solidarity in Poland. One article even referred to the problem of 'alienation' among Soviet workers (Ye. Kotelenets in *Pravda*, 20 April 1983, p. 2). The new law required regular meetings of the work collective, at which workers could be consulted about enterprise policies. The agenda for these meetings would be firmly in the hands of the Party and the Trade Union, the latter being merely a tool of the Party-state machine. Only consultation was envisaged. (For discussion of the measure see Berliner 1984, Teague 1988, Michel Tatu in *Le Monde* 20 April 1983, Teague 1983 – the last two addressing the law in its draft form). Whether the thinking behind the law was mainly about discipline or mainly about increased participation, it was certainly motivated by worries about low worker morale.

The measure designed to improve the introduction of new products and processes included amendments to pricing rules and bonus-forming indicators. It was designed to make profit margins larger for new products and products classified as of the highest quality, with benefits for bonus payments. The direction of the change in incentives was probably correct; whether the net effect of the change, given all the other considerations that impinged on Soviet management, was appreciable, was another matter (see Berliner 1984). The direct evidence of reported innovations suggests in fact a continuing slowdown in the rate of introduction of new products and processes (Kontorovich 1986).

The experiment in enterprise autonomy was limited in scope territorially and by branch of industry. This was only fitting for an 'experiment'. It was supposed among other things to entail a reduction in the number of indicators imposed on the enterprise by its branch ministry. It was also supposed to allow more flexibility for the enterprise management to reallocate the enterprise wage fund so that workers' earnings could benefit from savings in labour achieved through productivity gains. A much earlier experiment along the latter lines, started at the Shchekino chemical combine in 1967 and then turned into a national campaign, had fizzled out.

Such experiments, when introduced from above, tended to be associated with preferential resource allocations to the enterprises involved, to ensure success; moreover, the regime of shortage dictated that enterprises' and branch ministries' desire to maximise inputs was limited only by what central planners would allow them to get away with (Selyunin 1985). In any case, surveys found that branch ministries simply were not implementing the experiment in practice (Karagedov in 'Samostoyatel'nost' 1984). So long as planners' information was highly imperfect, and centralised supply of inputs was an essential part of the system, relaxation of control from above was scarcely possible (Dyker 1984).

Konstantin Chernenko was 72 when he took over the leadership in February 1984. In his first speech as leader he emphasised the need for the Party to stay out of the detail of economic policy and to concentrate, rather. on ensuring that the right people were in place to develop policy (*Pravda*, 14 February 1984, pp. 1–2). This was a venerable theme of Soviet speeches, but it seemed in this case to reflect his own approach.

It was agreed by analysts at the time that there was an identifiable top-level economic policy team of Mikhail Gorbachev, Vladimir Dolgikh and Nikolai Ryzhkov. Gorbachev, as a full member of the Politburo, was the senior in rank. He had been responsible as a regional Party boss for the heavily agricultural region of Stavropol', and had entered the Party leadership with responsibility for the farm sector – usually a political death sentence. Dolgikh and Ryzhkov both had track records in industrial administration. Ryzhkov, still active in Russian politics at the time of writing, had at one time managed the huge Uralmashzavod engineering complex.

At this point the Brezhnev Food Programme, allocating a large share of investment to agriculture and closely-related upstream and downstream industrial branches (the 'agro-industrial complex' – see the previous chapter), was still in place. So, notionally, were the discipline campaign and the organisational measures introduced under Andropov.

None of these initiatives directly addressed the slowdown in labour-force growth. Total employment grew at 2.2 per cent per annum in the 1960s, 1.4 per cent per annum in the 1970s but at an annual rate of only 0.7 per cent in the first half of the 1980s (derived from Rapawy 1987, Table 5). Employment levels in the Soviet Union were mainly a supply-side phenomenon and not, as they are in market economies, a reflection of aggregate demand. The excess demand for labour was built into the system. Voluntary unemployment was, for able-bodied people of working age, an offence. Involuntary unemployment was very small and almost all of a short-term, frictional character (Hanson 1986). For practical purposes, therefore, the level of employment was determined by the size of the working-age population, minus full-time students, invalids and a very small number of working-age women, plus working pensioners. Very nearly everyone who could work, was working. If the growth of the working-age population slowed, so did the growth of employment.

A measure designed to address this problem directly was introduced under Chernenko. It had probably been in preparation for some time. This was a scheme of Attestation of Work Places (*Attestatsiya rabochikh mest*; see *Ekonomicheskaya gazeta* 1984 no. 10, p. 5 and no. 20, pp. 11–14). A 'work place' or 'working place' was an employment position approved under the plan: a job slot. Not all work places were filled, but an enterprise director could seek to fill any that were vacant, and his basic salary was positively related to the number of work places at his enterprise, not to the numbers actually employed.

All the incentives therefore were to expand the approved number of work places at your enterprise. If you could fill them, that would help meet plan targets, and the costs of any extra workers would be incorporated in your plan. As usual, there was no incentive to economise. Even if the director could not fill additional work places, he would still be personally better off for having them. One of several perverse results of this was that existing work places were rarely cancelled. New equipment might come into operation in enterprise A and workers might not be found to man it; meanwhile older, less productive, even obsolete, equipment at enterprise B was manned. Shifting labour from B where it was less productive (and might not even be covering its costs) to more productive employment at A was impeded by the existing rules of the game. This could be one of the institutional arrangements that lay behind econometric findings suggesting a particularly low elasticity of substitution between capital and labour in Soviet industry (see the final chapter).

The attestation scheme was a vetting of existing staffing levels, with a view to cutting less productive work places, and thus freeing up labour to fill more productive slots. Within the enterprise twelve different departments, working with an (external) inter-branch commission, had to review each work place, referring to twenty-seven different regulations and applying fifteen criteria. One aim was to accelerate the scrapping of obsolete equipment. In current Soviet practice, this worked out at an annual retirement rate of about 2.3 per cent of the stock of machinery and equipment (*Pravda*, 12 November 1984, p. 2), compared with rates between 4 and 8 per cent in developed Western economies. It was also intended that new investment proposals would be assessed from the point of view of available labour supplies, to ensure that new capacity would be manned. Positive results from this scheme were not detectable.

The arguments in favour of a re-acceleration of investment growth (see above) seem to have had some effect, at least under Andropov. Resources committed to investment increased sharply in 1983; their growth then slowed appreciably. The commitment to heavy investment in the (broadly defined) agro-industrial complex was reaffirmed at an Extraordinary Plenum on agriculture of the Central Committee in October 1984. This meeting launched a major programme of investment in a land improvement programme, intended to last through the year 2000 (*Pravda*, 24 October 1984, pp. 1–3).

To sum up, there was a great deal of policy activity in 1983 and 1984, but not much real change.

Outcomes

Table 6.1 provides some of the key numbers for this brief period. It includes both Soviet official figures and CIA estimates. The former are included here to show the numbers with which (presumably) policy-makers in Moscow were presented, in the period just before Gorbachev's *perestroika*. As was mentioned in an earlier chapter, there is no evidence of a substantially different set of 'secret' numbers for macro-economic aggregates being employed.

Table 6.1   *The Soviet economy in 1982–85: selected indicators (% year-on-year change)*

	1982	1983	1984	1985
A. *Soviet official*				
National income produced	4.2	4.0	2.7	3.7
Investment	3.5	5.6	1.9	3.0
Industrial gross output	2.9	4.7	3.6	4.3
Agricultural gross output	5.1	6.7	0	0
B. *CIA estimates*				
GNP	2.6	3.2	1.4	0.9
New fixed investment	2.0	4.9	1.2	2.9
Agriculture	8.9	5.9	−2.1	−3.8
Industry	1.3	2.4	2.8	2.1

Note: the CIA series are in 1982 rouble prices; the Soviet figures are in 'constant' prices of a year not identified in the source, but 1973 in at least some of the series.
Sources: from or derived from (in row-by-row order) *Narkhoz 85*, pp. 410, 365, 100, 188; CIA *Growth* 1990, pp. 77 (first two rows) and 62 (last two rows).

The direction of year-to-year changes is similar in the two versions, with the CIA figures mostly significantly below the Soviet figures – but note the farm output figures for 1982. From longer runs of figures than these, we know that the year-on-year changes in national income, whether NMP as measured in Moscow or GNP as measured by the CIA in suburban Virginia, were heavily influenced by agriculture (20.6 per cent of GNP in the CIA estimates); agricultural output, in turn, was very much influenced by the weather. A bad harvest also affected the livestock sector and some branches of industry in that crop year (that is, mainly in the following calendar year).

With that circumstance in mind, one might suggest, very tentatively, that the overall level of economic activity revived somewhat in 1983, for reasons unconnected with the weather, but slower growth reasserted itself in 1984. One conjecture would be that Andropov's discipline campaign in late 1982 and 1983 did have some positive effect in stimulating growth, but that this effect petered out in 1984. If, in the CIA figures, farm output had grown by 2 per cent in 1984 instead of falling by 2 per cent, the direct arithmetical effect would have been to boost the GNP growth figure by 0.8 per cent; that would still be one percentage point below the growth rate of 1983. It is true that, by the same logic, if farm output had risen only 2 per cent in 1983, that would bring the 1983 GNP growth down to 2.4 per cent, only a fifth of a per cent above our hypothetical, adjusted growth in 1984: perhaps that small difference gives a better indication of the net effect of Andropov. To repeat, however, these are conjectures, not reliable measurements.

One final observation about these numbers: the CIA's picture of progress in 1985, relative to progress in 1984, is much less rosy than that of the Soviet Central Statistical Administration. This is probably because the Soviet official figures, produced in 1986, were tweaked to make Gorbachev's first year look better than Chernenko's last (full) year. This was standard behaviour. The Soviet authorities, in economic matters, preferred secrets to lies; but they were not dogmatic about it.

The period 1982 through 1984 was a fairly comfortable one for Soviet hard-currency trade. Financial caution had triumphed: machinery imports from the West were held down, with orders kept below $4 billion a year (McIntyre 1987). In real terms, Soviet imports of Western machinery and equipment had peaked in the mid-to-late 1970s, and continued to edge downwards, with imports of course lagging orders by a year or more. Imports of agricultural produce were higher: typically around $9 billion a year. On CIA estimates, the hard-currency current-account balance of payments was in surplus by $4–5 bn a year, even when gold sales are treated as a capital-account item (*ibid.*). Gross hard-currency debt was a manageable $21–23 billion; the ratio of debt service to all hard-currency earnings was below 15 per cent.

One consequence of the combination of agricultural difficulties and financial conservatism was that technology transfer from the West was playing a smaller part than it had in the 1970s. More precisely, the import of technology new to the Soviet Union and potentially productivity enhancing, insofar as it was embodied in imported hardware, was smaller than it had been. Policymakers had in effect decided that, at the margin, food imports had to have priority, under the constraint that debt to the West had to remain modest. Oil and gas, the largest hard currency earners, continued to have a high priority partly because of their foreign earnings; the energy sector therefore continued to absorb a large share of investment.

This set of priorities, and the flows associated with them, were more a holding pattern than a way ahead: arrangements for getting by rather than for getting on. In the mid-1980s, as Gorbachev began to take charge, events conspired to disturb that holding pattern. Bottlenecks in the oil sector held back oil export volume in 1985. Then in 1986 world oil prices fell. The new Party leader had a strategic problem on his hands: the long-term growth slowdown had not been halted; moreover, a way of getting by for the time being, via oil exports and grain imports, was under threat.

Notes

1   One Moscow rumour had it that he was a jazz fan. A superior class of rumour, supposedly emanating from a young man who knew Andropov's son, was that he was a Glenn Miller fan. No person of taste and discernment could possibly be both.

2   In late 1983 a young Marxist dissident (a member of a rare Russian breed) talked to me about Willy Brandt's reception in Moscow. He described with great scorn how senior members of the Institute of the World Economy had been besotted with the German leader. 'That showed what they really are,' he said, 'Social democrats!'.

3   '*Dokazhi, chto ty ne verblyud*' – 'Prove you are not a camel', as people described all demands for documents.

4   In the late 1980s an economist gave me his business card with his office address (an industrial-branch institute) and phone number. He then explained that he was not there very often, adding, 'As a matter of fact, I'm not really sure where it is'.

CHAPTER SEVEN

Gorbachev and Catastroika

Mikhail Gorbachev was the first Soviet leader who, if one may judge by appearances, did not understand the Soviet system. He was therefore the last Soviet leader. Gorbachev is also a man who has – judging again by appearances – a wide streak of human decency. He was at crucial moments unwilling to use military force to preserve communist rule. That compunction – for he was not forced by circumstances to eschew repression – makes his ever having become Soviet leader more surprising than the outcome of his rule.

This preamble may seem to personalise unduly the collapse of the USSR. There were of course factors contributing to that collapse that were beyond the leader's control. These will be considered in the final chapter, when we review the whole post-war trajectory of the Soviet economy. It is also true that the policies pursued under Gorbachev's leadership were introduced by a team, and not by an individual dictator. Still, it is almost impossible to imagine the Gorbachevian policies of *glasnost'* (roughly, openness) and *perestroika* (restructuring) being pursued by a leadership group headed by other potential leaders of the time: by the former Leningrad Party boss Grigorii Romanov, say, or by Egor Ligachev, by Heidar Aliev (at the time of writing the president of Azerbaijan), or even by the socialist manager Nikolai Ryzhkov, who had direct responsibility for economic policy through almost all of Gorbachev's time as leader.

Gorbachev held the Soviet leadership from March 1985 until the USSR dissolved into fifteen separate states in late 1991. The events of this period suggest a division into three sub-periods: an early emphasis on discipline and heightened priority for investment and the military (1985–86); a middle period of experiments with economic and political devolution, from 1987 until some point in 1989, when reformers could still, with some plausibility, hold out prospects of success; and an endgame from 1989 through 1991, when central control unravelled, the rules of both the economic and the political game became obscure, and middle-level officials saw their way to grabbing assets for themselves (on this process, see Solnick 1999).

This chapter is, accordingly, divided into two chronological sections that take the story into 1989. Chapter 8 will deal briefly with the end-game of 1989–91. That layout should not be allowed to obscure two themes that run through the whole Gorbachev period. The first is the progressive loss of control of the public finances, creating inflationary pressures over and above the repressed inflation endemic in a shortage economy. The second is the continuing interplay, at any rate after 1986, of political and economic liberalisation, eroding the standard operating procedures of the Soviet social system. That the USSR and the Soviet planning system ceased to exist at the particular time they did can best be accounted for by events in the political sphere: above all, the loss of the Communist Party's previously entrenched monopoly of power. The economic story shows why the economy was in exceptionally poor shape in 1991. It does not by itself account for the collapse in December 1991 of an entire social, political and economic order.

Acceleration, discipline and the alcohol campaign, 1985–86

Gorbachev's acquisition of the Party leadership, immediately upon the death of Chernenko, was attended with great expectations both at home and abroad. At last the long-awaited change of generations had occurred. True, Gorbachev had joined the Party before the death of Stalin; but his adult career had not taken shape under Stalin. While still only a plausible successor to the leadership, he had gained favourable reviews from Western diplomats in Moscow. He had been invited to London in late 1984, where the British Prime Minister famously declared that he was someone she could do business with. Surely he would bring change to the Soviet Union.

What kind of change that might be, was another matter. So far as the economy was concerned, there were, as the last two chapters have, I hope, made plain, two central problems. The Soviet Union needed to move to a higher long-run trend rate of growth if it was to remain a credible superpower into the twenty-first century. And it needed to resolve a core structural problem: a costly and ineffective farm sector that held back consumption levels so long as the Soviet leaders were unwilling simply to give up on agriculture and rely indefinitely on food imports.

Tighter discipline: the anti-alcohol campaign

Gorbachev and his team did not start with a clear economic strategy. Like all new leaders, Gorbachev began with personnel changes. These ranged from removing his closest rival, Romanov, from the Politburo to bringing in a defence-industry planner to head Gosplan. The early policy decisions were highly traditional. They were aimed at strengthening social discipline and shifting priorities back towards investment and the military. One of the earliest measures, two months into Gorbachev's rule, was the launch of the anti-alcohol campaign.

There was a lot to be said in favour of a national campaign to reduce drinking. Soviet – chiefly Russian, Ukrainian and Belorussian – drinking habits were of a particularly noxious kind, and all the evidence indicates that they had got worse since the 1960s. Consumption per head of the population of 15 years of age and above in the early 1980s is estimated by Treml (1986) to have been about 16 litres a year. This was less than contemporary alcohol consumption in France, but far more unhealthy. The Slavic tradition is to drink vodka, and to proceed in binges.[1] This has produced a high incidence of alcohol-related accidents and violence, as well as alcohol poisoning and alcohol-related cardio-vascular disease. Treml estimates that close to a third of alcohol consumption by the mid-1980s was illegally produced – mostly *samogon* (moonshine from illegal stills). That added to the risk of poisoning. Treml (*op. cit.*, p. 299) cites a remarkable statistic for the late 1970s: the Soviet annual death rate from alcohol poisoning was 19.5 per 100,000 population, compared with an average of 0.3 for nineteen other countries for which data were available. Soviet society, with its endemic labour shortage and consequent minimal work discipline, also allowed more drinking at work than would have been possible under capitalism. This contributed, along with poor safety arrangements, to an exceptionally high rate of accidents at work.

It certainly did not contribute to high productivity. The geographers Grigory Ioffe and Tatyana Nefedova recall visiting in 1985 the First of May farm in Yaroslavl' region. They found the cows had not been milked for three days. The reason was that the dairywomen had received their long-delayed pay three days before, and had been drunk ever since. The annual milk yield on this farm was about 1,000 kg, or about a sixth of North-West European levels (Ioffe and Nefedova 2001).

The increase over time in Soviet drinking was particularly worrying for the leadership. It had contributed to a decline in male life expectancy at birth from 67 years in 1964 to 62 in 1979. And by the mid-1980s spending on alcohol accounted for 15 per cent of household disposable money income (Treml 1986, pp. 299–300).

The latter figure also indicates a drawback to any sustained attack on Soviet drinking. The state had a large stake in the sale of alcohol, gaining 12–14 per cent of budget revenue from it (*ibid.*). It also gained revenue from a very high rate of turnover tax on sugar – an important ingredient in *samogon*. Furthermore, if the planners did not provide other consumer goods to mop up any reduced spending on alcohol, there would be even more frustrated spending power, that is, forced savings, in the household sector. Any sustainable anti-alcohol campaign would need to be carefully designed if collateral damage to the economy was to be contained.

There had been several earlier campaigns, under Khrushchev and under Brezhnev. These however had been limited to raising vodka and fortified-wine prices and imposing stiffer penalties on drunken misbehaviour. State production of alcoholic beverages had continued to rise. The Gorbachev campaign was more serious. State production of vodka and wine was reduced substantially. Vines were ripped out of some vineyards; some distilleries were closed. The minimum legal age for drinking alcohol was raised to American levels – twenty-one. Hours when alcohol could legally be sold were cut and the number of retail outlets selling alcoholic drink was reduced. The state production of vodka was cut by a third in one year, and then reduced further.

A rough calculation based on figures given by Treml (1986) suggests that state revenue from alcohol was reduced in 1986 by just over a quarter, equivalent (see above) to about 3.5 per cent of total budget revenue. (Consumption of legally produced alcohol down by a half; cumulative price increase in 1985 and 1986 about 47 per cent, taking median percentage increases from the ranges quoted by Treml.) The unanticipated revenue loss was equivalent to about 60 per cent of the health budget (*op. cit.*, p. 304). Illegal alcohol production is estimated by Treml to have increased substantially but (on my reading of his figures in terms of absolute alcohol) by only around half of the drop in legal production. Thus one effect was a diversion of funds from the budget to the bootleggers, and another was a real reduction in alcohol intake – with some beneficial effects on health.

Other factors will also have been operating. It is striking, all the same, that the crude death rate falls from 10.7 per thousand population in 1984–85 to 9.9 in 1986–87; that the death rate per 100,000 working-age population falls from 522 in 1985 to 480 in 1989 and that the murder and suicide rates are substantially lower in 1986 and 1987 than in 1985 (*Narkhoz 90*, pp. 90–93). Mortality and morbidity indicators began to edge up again in the late 1980s, and were to worsen substantially in the post-communist Russia of the early and middle 1990s. For a time, at least, the anti-alcohol campaign did some good; it also helped to destabilise the budget, expand the shadow economy and worsen repressed inflation.

Back to extensive growth: acceleration

The anti-alcohol campaign could reasonably be expected to have some beneficial effects on production. Insofar as it succeeded in reducing alcohol consumption – as it did – it helped to keep more working-age members of the population alive and, when at work, less inebriated or hungover, and less likely to cause accidents. Whatever the effects on the public finances, there should have been some positive net effect on output, as well as some savings in health expenditure. These effects, however, could hardly be of an order of magnitude that would transform Soviet economic performance. And they would essentially be one-off effects, not affecting the trend rate of growth.

On the all-important question of how to improve the growth rate, Gorbachev and his closer associates in the leadership (initially Egor Ligachev and Nikolai Ryzhkov, both of whom he brought into the Politburo less than two months after he became Party leader) were persuaded of the need to raise once more the share of gross fixed investment in national income: that is, to raise the growth rate planned for investment (see Chapter 5 for the earlier policy debate on this subject).

The early Gorbachev policy of acceleration (*uskorenie*) did not last long, and in retrospect is easily made to look foolish. For that matter, several Western analysts cast doubt on its feasibility soon after the Twelfth Five-Year Plan (1986–90) was published (for example, Hewett *et al.* 1987 and Hanson 1992, chapter 9, originally published in 1987). However, policy options short of the abandonment of socialism and central planning were few and far between. And Gorbachev seems never to have contemplated anything so radical as the abandonment of communism, even as he unintentionally led the Soviet Union precisely in that direction. The temptation to pursue something like an old-fashioned extensive growth strategy was in 1985–86 very strong.

Real GDP growth was by 1985 around 2 per cent a year or slightly less (Figure I.1 and Table 5.1). The population was growing at just under 1 per cent per annum. The United States was talking up its Strategic Defense Initiative (SDI or Star Wars). If Moscow was to respond with something similar (rather than rely on low-tech counter-measures, which would not have satisfied the military planners) defence spending had to grow rapidly and the technological level of associated production would have to be raised sharply: this applied particularly to information technology, where the Soviet Union lagged far behind. At the same time the Soviet leaders were worried that a deterioration in consumption levels might provoke serious unrest, akin to that already experienced in Poland (Teague 1988). Yet the margin for covering both these requirements was very small.

Table 7.1   *A schematic illustration of Soviet resource-allocation options for 1986–90 (% of GDP and % per annum rates of change)*

	1985 output shares (%)	Growth (% p.a., 1986–90 inclusive)	1990 outcome
A. Consumption per capita grows at 1% p.a.			
Cons	55	2.0	60.7
Defence + inv + other	45	2.0	49.7
B. Consumption per capita stationary			
Cons.	55	1.0	57.8
Defence + inv + other	45	3.2	52.6
GDP	100	2.0	110.4

Notes: The figures are stylised and illustrative, and take a prospect of 2 per cent annual growth as the given baseline scenario (in other words, what would happen in the absence of policy changes affecting overall growth).
Source: The illustrative 1985 end-use shares are loosely based on CIA *Measures* 1990.

Soviet output per head of population would on unchanged polices be growing at best by 1 per cent per annum or slightly less. Soviet official figures made the prospect look a little better than this, but there were people around Gorbachev who knew the limitations of those numbers. Abel Aganbegyan, whose uncensored 1965 outburst about the Soviet economy and its statistics was noted in Chapter 4, was already rumoured to be a source of advice to the leader (*Guardian*, 12 June 1985; memorandum circulated by the Bundesinstut für ostwissenschaftliche und internationale Studien, Köln, 6 September 1985), though he did not become an official adviser to Gorbachev until later.

In other words, the scope for switching priorities amongst consumption, defence and investment was narrow. No doubt the numbers were presented differently to the Soviet leaders, but this is likely to have been the bottom line. It would explain Gorbachev's referring as early as May 1985 to the need for the Soviet-style national income (NMP) growth rate to go up from the current 3 to 'at least 4' (speech in Leningrad, reprinted as Gorbachev 1985).

One way of illustrating some broad strategic options is shown in Table 7.1. This was to be achieved in the standard, traditional, Soviet way: by raising the growth rate of investment, and particularly of investment in research and development and in the engineering sector (in practice, both civilian and military). Gorbachev even hinted at a downgrading of the investment priority for agriculture in a June 1985 speech, when he said,

'We have reached here [in agriculture] the rational limits of building up investment,' (BBC *Summary of World Broadcasts*, SU/7976/C/7–19, June 1985; the texts of Gorbachev's speeches exist in a variety of forms: TASS texts, Soviet central press, subsequent publication in book form, and so on; the only reliable version of the words he spoke on the day of the speech is from broadcast monitoring; ideologically sensitive formulations were routinely sanitised in *Pravda* versions). This was understandable; high past investment in the farm sector over two decades had run into sharply diminishing returns, and room would have to be made for increased investment in engineering. In the event, the growth of investment in the agro-industrial sector (see Chapter 5 for the meaning of this term) was slightly moderated, but not halted. The grandiose scheme for diverting Siberian rivers, part of an earlier long-range plan for the sector, was abandoned. It would have taken forever and been an environmental disaster anyway.

The upgrading of the priority for 'science' (roughly, research, development, testing and evaluation, and dominated by military-related work) was dramatic. Nikolai Ryzhkov was now the Prime Minister and thus the leader's chief engineer or, in corporate terms, the CEO to Gorbachev's chairman of the board. It was Ryzhkov who announced in June 1986 that current spending on science was to grow by 5.9 per cent per annum in 1986–90 inclusive and capital spending on science by 11.2 per cent a year (*Izvestiya*, 19 June 1986).

The Twelfth (and last) Soviet Five-Year Plan was ambitious. It proved to be over-ambitious. Table 7.2 sets out the main aggregate targets in comparison with the preceding five years.

Two figures, both particularly misleading about reality, convey a great deal about the changes in priority. These are the figures for investment and for per capita real income. The former was set to grow faster than in the previous plan, the latter slower. Never mind that both grossly exaggerated real rates of change. The shift in intentions is clear.

This plan was based on highly optimistic assumptions. To begin with, it was assumed that the deceleration of the past twenty years could be reversed. The growth rates of the major aggregates shown in Table 7.2 were nearly all set higher than those planned, let alone those that materialised, in the previous five years. They were generally higher, indeed, than those planned for 1976–80.

The extent of the optimism involved is particularly clear when the more detailed outputs in physical terms (mostly in tons) are considered. These, as earlier chapters have I hope made clear, were the real building blocks of a Soviet plan. Output of crude oil had fallen at an average annual rate of 0.3 per cent a year in 1981–85; it was now planned to grow at an annual rate of 1.3 per cent. For coal the change was to be from 0.3 per cent growth to

Table 7.2   *Soviet medium-term plans, 1981–90 (% p.a. growth rates)*

	1981–85 plan	1981–85 actual	1986–90 plan
NMP utilised	3.4	3.2	4.1
Labour productivity[a]	–	3.1	3.7–4.2
Industrial output	4.7	3.7	4.6
Industrial lab prody	3.6	3.2	4.6
Agricultural output[b]	2.5	1.1	2.7–3.0
Investment[b]	2.0	3.4	4.3
Per capita real income	3.1	2.3	2.7
State retail sales	4.2	3.0	5.9[c]

Notes: General: the figures in this table are Soviet official figures, and tend to overstate real growth. Plan and actual data not precisely comparable.
a. in net material product. b. Between the averages of the five-year periods. c. Excluding sales of alcoholic beverages.
Source: Hanson 1992, Table 9.2, where the original Soviet sources are given.

1.8 per cent; for steel from 1.0 to 1.4–2.0; for grain from 0.3 to 5.6–6.1, and for meat from 2.5 to 4.2 (Hanson 1992, Table 9.3; original Soviet sources given there).

Meanwhile input growth was slowing. The planners apparently expected labour-force growth to average only 0.1 per cent a year (implied in Table 7.2; also stated directly by Ryzhkov in his speech to the XXVII Party Congress, *Izvestiya*, 4 March 1986) and capital-stock growth to be at a historically low 5.4 per cent a year (*ibid.*). The CIA estimates for the preceding five years were 0.7 and 6.3, respectively. In other words, an almost miraculous transformation was expected in the growth rate of total factor productivity.

Two Soviet economists, both of whom were to play prominent parts in *perestroika*, produced estimates of the extent of productivity improvement required. Aganbegyan estimated total factor productivity (TFP) growth in 1976–85 at 1.4 per cent a year and reckoned that it needed to accelerate to 2.1–2.7 per cent to meet plan targets in 1986–90. Stanislav Shatalin estimated an annual TFP growth rate of 0.6 per cent for 1981–85 and a requirement for that to rise to about 2 per cent a year to fulfil the plan (Aganbegyan 1986; Shatalin 1986). Being Soviet economists, they did not define clearly their main variables or explain how they reached their conclusions. At least they made it clear that they could see the problem.

Several Western analysts detected potential imbalances within the plan (Noren 1986; Leggett 1987; Hanson 1992, Chapter 9, originally published

1987). There were doubts about the adequacy of planned supplies of non-energy raw materials for industrial production and of equipment for the investment plan.

Part of the acceleration strategy entailed a sharp increase in the share of equipment within the total spending on investment. This was a belated attempt – or rather, a repeat of an earlier, failed attempt (in the 1976–80 plan; see Chapter 5) – to reduce the high share of building in total investment. By international standards, Soviet gross fixed investment was exceptionally construction-intensive. This may have made some sense in the forced industrialisation of the 1930s and the post-war rebuilding of the late 1940s. Its perpetuation after that was a characteristic of the shortage economy. Branch ministries and enterprises had every incentive to bid for as much in the way of inputs as they could get away with during the formulation of plans, and only weak incentives to economise on the use of inputs during plan implementation. New construction was a particularly attractive input to bid for because, once a construction project was in the plan, it could always suck in more inputs later: delays and cost overruns are a feature of public-sector construction projects the world over.

Equipment, however, is the ingredient of investment that, once installed, directly produces output. It was another characteristic of Soviet-type planning that old equipment was kept in use when it should have been scrapped: that is, at the very least when the hourly productivity of labour using the old equipment was below the hourly wage or, in an economy with excess demand for labour, when new machinery offering higher labour productivity was under-utilised while less productive equipment was fully manned. Therefore the Twelfth Five-Year Plan aim of increasing the rate of re-equipping at the expense of new construction of production capacities was entirely laudable.

Unfortunately, another characteristic of the Soviet economic system was that it was slow to absorb new technology. This applied not only to the date at which a new product or process was first introduced on a scale beyond that of pilot-plant or experimental production, but also to the rate at which an established new technology was diffused. Soviet makers of steel-making equipment continued to produce open-hearth furnaces long after electric-arc and oxygen steel equipment had become established in the West and after some of the newer generations of steel-making equipment had begun to be produced in the USSR. There are many similar examples (see Hanson 1981; Amann and Cooper 1982, 1986).

Gorbachev's Politburo ally, Aleksandr Yakovlev, later described the whole exercise bluntly: 'We allocated 12 billion roubles for new technology, which in those days was serious money, and it just disappeared. The system spat it out' (interview quoted in Mau and Starodubrovskaya 2001, p. 181).

Rapid modernisation of the Soviet equipment stock therefore would have benefited from a strong growth of machinery imports from the West. Whether that growth was measured in constant dollar prices or constant domestic rouble prices, it needed to be substantial. Given the targets for domestic machinery production, it could be calculated that total machinery imports would need to grow in real terms (in constant, domestic rouble prices) at about 5.4 per cent a year if the 1986–90 machinery investment targets were to be reached (for assumptions and details of this calculation see Hanson 1992, Table 9.5). Total machinery imports in 1985 were made up about 2:1 in favour of machinery from Central-Eastern Europe, but the key ingredient of Western machinery would need to grow at something like the same rate as total machinery imports if its contribution to raising productivity were to be maintained. Unfortunately, that ingredient of imported Western machinery had peaked in 1976 and was now stagnant or declining as external borrowing was cautious and preference was given, at the margin, to spending scarce hard currency on food.

This weakening of the rate of importation of advanced equipment was unlikely to be reversed. External circumstances were against it. In particular, the fall in world oil prices in 1986 was bad news for Moscow. Evgenii Yasin, a senior academic economist who was a mentor to some of the young reformers of the 1990s and himself for a time Minister of the Economy under Yeltsin, considers that there were two big setbacks at this time: advice from military intelligence that the Soviet Union could not cope with SDI, and the fall in oil prices (Yasin 2001, February issue, p. 68). The chances of meeting the 1986–90 plan targets, in other words, were slim.

Two other elements in Gorbachev's early economic strategy, apart from his hints about future organisational change, deserve a mention. A joint Party-Government decree of August 1985 required, among other things, that quality attestation commissions should be made more independent of branch ministries, and their grading of output should determine mark-ups and mark-downs from the basic price of a product (*Pravda*, 4 August 1985). Like the anti-alcohol campaign and the drive to raise the share of equipment in investment, this was not a new idea; nor was it a liberalising move: in a market economy, supply and demand should operate to reward product quality, with state regulation reserved for weights, measures, health and safety. This measure, however, like others introduced in 1985–86, was at first pursued more vigorously than similar measures had been in the past. For a few months, production figures were dented by the downgrading of low-quality products. Then there was a Soviet reality check. The primacy of numerical output targets was reasserted and the quality controllers were put in their place.

The second of these early organisational developments was the creation of 'superministries' to oversee large sectors of the economy. The better management of large production complexes and of groups of closely related economic branches was listed as an aim in the Party programme published in draft form in October 1985 (*Pravda*, 26 October 1985, pp. 1–7). Generally, this took the form of creating an umbrella organisation to oversee a group of branch ministries – another layer of bureaucracy, in the view of critics, but not necessarily doomed to ineffectiveness as a modification of a top-down system of management. A Bureau of Machine-Building, overseeing at least the eleven civilian engineering ministries, had already been set up (*Pravda*, 18 October 1985). A joint Party-government decree set up a formal merger of ministries in the (broadly defined) agro-industrial complex, into the Union-Republic State Agro-Industrial Committee (*Pravda*, 23 November 1985, pp. 1–2). A Politburo decision to set up a Bureau for the Fuel-Energy Complex was announced soon after (*Izvestiya*, 15 March 1986, p. 1). And so on – the chronological sequence seeming to reflect current priorities.

It would be easy to write off the superministries as a doomed experiment. But the branch ministries were at the time the favourite scapegoats of nearly all the internal critics of the economy. There was some justification for this: they combined a narrow, departmental view of what was desirable with a lack of detailed understanding of what was feasible. To attack this weakness, one could devolve powers down to enterprises or concentrate powers higher up in the hierarchy. So long as the organisation of the economy remained hierarchical, there was no obvious presumption in favour of the former. All that can be said is that if the superministries did any good at all, it was not enough to arrest the deterioration of economic performance.

Early policy conflicts

'Take Gosplan. For Gosplan we have no central authorities, no General Secretaries, no Central Committee. What they want, they do.' Thus Mikhail Gorbachev in June 1986, speaking (he thought) unattributably. He chose a strange audience for an off-the-record speech: the Union of Writers. His remarks duly appeared in *samizdat* and then in the Italian newspaper *La Repubblica* (7 October 1986, p. 13, translated in Foreign Broadcast Information Service, 9 October 1986).

This was one of his franker admissions about the resistance he was encountering, even at an early stage when he was not proposing radical changes in organisation. And it came eight months after he had changed the leadership of Gosplan. Probably officials in Gosplan found the Twelfth Five-Year Plan targets over-ambitious. They probably also resisted the attempt to ratchet up the priority for investment. Hints of such scepticism appeared in a round-table discussion of the plan in the Gosplan house journal (*Planovoe khozyaistvo*, 1986 no. 1, pp. 9–45).

Gorbachev went on to tell the Union of Writers that he was getting on top of the resistance to his plans in Gosplan. But he may have lost on some matters. Having said that further heavy investment in the agro-industrial complex might be pointless (see above), he ended up presiding over a five-year plan in which investment in that sector was yet again scheduled to grow faster than total investment (Hanson 1992, Table 9.3).

Disputes about priority changes and feasible rates of improvement were sharpened, no doubt, by the rate at which Gorbachev was moving to sack senior officials. Brezhnev had presided over a long period of 'stability of cadres'. Andropov had begun a personnel shake-up; under Chernenko this had slowed down; now it was accelerating again. New bosses, like Talyzin at Gosplan, were seeking to impose themselves on their new subordinates; old bosses were anxious to stay in place. Nobody could be sure that the new and comparatively young leader was not opting for a long-run regime of 'instability of cadres' as a way of intimidating all senior officials into compliance with his wishes. More was at stake than mere plan numbers.

At the XXVII Party Congress, Gorbachev criticised the kind of officials who feathered their own nests, and said there would be no compromise with them (*Pravda*, 26 February 1986, p. 5). This may have gone down well with the rank and file, but it must have made most middle-level and senior officials uncomfortable.

In the background lurked the question of resource priorities for the military. In assigning high priorities to research and development, engineering and information technology, Gorbachev was in harmony with the military leadership. But Condoleezza Rice noted at the time (Rice 1987) that there were conflicts within the military leadership over priorities, and military programmes were due to become controversial before long. In general, Gorbachev's early stance was that the 'success of socialism in the world' rested on its long-term economic performance, and the latter had to improve. The military leaders would have gone along happily with that formulation. But questions of methods and priorities in the medium term – about how to reach that long-term goal – were sensitive.

There were also strains on the public finances. These were not revealed at the time. The state budget was routinely presented until 1988 as having a small surplus. Official data supplied in 1990 to the IMF-World Bank-OECD-EBRD study of the Soviet economy, however, show a modest deficit equivalent to 2.4 per cent of GDP in 1985, rising to 6.2 per cent in 1986 (IMF *et al.* 1990, Table 2). The CIA's Russia-watchers were in the process of identifying the problem before that, estimating a large deficit in 1987, though slightly lower than the figure the IMF study came up with two years later (CIA 1988).

The Agency's list of reasons for the widening deficit was as follows: the big increase in budget-financed investment (part of Gorbachev's acceleration plans), the loss of revenue from alcohol (his anti-alcohol campaign, already described), reduced revenues from retail mark-ups on imported consumer goods as imports were cut back (see below) and slower growth of revenues from profits taxes as reforms left more discretion to enterprises for self-financed investment (the last of these influences came into effect only from 1987). In short, it was Gorbachevian policies, for the most part, that created the problem. Ryzhkov, discussing the problem in 1989, loyally cited 'economic shortfalls' and, plausibly, the costs of the war in Afghanistan (*Izvestiya*, 8 June 1989, pp. 1–3). In fact, that speech also made it clear that defence spending had been planned to grow faster than net material product in the 1986–90 plan. Accelerated defence spending in general, in other words, was also part of the problem.

General government deficits were largely financed, for want of less inflationary means, by borrowing from the central bank: that is, by printing money. The growth of currency emission and credit accelerates around this time (IMF 1990, Appendix Table II).

Within the Politburo, unity was far from guaranteed. For example, at the Party Congress Egor Ligachev sought to moderate criticism of allegedly venal senior and middle-level officials (*Pravda*, 28 February 1986, p. 4). He also denied publicly that market reforms were ever going to be on the cards (Tanjug in English, 28 June 1985). At this time, and indeed until well into 1987, Gorbachev was not espousing proposals that could be construed, even with a great effort, as market reforms. But he was keeping reform options open.

On the basis of his speeches and policy measures in 1985 and 1986, one would have to conclude that Gorbachev was at most considering a streamlining of economic organisation along East German lines, with perhaps some loosening up on very small-scale private provision of services; not a more systematic decentralisation to enterprise decision-making on Hungarian lines (a kind of limited market socialism) and certainly not anything more radical than that. But he was acquiescing, as Party leader, in a striking liberalisation of public discussion of the economy.

Early reform discussion

One early public proponent of serious decentralisation was B.P. Kurashvili, not an economist but a specialist on state administration in the Institute of

State and Law. Reputedly, Kurashvili had a background in intelligence; he also had a reputation as a man of principle. He certainly stuck to a market socialist vision, from a time when it seemed risky to go so far to a time when it was seen as passé. Work by him was cited approvingly by Zaslavskaya in the 1983 Novosibirsk report (see Chapter 6), with the implication that it was mostly unpublished. In May 1985 he came out with a clear set of arguments for a market socialist system (Kurashvili 1985).

'The choice of suppliers and customers,' Kurashvili wrote, 'and the content of relations with them [would be] guided by the regulating power of the market.' Instructions to enterprises from above would be abandoned. Most prices would be left to the market. Branch ministries would be abolished. There would be a general 'ministry for the national economy' and ministries for energy, for housing and for communications – roughly the arrangement to which Hungary had evolved more than a decade after the original establishment of the Hungarian New Economic Mechanism in 1968.

State enterprises in this set-up, he claimed, would be motivated to economise and therefore to shed, not to hoard, surplus workers. Will this (he asks) create unemployment? 'No. It would be strange if the absence of unemployment under socialism was based on the fact that enterprises hold on to surplus people, ignoring the need to assimilate new technology and thereby raise labour productivity.'

Socialists, anti-socialists and non-denominational pedants could all agree that this is an odd way of answering the question. The implication is that socialism has other ways of ensuring full employment, however that happy state of affairs might be defined. 'It would be strange if . . .' sounds ironic. Perhaps Kurashvili suspected that this was precisely how Soviet socialism had so far ensured that unemployment was tiny. If so, he was not alone in holding this view (see, for example, Hanson 1986).

On 19 August 1985 *Izvestiya* published an article explicitly and straightforwardly arguing that the large black economy in personal services (hairdressing, repairs, etc.) should be legalised rather than repressed. And the distinguished economic journalist Vasilii Selyunin wrote a withering critique of halfway-house reforms, and said that, even with some modifications, the current economic system was incapable of generating the inter-sectoral re-allocation of resources and the rate of innovation that had been achieved in recent years in a country like Japan (Selyunin 1985).

The more academic reformers, such as Zaslavskaya and Gavriil Popov, were at this time more discreet in what they published. Favourable references to the (Leninist) New Economic Policy of the 1920s, a rather fragile mixed economy, were a popular device. Writers and journalists were more robust. One writer produced a spirited article in praise of the small private firms that remained in services and crafts in East Germany. Their bosses, he wrote, did not behave like Soviet enterprise directors, but worked alongside their own staff (Levikov 1986).

It was in the treatment of small-scale production activities that the Gorbachev leadership showed the first sign of organisational radicalism. In March 1986 the Politburo outlined plans for new and clearer legislation on 'individual labour activity envisaged in the constitution' in crafts, services and agriculture, 'based exclusively on the personal labour of citizens' (*Izvestiya*, 29 March 1986). Just to assist this clarification, the same Politburo meeting also called for tougher regulation of 'non-labour incomes'. The resulting legislation in November 1986 allowed only people of pensionable age to work full-time on their own account (in a specified range of activities); people of working age could do so only part-time; in other words, the state would not let them go altogether (text in *Izvestiya*, 21 November 1986, p. 2).

This is a rare example of legislation that restricts entrepreneurship to senior citizens. It was accompanied by legislation on 'non-labour incomes' that gave the green light for a witch-hunt for entrepreneurs. Such are the ways of committees. By mid-1989 there were only about half a million people registered under the Law on Individual Labour Activity (*Ekonomicheskaya gazeta*, 1989 no. 42, p. 4). To be fair, it had by then been largely superseded by the more liberal 1988 Law on Cooperatives (see below).

The external environment in 1985–86

One important outside influence was President Reagan's Star Wars initiative. Whether the policy of 'forcing the Soviet Union to arm itself to death' really had a large influence on the Soviet economic collapse, is a question that will be left to the final chapter. But we know that it was something that concerned Soviet policy-makers in the mid-1980s, and contributed to the acceleration policy – which in turn was unsuccessful and economically damaging.

Meanwhile the difficulties in crude oil production in 1985, with consequent losses in export earnings, were followed by a decline in world oil prices in 1986. The Soviet Union's convertible-currency situation deteriorated. The estimated current-account surplus (estimated, that is, by the CIA) was not eliminated, but it fell from $4.6 billion in 1984 to a mere $12 million in 1985, improving slightly to just under $1 billion in 1986. The large negative errors and omissions item in the CIA calculations increased from $3.8 to 5.8 to 7.2 billion during the three years. This would have included convertible currency payments to Central-Eastern countries, Third

World countries and others. It helps arithmetically, if somewhat enigmatically, to account for the steep rise in net foreign borrowing over the three years from $274 million to $7.4 billion to $8.0 billion and of gold sales from $1 to 1.8 to 4 billion (McIntyre 1987, Table 4).

Gross sovereign external debt (as estimated by the Agency) therefore rose, from $22.8 to 30.2 to 38.2 billion. By 1986 the ratio of debt service to convertible-currency exports of goods and services was 23.2 per cent – not necessarily unmanageable, but 8–10 per cent higher than the USSR's cautious financial managers had been used to (data from *idem*, Table 5).

For a country that derived about a tenth of its population's food intake (in calories) and perhaps a tenth of its new equipment from the West, and whose planners were not willing to increase their foreign borrowing, all this was bad news. It added to the constraints operating on Soviet economic performance.

Forward to reform, 1987–89

The trial-and-error character of Gorbachev's reforms

The major reforms introduced in the middle years of Gorbachev's leadership were of three kinds: measures to decentralise decision-making in what was still presumed to be a state-owned economy; measures to legitimise the unplanned, non-state economy; and measures to facilitate trade and investment links with the outside world.

In calling these measures 'reforms', I do not wish to convey approval of them. To repeat a point made in Chapter 2: the conventional sense of 'reform' in Soviet-type economies is reorganisation or reassignment of decision-making powers so that some devolution of decision-making is supposed to follow. Whether such measures are internally coherent, compatible with the ownership system, compatible with the political system, capable of being implemented and likely, if implemented, to improve economic performance, are separate questions. So far as Gorbachev's reforms are concerned, history has returned a dusty answer to all of them. One interesting question remains: why was the outcome so far removed from the aspirations of the leadership?

The Gorbachev team embarked on this legislation, not as part of a plan already conceived in 1985 but in an evolutionary, trial-and-error way. Public discussion had been allowed to be more open from the start, and the reform debate unfolded rapidly into proposals that would earlier have been censored, never mind legislated. Meanwhile it was becoming increasingly clear that discipline plus quality controls plus accelerated investment growth would not secure a significant and sustained improvement in economic performance.

The former Politburo member Vadim Medvedev recalls that the fall in industrial output in early 1987 was the key event. This shifted the balance of arguments among top policymakers towards reform (Medvedev in Ellman and Kontorovich 1998, p. 134). Medvedev stresses the political impact of a poor monthly report for January. But the weakening was more than a statistical hiccup. Industrial output in the first four months of the year was reported to be 2.8 per cent above the same period of 1986 (*Izvestiya*, 27 May 1987, p. 1). This was the Soviet official gross industrial output series, containing concealed inflation as well as real change. Compared with previous official annual rates of change, 2.8 per cent was not good.

To many, it was obvious that the industrial sector was back in trouble after some improvement in 1986. From more detailed data for the same period of January–April 1987 (*Ekonomicheskaya gazeta*, 1987 no. 21, p. 2) it is possible to calculate an unweighted average output growth year-on-year of the 38 industrial products given in physical terms (tons, etc.): 0.8 per cent. Even that was in one sense unduly flattering. The year 1986 had seen an improvement in agriculture because of better weather (1987 was to see another decline), so part of that growth in early 1987 came from food processing. If the five food-industry products are excluded, the rate of increase calculated in this way goes down to 0.1 per cent. Properly weighted, the real growth of industrial output was probably a bit better than this, but not much.

Gorbachev later recalled that at this time he was learning, also, of the ineffectiveness of his own measures. His travels round the country and letters coming 'from below' were all conveying the message that, on the ground, nothing was changing. The same local officials were behaving in the same way as before (quoted from an interview with Gorbachev in Mau and Starodubrovskaya 2001, p. 137). It was in early 1987 that he began to seek support from the grass roots, appealing over the heads of Party officials – a process that was to lead to the undermining of the whole established system of economic control.

The top policy-makers were facing once more the prospect of economic stagnation. The previous year, Gorbachev's first full year in office, had seen some improvement (according to the CIA estimates at 1982 factor cost, GNP growth at 4.0 per cent, compared with an average growth rate of 1.8 per cent a year in 1981–85; CIA *Measures* 1990, Table A-6). This was in part the result of a good harvest and perhaps in part the initial impact of the anti-alcohol campaign and a shake-up of leading personnel. In early 1987 it looked as though they were back to square one.

What they did about it was, I suggest, a reflection of the generational change in the leadership. The economist Evgenii Yasin suggests that top-level recognition that the old system was failing was nothing new. Such an arch-traditionalist in the elderly Brezhnev Politburo as Mikhail Suslov, he says, knew both that economic reform was necessary and that its conse-quences would be unpleasant (in precisely what way, Yasin does not specify). Suslov and others like him, Yasin says, probably thought, 'Well, it can happen without me. *Après moi la deluge.*' (Yasin uses the Russian translation: *posle menya – khot' potop*; Yasin 2001, February, p. 68.) Suslov died in 1982.

Actuarially, Gorbachev had no such easy way out. He had a reasonable prospect of presiding over the Soviet Union into the twenty-first century. In early 2001 he celebrated his seventieth birthday. At the birthday party he was still dancing in the small hours. Admittedly, continuing to run the Soviet Union might have worn him down a bit, but the indications are that physically he could have stayed in charge to this day.

A stagnating economy would, for him, have unpleasant consequences. He would be leading a country unable to maintain the status of a superpower. Its social system would have lost the last remnants of international respect. And what of domestic unrest? Soviet workers might even, eventually, begin to behave like Poles. It was time for serious changes in the economic system.

The reform process

The reform process was messy. No politically sensitive reform anywhere can ever go unblemished from think-tank to policy implementation. Incre-mental and somewhat disorderly reform processes are not necessarily doomed. The process of change in China from 1978 was far more *ad hoc* and trial-and-error than the Hungarian New Economic Mechanism from 1968, but the former improved performance dramatically while the latter did not. Even so, the Soviet reform process from 1987 was more confused than was good for it.

Medvedev recalls that at a March 1987 Politburo meeting Gorbachev proposed that a radical economic reform programme should be prepared (Medvedev, *loc. cit.*). Medvedev describes (pp. 134–6) a process of policy formation driven and coordinated by Gorbachev himself but without, it would seem, a single reform architect with an overall vision of the sort of changes needed. There was no Reszo Nyers (Hungary 1968), Leszek Balcerowicz (Poland 1990), or Egor Gaidar (Russia 1992). Senior Soviet academic economists such as Abel Aganbegyan and Leonid Abalkin played a part as critics of the existing system and sources for particular ideas, but there was no chief designer.

Looking back fourteen years later, Yasin observed, 'Soviet economists had their chance: we'll do whatever you propose. And we had nothing to propose' (Yasin 2001, March, p. 81). That is one way of putting it. Certainly there was no senior Soviet economist with a coherent and convincing vision of how to transform the performance of the Soviet economy. But there is no reason whatever to believe that, if there had been such a genius, he would have had his way. And the academic economists did, alas, make proposals; some of them, unfortunately, were acted upon. Aganbegyan is generally credited with the authorship of the acceleration proposals, which were already failing. Another view is that of Gennadii Zoteev, then in the Gosplan Research institute: it would have been better if the leading Soviet academic economists had admitted their ignorance (Zoteev in Ellman and Kontorovich 1998, pp. 141–3).

In the event, different groups worked on different parts of the programme, with different ends in view.

Vladimir Mozhin, then the first deputy head of the Economics department of the Central Committtee of the Party (that is, a senior member of the central policy staff) had proposed in March 1986 a shift to enterprise autonomy. He recalls that he, Gorbachev and Vadim Medvedev were arguing in early 1987 for the abolition of mandatory output targets for enterprises, while Ryzhkov (Prime Minister and a full Politburo member), Vladimir Dolgikh (still only a candidate member of the Politburo, but also the Central Committee secretary with oversight of heavy industry, energy and transport) and Aleksandra Biryukova (then Central Committee secretary with oversight of consumer-goods supplies and family matters) were against. (Mozhin in Ellman and Kontorovich 1998, pp. 136–8). Mozhin and Yasin agree in their recollections that in the top policy discussions of 1987 the word 'market' was still not acceptable (Mozhin in *op. cit.*, p. 137; Yasin in Ellman and Kontorovich 1998, pp. 143–51, at p. 144). Mozhin suggests also that even the Aganbegyans and Abalkins were 'not as yet ready' to consider a system based on private ownership.

What emerged from this process in the middle Gorbachev years was a series of organisational changes that weakened central planning but did not replace it.

The main reform measures were government decrees allowing joint ventures with up to 49 per cent foreign ownership on Soviet soil in January 1987 (*Ekonomicheskaya gazeta*, 1987 no. 4, pp. 3–4; no. 6, pp. 15–18; no. 9, p. 23; no. 10, p. 23; no. 11, p. 23); the law on the state enterprise of June 1987 (*Pravda*, 1 July 1987, pp. 1–4), and the law on cooperatives of a year later (*Izvestiya*, 8 June 1988, pp. 1–4).[2]

There were of course a great many more laws and decrees bearing on the organisation of the economy. Many supplemented, modified or provided enabling legislation in support of the major laws and decrees listed above.

In addition there was a flurry of further, and potentially far-reaching, legislation in 1989–91: on leasing of assets (*Izvestiya*, 1 December 1989, p. 3); on property (*Izvestiya*, 10 March 1990, pp. 1, 2); on land (*Ekonomika i zhizn'*, 1990 no. 11, pp. 17–20); a decree on anti-monopoly policy (*Ekonomika i zhizn'*, 1990 no. 38, supplement, pp. 2–3); laws on banking and on the State Bank (both in *Izvestiya*, 18 December 1990, pp. 3–4); on currency regulation (*Ekonomika i zhizn'*, 1991 no. 12, pp. 18–19); on inventions (*Izvestiya*, 14 June 1991, pp. 4–5) and the foundations of civil law (defining a legal person, property, liability and contract; *Izvestiya*, 25 June 1991, pp. 3–7). This was a serious attempt to begin to create a legal framework for a mixed, market economy, but it came too late. Republics, notably the Baltic states and Russia, were putting through their own, rival laws. The outline legislation covering property, liability, contract and other basic elements of commercial legislation never even came into effect. It was due to come into force on 1 January 1992, and the Soviet Union ceased to exist the week before.

So far as the main legislation of 1987–88 is concerned, the sad truth is that it was in one way or another unworkable. Central planning of output, centralised supply allocation and central control of prices remained in place. Within those arrangements, any foreign joint ventures faced enormous difficulty in functioning; the autonomy of state enterprises was largely fictitious, and unplanned activity by cooperatives was likely to produce transactions not designed to meet the wishes of consumers but harnessed to plan evasion by state enterprises.

The centrepiece was the 1987 law on the state enterprise (henceforth the enterprise law). This was put forward at the June plenum of the Party Central Committee, which Evgenii Yasin regards as the turning point in *perestroika* (Yasin 2001, March, p. 80). At this plenum Gorbachev spoke of the 'pre-crisis state' of the Soviet economy (*Pravda*, 26 June 1987).

The enterprise was to have more control over its own finances. That was the main provision of the new law. Deductions from its revenue for state and local budgets were to be fixed in advance for five years at a time: fixed, that is, as percentages of net income (revenue less payment for material inputs). Then it was required to cover wages and bonus payments and also to pay fixed proportions ('stable long-run normatives') of post-tax net income into production-development, research and social-development funds nominally of its own. The branch ministry was not to interfere by way of changing any of the tax or fund-forming normatives.

The idea was to provide state enterprises with incentives to develop their own activities, secure in the knowledge that there was a fixed set of rules about the disposal of net revenue, at least for five years at a time.

Thus far, as readers with exemplary powers of recall will realise, the provisions of the enterprise law were a rerun of the 1965 reform plus 1970s counter-plans. The novel ingredients in the 1987 law were to do with who decided output levels, and how. The enterprise was now to be free to set its own annual and five-year plans, but subject to branch objectives, 'control' (guideline) figures and state orders (*goszakazy*) for output from the central authorities. The *goszakazy* were to be for items needed for state priority programmes. In principle, therefore, there could be capacity the use of which was not entirely pre-empted by state orders. That meant, in turn, that there could be some decentralised, even in due course competitive, buying and selling of output not covered by *goszakazy*.

Therefore the reform envisaged some development of wholesale trade between enterprises, which, in the case of consumer goods, would include trade between producers and the distributive network. Accordingly, enterprises were explicitly given some organisational leeway: they could form joint ventures with one another, merge, establish their own research divisions and sign agreements with individual entrepreneurs (operating under the law on individual labour activity described in the previous section) and cooperatives (some outline legislation on cooperatives already existed, though the main law on cooperatives was still to come). They could also, 'if necessary', arrange contracts with groups of their own employees for additional production on terms to be negotiated between the two parties. This last device had been developed in Hungary.

Remarkably, the law also allowed for enterprises to go to arbitration courts against their superior ministry and seek compensation for ministry decisions that were to their detriment. The text of the law also said that the share of decentralised price-setting would rise. Soviet laws were unusual documents; they included sentiments and predictions as well as many loose ends. The loose ends were in Kurashvili's view deliberate; they were 'conservative-bureaucratic traps'.

One other element in this reform was also novel: the employees of the enterprise were to have the right to vote on candidates for enterprise director. As in Yugoslav self-management, they did not have clear sovereignty in the appointment; it was also subject to approval by the authorities – in this case, the branch ministry.[3] This was an instance of Gorbachev's optimism about the role that could be played by popular initiative; it was one of his 'human factor' policies (see Teague 1987). These did not extend to submitting himself to election.

It is easy to pick holes in this reform from the standpoint of 2001. In fact, it was very easy to do so in 1987. Many cynical, old, *Pravda*-scarred, decree-weary, Sovietological hacks did just that (for instance Hanson 1992, Chapter 10, originally published in July 1987).

The law did not change the state enterprise's position in the economic hierarchy. It still had a superior branch ministry, which amongst other things appointed enterprise directors. The law did not specify that the normatives to be applied to net revenue to determine how much would be remitted to the budget and how much retained, would be the same across branches or even across enterprises within a branch. Discretionary treatment of individual enterprises 'from above' could remain the norm. The provision for suing the ministry was not, so far as I know, ever employed. You could always sue the boss if you didn't want to keep your job. The legal framework that allows some people in the West to sue their bosses for (say) sexual harassment and enjoy some legal protection against retribution was not available. (Even in the most litigious Western countries, legal protection seldom saves whistle-blowers.)

Branch ministries and central planners still had targets to meet and needed to be able to allocate equipment, raw materials, semi-fabricates, components and sub-assemblies among producers. Moreover, the five-year plan gave them high targets to meet and, even as the prospects of achieving the ambitious 1990 targets withered away, there were still annual plan targets covering just about everything. The reform was to come into effect at the start of 1988. The chances that branch ministry, Gosplan and Gossnab officials would prepare an annual plan that left any significant amount of production capacity to be used at other people's discretion were remote.

If they had done so, the chances of decentralised production, investment and supply conditions producing a more efficient allocation of resources were also remote. Prices were still centrally fixed and were a long way from reflecting relative scarcities.

At the time, Aganbegyan voiced the aspirations of the halfway-house reformers on the fringe of policy-making. The *goszakazy* should initially cover 50–60 per cent of industrial output, shrinking to only 25 per cent in 1990 – at which point a price reform would have been introduced (Reuters from Moscow, 27 June 1987). Whether he hoped for price decontrol or a mere revision of centralised prices, is not clear: from other things he has written it seems likely that he envisaged only limited decontrol.

In due course Gosplan put all this chatter in its place when the 1988 annual plan targets were announced. National income (NMP) produced was to increase by 6.6 per cent over 1987 (*Izvestiya*, 27 April 1988, p. 1). The previous year's actual increase had been 1.6 per cent (*Narkhoz 90*, p. 7). The 1988 plan was, to put it mildly, taut. The *goszakazy* would have to cover everything. They duly did. The notion of increased enterprise autonomy faded away.

The enterprise law, it should be said, was introduced at the June 1987 plenum as the first instalment of a package of measures. At a meeting ahead of the plenum, Gorbachev explained that other legislation was in the pipeline, to amend other parts of the system (*Pravda*, 13 June 1987). A Central Committee resolution made public two weeks later (*Pravda*, 27 June 1987, pp. 2–3) outlined what these measures would cover. That included price formation, the supply system and Gosplan. But what was said there was vague. In the event, prices were not generally decontrolled and Gosplan and the supply system were not reorganised.

On the evidence available in late 1987 it was clear that Gorbachev and his allies were seeking only limited changes, and that even these encountered great resistance among top policy-makers. Thanks to the efforts of Michael Ellman and Vladimir Kontorovich in eliciting and assembling the memoirs of insiders, we now know more about what was going on behind the scenes.

Mozhin describes how policy developed on the reshaping of the central administration (including Gosplan and the branch ministries): a highly sensitive subject. A commission chaired by Ryzhkov met, often twice a week, over a year from the autumn of 1987, and produced no real changes (Mozhin in Ellman and Kontorovich 1998, pp. 151–3). Medvedev recalls that, in preparing the 1988 annual plan, the central planners sought to make ministry control figures mandatory, contrary to the letter of the enterprise law, and to subject almost all output to *goszakazy*, which was contrary to its spirit (Medvedev in *op. cit.*, pp. 153–4). He also (p. 158) says that resistance to an early, comprehensive revision of prices united the government (that is, the Council of Ministers, as distinct from the Party leadership), Gosplan and the State Prices Committee. Gorbachev gave in. What was at stake, though Medvedev calls it a price reform, was a systematic revision of centralised prices plus some limited decontrol, not a general decontrol of prices.

Reforms in foreign trade and investment attracted far less attention. In allowing direct ownership by foreign private firms of assets on Soviet territory, they were ideologically more of a departure than the enterprise law. But the evidence from the Soviet Union's last years is that very few people in the USSR at this time cared two hoots about Marxism-Leninism. In 1988–89 Alexander Tsipko published a series of articles attacking Marxism. He was at the time working as a consultant to the Party Central Committee International Affairs Department. He describes a Central Committee official saying to him in the cafeteria: 'Sasha, you are a genius. It took you four articles to say what could be said in a single sentence: "Marxism is bullshit and the Bolsheviks led by Lenin are a bunch of criminals."' (Tsipko in Ellman and Kontorovich 1998, pp. 169–87, at p. 185.) Such conversations in the Central committee cafeteria, Tsipko adds, were not, by late 1988, out of the ordinary.

Joint ventures had in any case been long established in several other CMEA countries: for over a decade in Hungary and Romania, for example. Also, foreign economic activity was widely believed to be peripheral to the Soviet economy. That this was a misapprehension (see Treml 1983 and the discussion in Chapter 5 above) was neither here nor there. Foreign-trade rights and joint ventures were of little interest to most Soviet citizens, including most members of the elite.

From 1987 foreign companies could set up joint ventures in the USSR, and some branch ministries and large enterprises were given the right to engage directly in foreign trade – formerly a monopoly of foreign trade organisations mostly under the Ministry of Foreign Trade. The joint ventures, as has already been mentioned, had to be majority owned by a Soviet entity. They also had to be headed by a Soviet chief executive.

These requirements were not too onerous for foreign business. Even equity stakes well below 49 per cent can convey considerable powers of control. The most widely used definition of 'direct' in measurements of foreign direct investment is that it entails an equity stake of 10 per cent or more; this is held to entail both a significant degree of control and a long-term commitment to the business in question. The appointment of a Soviet chief executive could be balanced in a variety of ways through his or her contract, the statute of the new company and so on. In any case, foreign executives could not hope to operate successfully in such an exotic business environment without a local person in a position of some authority in their team.

The real difficulties were non-statutory. How did you assess your costs and revenues in a country where prices were fixed and often misleading? How did you obtain material inputs in a country where almost all inputs were centrally allocated and your joint venture was outside the plan? Could you credibly threaten any of your local employees with the sack? If you fell out with your Soviet partner enterprise, could you protect yourself against legal and administrative manoeuvres on their part to get control of joint venture assets?

Some problems were covered by the legislation on paper, but turned out to be hard to resolve in practice. One example was the importation of materials for joint venture production, which was supposed to be duty-free but was not necessarily so in reality. Another was repatriation of profits: could it be done only out of export earnings, as the legislation stipulated, or were there ways of repatriating profit from domestic sales? The country of operation was the USSR, so the answer usually was: it depends . . .

Nonetheless, there was no lack of Western interest. The Soviet Union had a very large population (283.1 million in mid-1987), starved of good-quality goods and services, rather cheap to employ and fairly well educated;

it also had huge natural resources, often extracted and processed in ways that could be made a great deal more cost-effective than they currently were.

The first joint venture, signed before the end of 1986 under sketchy initial legislation, was with the German fashion magazine *Burda*, to produce a Russian edition of 100,000 copies, earning convertible currency by selling advertising (Lavigne 1987). By the end of 1990 there were 2905 joint ventures registered (*Narkhoz 90*, p. 65), though many were not active and almost all were small.

The attempt to link Soviet production to world markets by encouraging direct trade by enterprises was bound to be problematic. The central authorities wished to keep control of the country's external finances. They lacked the indirect means appropriate to a market economy. Monetary policy did not influence aggregate demand. Changes in the exchange rate were of no practical importance. So they had to keep some sort of administrative control of trade. The producers wanted to retain hard currency in order to purchase imports of their own choice, but Gosbank, the Foreign Trade Bank and the Ministry of Finance were used to controlling all the *valuta* (foreign currency) and had good reasons for continuing to do so. And if enterprises traded abroad at world prices, the results would bear no systematic relationship to domestic prices or to the cost-effectiveness of the foreign transaction. The Soviet trade specialist Vladimir Kuznetsov assembled the following price data that underline this point (Table 7.3 contains only part of a longer list of goods in the original source).

Table 7.3   *External and internal prices for selected Soviet products, 1987 (domestic wholesale price = 100)*

Product	CMEA price	Soviet export price in West
Oil	510	267
Gas (000 cu. metres)	423	173
Quality steel	167	122[a]
Ammonia	129	45
Sawn timber (cu. metre)	154	93
Screw-cutting lathe (unit)	170	68
VAZ 2108 car (unit)	103	47
Colour TV Ts-380D (unit)	79	17

Notes: General: conversion at official exchange rate; prices are per ton unless otherwise specified. a. Import price from the West.
Source: derived from Kuznetsov 1990, p. 161.

The difference between the structure of domestic wholesale prices and of world prices, as illustrated in Table 7.3, was huge. Soviet domestic prices for energy and materials had been kept low (relative to domestic marginal cost and also to the market-driven prices in world trade), while the prices of manufactures were relatively high (at least in comparison with world market prices).

The domestic price quoted for a VAZ car (of the type marketed in the West as a Lada) includes a large element of turnover tax, while that for a lathe does not. In any case, a general point is exemplified here: given the exchange rate, Soviet manufactures could be sold in free markets only by cutting the prices drastically. Conversely, fuel and materials made large paper profits if sold in the West. The CMEA prices reflect, in principle, the average of the previous five years' prices on world markets; in practice, this worked fairly well for simple products like crude oil and natural gas. For these, the higher price in the CMEA than in the West was the result of the recent fall in world prices. The other prices were more heavily influenced by bilateral bargaining in what amounted to barter deals.

In this set-up, Soviet foreign trade organisations (FTOs) characteristically recorded a rouble profit when selling energy and raw materials on world markets. Often, though not always, they would record a loss in selling manufactures. They tended to record a paper profit from the domestic rouble transfer price of imports. Surplus European Community farm products, for example, exported at prices that could be below cost, were resold within the USSR at rouble prices well above the convertible currency price paid for them times the exchange rate. Normally the FTOs as a group made, in this way, a substantial net rouble profit. This could happen even when the convertible currency trade balance in dollars showed a deficit. These 'earnings from foreign trade' went into the state budget.

If individual enterprises and production-branch ministries were to trade directly with the outside world, bypassing the FTOs, the central authorities had to ensure not only that the great bulk of convertible currency earnings continued to be controlled by the government, but that exporting entities, despite surrendering nearly all their hard currency, found exporting what they were instructed to export attractive. In the face of the exotic structure of Soviet domestic prices, this could be done only by applying multiple rouble–dollar conversion rates, differentiated by product. Differentiated currency coefficients accordingly were used, and they were differentiated not merely across product lines but across individual production enterprises in a given line of production. According to Kaser and Maltby (1988), there were originally 1,500 of them, but the number rapidly grew to 3,000. They were applied for calculating rouble returns from exports.

In 1988 the authorities in Moscow were greatly exercised, just as they were thirteen years later, about their reliance on exports of fuel and raw materials. Manufacturing branch ministries were given export targets, while at the same time the *goszakazy* pre-empted all their available capacity in order to meet planned domestic usage. This point was repeated by several contributors to an *Ekonomicheskaya gazeta* round-table discussion of the first year of the foreign-trade reforms (1988 no. 25, pp. 19–21).

A deputy minister of the motor industry, who could boast that his industry was exporting a quarter of its car production, pointed out that there was still a shortage of spare parts (for exported vehicles, for which requirements were more demanding), and a lack of incentives for producers to supply them. He wanted more freedom for the ministry to alter export prices. Others called for a devolving of powers to set the differentiated currency coefficients (the multiple exchange rates).

The man from the Ministry of Farm Machinery complained of the intense competition for sales on world markets, amidst falling world demand, and lamented that his industry's hard-currency earnings plan had been increased by 450 per cent in 1987. 'Is that really planning?' he asked plaintively. (Nobody gave the correct answer: 'Yes'.) The man from the Electrical Equipment Ministry went one better: his branch export plan was set 600 per cent above 1986 export earnings.

The man from the new State Commission for Foreign Economic Relations (GVK), the organisation with oversight of the new arrangements, said he thought export deliveries should in 1989 be included in the *goszakazy*. This was a logical response to the complaint that state orders were crowding out export supply capacity. It was also another nail in the coffin of Aganbegyan's hopes for the development of unplanned wholesale trade.

One problem with devolving foreign-trade rights to selected producers was that many of them, select though they might be, were outside Moscow. To negotiate foreign-trade contracts required specialist knowledge, all of which was in Moscow. No normal Muscovite would voluntarily leave Moscow. The Soviet provinces had none of the advantages relative to the capital city that can reconcile Western professionals to life in second-rank cities outside the metropolis: not better schooling, cheaper housing, less pollution and so on. They simply had less of everything except pollution, at much the same price. The man from the GVK suggested an answer: allow foreign-trade specialists who are prepared to move to 'the periphery' to keep their Moscow apartments (and by implication their Moscow residence permits).

The man from the Ministry for Foreign Economic Relations (the new name of the Ministry of Foreign Trade, now subordinate to the new GVK) declared that the results of the diffusion of foreign-trade rights to production branches had in 1987 been unsatisfactory. His grounds for saying this were simple: ministries and enterprises with foreign-trade rights had imported 17.5 billion roubles' worth and exported 8.2 billion. Both measures were probably in *valuta* roubles, that is, they were foreign-currency totals converted to roubles at the official exchange rate. There is nothing in these numbers to suggest that the predominance of decentralised imports over decentralised exports was necessarily inefficient. But the effect on the trade balance was the opposite of what the central planners wanted.

In short, the attempted, partial decentralisation of foreign-trade activity greatly complicated Soviet trade and added to the internal inconsistencies in the operating arrangements of the Soviet economy.

The third major piece of legislation in this period was the 1988 law on cooperatives. This was the most radical of all Gorbachev's economic measures so far. It provided for people to be able to establish a cooperative of any size in any legal form of economic activity. Cooperatives would have to be registered with the local council and report their financial outcomes for tax purposes. Members of a cooperative could be few or many, and they could employ non-members. A cooperative was therefore capable of being a capitalist partnership, with the members exploiting, in Marxist terms, the labour of non-members. The members were required to work in the cooperative themselves, so they could not be pure, coupon-clipping *rentiers*. But they could be, in effect, private employers of other people. There was an attempt in the legislation to require that people employed in a cooperative should be employed only part-time and not entirely detached from state service; but this requirement was never very clear.

If Marxist-Leninist doctrine had mattered deeply to any large part of the population or to any significant elite group, the law on cooperatives would have created an uproar. It did not. Appearances had been preserved. The word 'cooperative' sounded vaguely socialist. Lenin had spoken warmly of cooperatives. So the term was used to cover the new private firms, and all was well.

The practical difficulties were another matter. The cooperatives would be outside the planning system; they would have to buy material inputs and equipment in the 'wholesale trade' that the 1987 enterprise law had been supposed to create, but had not. They could set their own prices, though there was to be some sort of checking to ensure they were not price-gouging. They could be either free-standing or attached to (*pri*) a state enterprise.

The cooperatives developed fast. Cafés, small building and transport firms, hairdressers, and so on began to appear as cooperatives. So did the first non-state banks and market research firms. The development was assisted by two things: new powers for members of the Young Communist League (Komsomol) to set up youth 'creative' teams that could engage in technology development and consultancy, and the acquisition by semi-official means of foreign computers.

The development had begun even before the law on cooperatives was passed, on the basis of some rather sketchy legislation in 1987. Thus by July 1987 in the Ukrainian town of Zaporozh'e, with just under one million inhabitants, there were 127 cooperatives included in an official listing, including 15 engaged in building work, 14 in motor repair and the Stiks Ritual Cooperative, which after a moment's reflection can be translated less literally as the Styx Funeral Parlour (*Kooperativy* 1988).

A number of young people, mostly from privileged backgrounds, set up banks and information agencies whose objectives were highly ambitious. Vladimir Yakovlev, the 28-year-old son of the editor of *Moscow News*, opened the Fakt cooperative in November 1987 to sell information of all sorts. In a country where telephone directories did not exist, he had several advantages. Fakt was the ancestor of, among other business concerns, the *Kommersant* newspaper. Gleb Pavlovsky, one of Fakt's co-founders, is at the time of writing a political adviser to the Russian President, Vladimir Putin. Copetas (1991) tells the story of the Fakt cooperative, of the authorities' attempts to close it down, of the bribery needed to keep the firm going, of the acquisition of foreign computers and the obtaining of American investment. According to Copetas, Fakt soon had people queueing every morning for information. One of Yakovlev's instructions to the receptionists was that anyone in search of clowns to perform at parties should be advised to phone the Council of Ministers (Copetas 1991, p. 92).

Early banking legislation in 1988 had formally separated the State Bank (Gosbank) from five specialised banks which had been parts of the single monobank system: a savings bank, an industrial construction bank, an agricultural bank, a housing and social infrastructure bank and a bank for foreign economic relations (Sberbank, Promstroibank, Agroprombank, Zhilsotsbank and Vneshekonombank, respectively). These still reported to the Council of Ministers, as did Gosbank itself (through the Ministry of Finance). They were still part of the single planning hierarchy, and there was no overlap and therefore no competition between them (Robbins 1991, pp. 38–40). By the end of 1988 there were 24 banks registered as cooperatives and 17 so-called joint-stock banks formed by state enterprises or ministries (*Ekonomicheskaya gazeta*, 1989 no. 2, p. 9). A listing of banks published in the same weekly (1989 no. 25, p. 10) includes the following (the capitalising of initial letters follows Russian practice).

Khimbank, founded by enterprises of the USSR Ministry of the Chemical Industry.
Progressbank, founded by the Centre for scientific-technical activity,

research and social initiatives attached to the USSR Academy of Sciences and Academy of Sciences enterprises and organisations.
Stroiinvest commercial bank, founded by enterprises of the production association Mosspetszhelezobeton (Moscow specialised reinforced-concrete production association).
Stolichnyi bank, founded by the Cooperative development union and cooperatives.
Molodezhnyi commercial bank, founded by the Komsomol Central Committee and komsomol enterprises and organisations.

This growth of new banks from below did not happen in most other communist countries. In Hungary, Poland and Czechia, for example, the development of the banking system has come about chiefly through the commercialisation and then privatisation of state-owned specialist banks, plus the entry of foreign banks. Bulgaria may be the only country outside the former Soviet Union to show a similar growth of *de novo* banks.

In the Soviet case, the development was unhealthy. The business environment, if it could be called that, was entirely unsuitable for the development of financial intermediation: for the development of banks that collected deposits from savers and lent to business to finance investment. Not only could most producing enterprises exercise little initiative in production or investment; even if they had been able to make use of banking services, the available financial information provided no reliable information on costs and returns.

What did develop was pocket banks used by their founding enterprises to move funds around discreetly and cooperative banks that were able, when foreign-currency and government debt markets developed, to make large profits from playing very thin financial markets. Most of the very wealthy Russians of the 1990s started as bankers. At the time of writing, in summer 2001, Russian banks still do very little intermediation. In Estonia, on the other hand, the post-communist banking system is now well developed. The origins of both lie in the period of *perestroika*.

The number of cooperatives of all kinds grew fast. At the beginning of 1988, according to the official statistics, there were 13,921 of them, employing 155,800 (including part-timers). Three years later there were 245,356, employing just over six million people (*Narkhoz 90*, p. 58).

Behind this rapid expansion there was a very mixed picture: some real improvement and some highly distorted development. For foreigners and for a small layer of the Soviet population in the larger cities, the growth in number and quality of restaurants, for example, was a boon. So, in a much broader way, was the development of alternative, non-state sources of information. The cooperatives could be businesses that really had to meet a payroll – to sink or swim by their own endeavours. Cooperatives of this kind tended to have a level of operating efficiency that was far above that of state enterprises. The state often contracted out work to cooperatives for that reason. The guide to cooperatives in Zaporozhe, mentioned above, was produced jointly by the city council and an information cooperative. Later, when the government was trying to develop the basics of a proper customs regime, it farmed out the printing of customs forms to a cooperative. But this was far from the whole story.

Cooperatives providing consumer goods and services, which had to be readily visible to function, soon ran into difficulties from criminal gangs. Protection rackets developed, and the police were unable or unwilling to stop them. If, in the late 1980s, a restaurant was firebombed or its manager murdered, it was always a cooperative, not a state restaurant, that was being fought over. State officials also oppressed the new cooperatives, extorting bribes for registration, safety certification, authorised use of copying machines and everything else for which there were state gatekeepers (Copetas 1991 gives many examples).

Contrary to initial expectations, cooperatives developed rather less well in consumer services, where the scope for them to improve things was enormous, than in business services. In the latter, the opportunities may have been no less great, but the important difference was the lower visibility of the business: this provided more protection. It has been possible to run a specialised business consultancy in Moscow for years without attracting the attentions of the *mafiya* (personal communication from a Russian friend who has done so).

The state-economy environment, however, created massive distortions in the development of cooperatives engaged in business services. The enterprise law allowed state enterprises to have cooperatives attached to (*pri*) them. The cooperative law, accordingly, provided for cooperatives to be formed *pri* state enterprises. This close linking of a state enterprise and a cooperative provided great opportunities for evading controls on the former. Two channels for weakening state control deserve special attention.

The first had to do with monetary control. The traditional Soviet system operated with two rigidly separated monetary circuits. Cash was used to pay wages but enterprises were not allowed to make other routine payments in cash. The traditional monobank system was not a banking system so much as a giant, in-house accounting establishment. Payment for planned deliveries from one state enterprise to another was made by offsetting alterations to the accounts of the two enterprises with the State Bank. They were not allowed to settle up in any other way. Cash dispensed as wages (which were always paid in cash) either went into the Savings Bank or directly or indirectly to state retail outlets that banked the cash: either way the cash came back into the monobank system. The separation of cash money from bank money meant that inflationary pressure could exist in one of these two monetary circuits without spilling over into the other. It also meant that managers in state enterprises could not easily enrich themselves without risking being caught making unauthorised uses of cash.

The cooperatives were not subject to financial monitoring in this way. If, therefore, a state enterprise could arrange to pay a cooperative for (say) consultancy and training, it had an avenue by which it could produce an unmonitored circulation of cash. This had potential advantages, including for asset-stripping. A closely tied cooperative *pri* the enterprise, run by the enterprise director's wife, son, brother-in-law or other trustworthy person, was the best way of arranging this.

The second had to do with price control. As with money, so with prices. Cooperatives, though subject to some monitoring for possible monopoly exploitation, could charge prices set by themselves. If a state enterprise sold, say, building materials at the controlled state price to an associated cooperative, that cooperative could sell on at a much higher price, and the profit could be shared.

These two ways round the traditional control system were widely used. Their use contributed to the loss of financial control in the late 1980s and the development of open inflation alongside the more traditional concealed inflation (for instance through phoney new-product prices that raised the price level but did not show up in the official price index) and repressed inflation, expressed in worsening shortages rather than price rises.

All in all, therefore, the cooperatives proved to be a mixed blessing. Their development marked the real renaissance of legal private enterprise in the USSR. But their operation in a predominantly state-owned, planned economy produced many anomalies. Halfway-house reforms, it began to be seen, could make things worse. The development of the main new economic entities is shown in Table 7.4.

The numbers in Table 7.4 suggest that by 1990, out of the new economic creatures established under the 1987–88 legislation, only the cooperatives were of more than minimal consequence in the economy. Using (officially) 4.4 per cent of the workforce, they generated sales equivalent to 4.1 per cent of gross social product and 6.7 per cent of GNP. Neither indicator of the importance of their output is satisfactory, even if we make the heroic assumption that the measurement of their sales is reliable. The sales are turnover, not value-added figures. They would include value added in the state sector, in the case of goods processed from state-produced materials and components, or simply sold on from state supplies. Therefore 6.7 per cent is too high. Gross social product, an old-style Soviet measure, is comparable in that it is the sum of all entities' turnover; but it is not comparable in that it excludes most services.

Table 7.4 *Individual labour activity (ILA), joint ventures (JVs) and cooperatives: the state of play in 1990 (according to official Soviet estimates)*

Type of business	Number[a]	Workforce (000)	Sales (bn roubles)
ILA[b]	–	200	–
JVs	2,905	100	4.8[c]
Cooperatives	245,356	6,098	67.3
Memorandum items			
Total workforce (m)		138.5	
Gross social product			1,631.6
GNP (Soviet estimate)			1,000

Notes: a. at end-year. b. excluding individual peasant farms and household private plots. The source also gives (p. 97) a substantially higher figure, without explanation. c. approximate; the source gives hard-currency sales measured in *valuta* roubles, that is, converted at the official exchange rate, separately from ordinary rouble sales. I have doubled the *valuta* rouble figure for comparability, but no reliable multiple for making the two numbers comparable is available for this period of multiple, non-equilibrium conversion rates.
Source: derived from *Narkhoz 90*, pp. 5, 58, 65, 66, 97.

The bottom line can only be guesstimated. Altogether, the new, legal private sector – though its private-enterprise character was not officially acknowledged at the time – probably amounted to around 4–5 per cent of the economy in 1990. This was smaller than the established private sector of household allotments and the black economy. Grossman (1989, note 4) estimated that in the late 1970s about 40 per cent of urban household expenditure, including self-supply of food products, was spent in the informal or second economy. Extending that to the whole population and converting it into an estimate of shadow-economy value added is impossible, but it strongly suggests that the shadow economy plus subsistence food production had recently been a significantly larger part of the total economy than 4–5 per cent. It probably still was.

The most important features of the organisational reforms of the middle Gorbachev period are two. They shattered the traditional taboos about ownership and the plan, and they hastened the disintegration of the old economic system. What they did not do was improve the performance of the economy.

Economic performance through 1989

Table 7.5 shows selected economic developments from 1985, when Gorbachev came to power, through 1989.

Table 7.5 *Soviet economic developments 1985–89 inclusive (% p.a. changes unless otherwise indicated)*

	1985	1986	1987	1988	1989
GDP	0.9	4.1	1.3	2.1	1.5
Population	0.9	1.0	1.0	0.8	0.8
Labourforce	0.7	0.6	0.4	0.1	0.6
Govt balance (% GDP)	−2.4	−6.2	−8.4	−9.2	−8.5
Credit to govt	8.7[a]	18.8	40.3	46.0	30.0
Broad money	7.5[a]	7.6	15.7	15.4	14.8
External debt-service ratio (%)[b]	–	27.7	28.5	23.1	24.2
External short-term debt ($ bn, end-year)	6.9	7.4	8.6	11.2	17.7

Notes: a. 1981–85 annual average growth. b. principal repayment and interest payment as % revenue from goods and services, convertible-currency trade only.
Sources (in row order): Maddison 1995, Table B10-c (GDP in 1990 international dollars); Maddison 1995, Table A-3c; *Narkhoz 90*, p. 6 (derived from mid-year official absolute figures; known to be imperfect); IMF *et al.* 1990, App. Table I; *ibid.*; IMF *et al.* 1990, App. Table II; *ibid.*

The picture is one of continued growth, but only just. Output per head of population was rising only very slowly. The better-looking figures for 1986 and 1988 reflect farm-sector recoveries after bad harvests. For reasons given earlier in the chapter, the public finances were deteriorating: a growing general government deficit was being financed by printing money. The effects on inflation were not readily visible. Prices were still predominantly controlled, but shortages were worsening. Meat and butter sales were being rationed in about one third of the Russian Republic (RSFSR) in late 1988 (*Financial Times*, 24 December 1988, citing *Sovetskaya Rossiya*).

There were shortages, not because output or output per head of population had fallen but because personal money incomes were allowed to expand faster than consumer supplies at (mostly) fixed prices.

Two Gosplan Research Institute economists had a stab at estimating both open and repressed inflation for 1981–88 (Shmarov and Kirichenko 1989). They did not explain exactly how they arrived at their estimates, but the general idea was clear: they estimated increases in involuntary saving by households (spending power frustrated by shortages), measured it as a proportion of household disposable income, and then asked what open increase in the general price level for consumer items would produce a reduction in real income of the same proportion.

They came up with open inflation at 1.6 per cent a year in 1981–85, rising to 4.1 per cent in 1988 as some *de facto* decontrol of prices occurred (e.g. through the growth of cooperatives). They estimate their proxy for the rate of repressed inflation at 4.1 per cent a year in 1981–85, dipping in 1986 and then increasing again, to 4.3 per cent in 1988. Their overall inflation rate (open plus repressed) is therefore 8.4 per cent in 1988. This was far below the open inflation already under way in Poland (60 per cent); it was still something that worried Soviet policymakers. Meanwhile, as Table 7.5 shows, the authorities were able to deploy traditional administrative controls on imports to keep external debt in bounds after the fall in world oil prices. But the external liquidity position still deteriorated as short-term foreign debt kept rising.

The first signs of retreat from reform appeared. A government decree of February 1989 was aimed at strengthening price controls (*Izvestiya*, 3 February 1989, pp. 1, 2). The same pressures also produced more openness. Boris Gostev, the Minister of Finance, finally admitted there was a budget deficit, and indeed that there had been one for several years, when all official sources had said there wasn't (*Pravda*, 28 October 1988). In the West, the one analyst who had been arguing for some time that this was the case, was vindicated (see Birman 1981).

Among the measures announced by Gostev were cutbacks in centralised financing of investment in 1989 and 1990: the final abandonment, in fact, of Gorbachev's acceleration policy.

There were two macro-economic problems to be tackled: the cutting back of the overhang of purchasing power in the hands of the population in cash hoards and savings bank accounts and the reduction of the budget deficits that generated the excess cash in the first place. The first problem entailed a once-and-for-all reduction of a stock. The second amounted to a reduction in the flow that, if unattended to, would simply build the stock (the monetary overhang) up again.

The monetary overhang might be dealt with by a confiscation of cash and savings accounts, as in the 1947 financial measures. But that was the kind of harsh measure that latter-day Soviet governments were nervous about. Decontrolling many consumer prices would also erase the monetary overhang – as it eventually did in 1992 in Russia. But that, too, was a frightening option. What would be the popular response? And how could the centrally planned economy continue to operate, without fixed prices? The choice was beginning to look like a choice between a return to authoritarian measures or a lurch forward to much more drastic, market reforms.

Reform debates in 1987–89

On 9 June 1987, Gorbachev set out the limits for the debate on economic reform (*Izvestiya*, 13 June 1987):

> We must ensure that there is an atmosphere such that all points of view can be taken into account. This does not mean that there should be no sense of responsibility in the discussion. . . . we need discussions and speeches that are permeated with concern for socialism . . . We must rebuff anyone who offers us anti-socialist alternatives.

This was a politician's fudge. All points of view were acceptable as long as they were socialist. If nobody had been offering anti-socialist alternatives, Gorbachev would not have warned against them. In fact, the debate was just on the brink of attacking socialist ownership.

As we have seen, there was already advocacy of small-scale private enterprise to be found in the media. At the pre-plenum meeting at which Gorbachev's speech was delivered, Oleg Bogomolov had argued that reform should start in the farm sector – as it had in China. There was little doubt that, for many, reforming agriculture meant scrapping the collective farms. The writer Anatolii Streliannyi had already said this with remarkable clarity (Streliannyi 1986).

At a round-table discussion in the weekly *Literaturnaya gazeta*, published just before Gorbachev's speech, other remarkable things were said (*Ekonomika na pereput'e* 1987). V. Krivosheev of Bogomolov's institute suggested that the country was 'at a stage of eclectic interpretation of *perestroika*' but eclecticism would lead nowhere. 'Without the market we shan't move.' More radical reforms, he said, were being blocked by fears of social unrest. The most striking statement, out of many, at this round-table, came from Anatolii Zlobin.

> More and more often you hear 'more socialism'. Does that mean we haven't had much socialism up to now? I reckon we have 100 per cent socialism . . . For years and years we've talked about the advantages of [our] advanced social order. With all these advantages, we spend our time trying to catch up. And whom are we trying to catch up? Those who haven't had our advantages.

Oleg Bogomolov, in an interview the previous month, had argued that family or individual businesses should be allowed wherever they were 'natural and economical' (*Izvestiya*, 14 May 1987; see also Bogomolov 2000, where he discusses the historical context). He made the point, elementary in Western understanding of property rights but usually skated over in Soviet publications, that ownership is not one-dimensional: it can, he said, be broken down into the right to enjoy the return from an asset and the right to control how the asset is used (he did not add anything about the right to dispose of an asset, but he and others were proceeding in stages).

Around the same time, the economist Larissa Piyasheva let the capitalist cat out of the market bag. In a piece that appeared as a long letter to a literary journal from L. Popkova (Popkova 1987), she pointed out that people in market economies tended to be better off than people in non-market economies, and she questioned whether socialism and the market were compatible. The piece was entitled 'Gde pyshnee pirogi?' ('Where are pies bigger and better?'). The market mechanism, she declared, was not in decline but at the beginning of its historical path. It had been stifled by the relics of feudalism and 'by the activities of all manner of utopians – as a result of which the twentieth century has been so bloodstained'.

Piyasheva and Boris Pinsker (her husband) had come across Hayek and become devout Hayekians (author's interview with them, July 1990). Instead of pragmatic winks and market-socialist nudges, Piyasheva had a whole oppositionist philosophy to offer. Piyasheva and Pinsker were not alone in their thinking, but she was, to the best of my knowledge, the first to offer Hayekian conclusions in print in Russian inside the USSR. 'L. Popkova' was attacked in *Pravda* (7 June 1987, by V. Lipitskii). If she had not been attacked, we would have known the sky was falling. But even so, the Soviet establishment's confidence was ebbing. She did not otherwise suffer.

Alexander Zinoviev's formulation, that socialist ownership is a contradiction in terms (Zinoviev 1981), never caught on. A simpler, less epigrammatic, version of it did. This was that state property was nobody's property. This phrase was widely used in 1987–88. It did not necessarily imply that the ultimate reform of the socialist economy was capitalism. It could mean that there was another, better socialism available, perhaps people's (*narodnyi*) socialism.

Some Soviet intellectuals appeared genuinely to believe that something under that heading was worth campaigning for. One was Valerii Rutgaizer, previously in the Gosplan research institute and then a deputy head of Zaslavskaya's Institute of Public Opinion Research. He sought arrangements whereby work collectives' leasing of state enterprises could be a vehicle for worker ownership (*Ekonomicheskaya gazeta*, 1989 no. 36, pp. 17–18). A few others, such as Kurashvili, remained faithful to the notion of market socialism. In general, the questioning of traditional Soviet state ownership was in the air, and the discussion of alternatives was open-ended.

Bogomolov's institute, IEMSS (see Chapter 6) was in the forefront of this discussion. In a collective monograph published (if that is the right word) in only 200 copies in 1987, they raised 'problems of ownership' including defective incentives and divergences of interest among Soviet social groups (*Problemy sobstvennosti* 1987).

One immediate reason for the leading role of IEMSS was that the influence of Central-Eastern European experience on Soviet thinking was, as before, very great. This does not appear explicitly in print: the paucity of references to Central-East European authors in Soviet reform writings is striking. Some combination of censorship and chauvinism made a constant harking back to the NEP economy of the 1920s more acceptable. Very little of the work of Janos Kornai, the most widely influential Central European economist of our period, was translated into Russian. But it was the business of Bogomolov's institute to follow and try to understand what was going on in these countries.

One thing that was going on there was the collapse of market socialist thinking in the face of Hungarian and Yugoslav experience. In March 1988, 170 economists met in Györ, in Hungary, for a conference on 'Alternative Models of Socialist Economic Systems'. Participants included émigrés from the Soviet Union and Central-Eastern Europe now based in the West. Wlodzimierz Brus, one of the leading proponents of market socialism in Poland in the late 1950s and 1960s, and since then based in Oxford, gave a paper in which he accepted that his earlier reform ideas had not gone far enough; the Hungarian New Economic Mechanism showed that doing away with mandatory output targets for enterprises did not free them from the influence of the state. There needed to be a market in capital, as well as a market in products, if producers were to have incentives to be efficient (Brus 1988).

Tamas Bauer, in his paper, concluded that such real improvements as there had been in Hungary came from the development of the private (small-scale) sector, rather than from the attempts to decentralise the state sector (Bauer 1988).

Bogomolov did not attend this conference, but several of his IEMSS staff members did, and they transmitted a paper from him that advocated the development of small and medium-size private and cooperative firms (see Hanson 1992, Chapter 13).

In these debates, both in and outside the USSR, reformers from the socialist countries did not say in so many words that a general regime of free markets and private enterprise would be better than any conceivable socialist reform. Even Piyasheva/Popkova had implied this rather than spelt it out. However, they were edging towards saying it.

Putting together serious reform proposals was monstrously difficult. The comparative weakness of the Soviet economic system showed up most clearly in two practical ways. There was a structural problem of especially low productivity (compared with the West) in agriculture, constraining consumption levels. And there was a general lack of technological dynamism, impeding the introduction and diffusion of new products and processes and thus constraining the overall growth of productivity. What reform could tackle both these problems?

The channels by which the fundamental systemic defects of information and incentives produced these symptoms were clearer by the late 1980s than they had been in the 1960s – partly because Hungarian experience of market-socialist reform had been so instructive, and partly because all European socialist countries had experienced a slowdown. Kornai's shortage economy analysis, distinguishing between hard-budget-constraint and soft-budget-constraint producers, was one way of presenting the systemic basis of the region's comparative economic weakness. Unless producers were left to sink or swim, financially, by their own efforts, the problems would persist. That meant that the expectation that the central authorities would always bail out failing enterprises had to be broken. But how?

A sector of small private firms might do a great deal for farming and the service sector. That was increasingly widely accepted among Soviet policy-makers. But why not have small private producers in manufacturing as well? What was supposed to happen if successful small, private firms grew? Could a small private firm be allowed to become a big private firm? If core, larger-scale production remained exclusively in the hands of the state, productivity growth would presumably remain sluggish.

Gorbachev himself seems to have accepted quite readily that the small-scale private sector was desirable. In a speech in March 1988 to the Kolkhozniks' Congress he spoke approvingly about Chinese farm reforms. He summarised them as 'they gave the land to the families'. The sensitivity of the reform process is indicated by the fate of this phrase: he said it on the day (as broadcast), but it was excised from, or had never been in, the text as published (e.g. *Ekonomicheskaya gazeta*, 1988 no. 13, pp. 1–7).

There is no evidence, however, that Gorbachev accepted a more radical, general privatisation as the way ahead. Allowing private enterprise on a small scale in selected activities was at this stage as far as he would go.

In any case, what was the environment needed for new private firms to develop, whether in a restricted range of activities or more widely? Decontrolled prices were accepted as desirable by many reformers; but what about all the supporting institutions of a market economy, including the legal framework, capital markets and everything else?

In 1989, efforts to grapple in public with these questions often involved strenuous word-games. Large corporations, for example, were made to look quasi-socialist. The Prime Minister, Nikolai Ryzhkov, in a speech to the Supreme Soviet (parliament) in October adopted a line of argument that said that joint-stock companies with numerous shareholders were not really quite private property in the old (and bad) sense (*Izvestiya*, 3 October 1989, pp. 1–3). Fedor Burlatskii (once described as 'a dissident who happens to be an adviser to the Party Central Committee') characterised current policy, in another speech to the parliament, as 'returning to the mixed economy' (*Izvestiya*, 17 October 1989, p. 1).

Bur what was a mixed economy? No leading politicians in 1989 said that it was more or less what the West already had. Some mixture of private and public ownership and of plan and market was vaguely indicated. The term de-stateification (*razgosudarstvlenie*) came into use, but was not to be confused with *denatsionalizatsiya*. The latter, according to those disinclined to stick their necks out, was a bad word (e.g. S. Alekseev in *Izvestiya*, 23 October 1989, p. 2).

In the middle of all this intellectual confusion, preparations were being made for a law on, among other things, joint-stock companies. Leonid Abalkin, a political economist not from one of the usual reform stables – the Bogomolov institute and the Central Economics-Mathematical Institute – but from the staid old Institute of Economics, had become a deputy prime minister responsible for reform policy. Despite his provenance he was an open-minded and thoughtful man. It seemed just possible in late 1989 that the Soviet Union might stumble, step by unintended step, into a sustainable process of real market reform.

By then, however, the political and social framework was coming apart.

Notes

1   It is sometimes alleged that conventional Russian drinking is all the more unhealthy because it is not accompanied by food. This is a half-truth. Serious Russian drinking is an end in itself rather than an accompaniment to food, but there is an etiquette of consuming *something* solid. My personal introduction to the culture came when I got talking to two Russian factory workers at the Moscow racecourse in the 1960s. We formed the classic drinking *troika*, sharing a bottle of vodka three ways, each downing a third of the bottle in one. But each of us ate a hard-boiled egg first.

2   The sources listed here are those in which the text of the new decree or law was most widely promulgated. The official sources are for laws *Vedomosti Verkhovnogo Soveta SSSR* and for decrees *Sobranie postanovlenii SSSR*. A peculiarity of even these official sources is that, in the grand old Stalinist tradition, there were often articles of the laws that were not published at all.

3   In 1989, along with several other Western economists, I spoke at a round-table on the Soviet economy at the Academy of the National Economy in Moscow. The Academy was the Soviet economic staff college, attended by mid-career managers heading for deputy branch minister positions. The course members

listened to us with the studied air of boredom that was *de rigeur* for all official Soviet meetings, with a little bit of extra sullenness added for the dumb foreigners. During question time someone from the floor asked what the panel thought about the election of managers by workers. Suddenly the boredom vanished. They were not ashamed now to betray a certain interest in the proceedings. Several of us said (in a suitably academic way) that it was a daft idea. At that, the audience turned friendly.

CHAPTER EIGHT

The End-game, 1989–91

Accelerating political change

From the mid-1950s to the late 1980s the political environment in the USSR did not change dramatically. It is possible, as a result, to tell the Soviet economic story without constantly bringing in political developments. For the period of collapse, this is no longer true.

Throughout the period from the mid-1950s to the late 1980s the Soviet Union was a society with a single chain of command but without mass terror. The chain of command was operated by the Communist Party of the Soviet Union. It stretched from workplace Party committees to the Politburo of the Central Committee. Appointment along that chain of command was exclusively from above. The Party controlled the machinery of state. Through its *nomenklatura* arrangements the Party made all government and other public appointments of any consequence. There was no legal opposition, almost no illegal opposition and no independent judiciary. The Party leadership used force where necessary to control people. Most Soviet citizens most of the time policed and censored themselves. Informing on others was widespread. A dissident was a dissident, liable to be exiled or sent to the camps.

The regime softened in some respects, through Brezhnev's policy of 'stability of cadres' and a loosening of plan discipline. Individuals could and did find room to do unofficial things: the early environmental movement to protect Lake Baikal and the semi-underground art and music scenes, for example, or Tarkovsky's films. After Stalin, terror was limited and no longer arbitrary. But there were well-understood limits. Even if some people devoted most of their energies to finding ways round those limits, the established system still governed their lives. That was the domestic political framework. Its main features were unchanged for at least thirty years after Khrushchev's (limited circulation) denunciation of Stalin.

The external political framework was also fairly stable. The USSR led the Warsaw Pact military alliance. Its military leaders might not be too confident about the reliability of Polish soldiers, say, in the event of a NATO–Warsaw Pact conflict. But if any of the allies in Central-Eastern Europe showed a tendency to misbehave, the Soviet army could and did invade to put a stop to it. Poland's martial law of 1981 was self-imposed, but under the threat of Soviet invasion. The arms race against the West was a fact of life throughout the period, even if there were periodic easings of tension, and disarmament negotiations.

In the last two to three years of the existence of the Soviet Union, all this changed. What follows is a brief catalogue of the main developments. What happened in the economy is incomprehensible without some understanding of them. (I have drawn heavily on the chronology in Ellman and Kontorovich 1998, pp. xix–xxiv.)

In March 1989 a limited amount of competition was allowed in elections to a new parliament, the Congress of People's Deputies. People unacceptable to the authorities were kept out, and the powers of the Congress were merely advisory. Even so, what followed was important. Gorbachev and his closest allies such as Aleksandr Yakovlev had come to the conclusion that desirable political and economic change was blocked by Party officials. Many Party officials lost what would in earlier times have been single-candidate elections to a parliamentary body: in effect, *ex officio* appointments. The *nomenklatura* appointment system had already been criticised at the January 1987 Party Central Committee plenum. Gorbachev was trying to reach over the heads of the Party officials to mobilise popular support for change (Gorbachev 1995, vol. 1, p. 281).

The proceedings of the People's Congress were televised. Remarkable things were said at them. One example of many that could be cited is a speech to the Congress on 2 June by the novelist Chingiz Aitmatov (*Izvestiya*, 4 June 1989, p. 2). He described the 'flourishing, law-abiding societies of Sweden, Austria, Finland, Norway, Holland, Spain and, finally, across the ocean, Canada' as having social welfare provision and average levels of workers' welfare that 'we can only dream about. What they have is real – workers' trade-union socialism, if you like, though these countries don't even call themselves socialist, but they're none the worse for that.' Of the USSR he said, 'We've done them a favour by showing them how not to build socialism.'

In July there was a miners' strike, led by unofficial unions.

Next there was a rapid collapse of communist power in Central-Eastern Europe. After partly-free elections, a non-communist government, led by

Tadeusz Mazowiecki, the former editor of a Catholic newspaper, came to power in Poland in August. The last communist government in Hungary, after deliberately allowing people from East Germany to move to West Germany across its borders, fell from power in October. The Berlin Wall was knocked down in November; unification of Germany (and thus the disappearance of communist East Germany) followed quickly. In Romania the Ceausescu regime was violently overthrown in December.

These changes came about in the Warsaw Pact countries after the Soviet leadership had let it be known that the Soviet army would not invade if communist power there were threatened. The Warsaw Pact was dissolved in March 1991. After an attempt to maintain CMEA as a trading bloc but with convertible-currency settlement, the organisation was dissolved in June 1991.

Street demonstrations, usually peaceful, reappeared in Moscow. There was a demonstration against radical economic reform plans in November 1989 (see below). In February 1990 there were demonstrations by people demanding political democracy.

In March Gorbachev had himself appointed President. He now had a position of authority independent of the Party. Article 6 of the Soviet constitution was revised to allow, in vague terms, organised political competition: the CPSU no longer had a constitutionally entrenched monopoly of power. Gorbachev, however, never submitted himself to a popular vote. By now, he would probably have lost if he had done so.

Yeltsin's rise was based on risk taking, including engaging in electoral processes that were not predetermined. In May 1990, contrary to Gorbachev's wishes, he was elected chairman of the Supreme Soviet of the Russian republic (by its deputies, and narrowly). In June the Russian parliament declared Russia to be sovereign – whatever that might mean. The Party itself, at Union level (the CPSU) responded in July to the growing power of the 15 Union republics by restructuring itself along federal lines. Yeltsin left the Party anyway, finally coming out as an anti-communist (he later banned the communist party in Russia for a time). In June 1991 he was elected President of Russia by popular vote.

In July Gorbachev requested financial assistance from the Group of Seven (G7) leading industrial nations. The G7 in turn tasked the IMF, the World Bank, OECD and the newly created European Bank for Reconstruction and Development (EBRD) to make a study of the Soviet economy and recommend possible forms of assistance. This report (IMF 1990), delivered in December, will be referred to below.

In September preparations for a new Union Treaty were launched. There were mass demonstrations in Ukraine against the idea. The following month the Ukrainian parliament declared it would not sign a Union Treaty until Ukraine had a new constitution.

In December 1990 the Foreign Minister, Eduard Shevardnadze, resigned. So did the Prime Minister, Nikolai Ryzhkov, who had served Gorbachev loyally but had found himself increasingly at loggerheads with the radical reformers, with Gorbachev failing to act decisively on one side or the other.

In the winter of 1990–91 there was an attempt to impose more central control. This included suppression of demonstrators in Vilnius by the military. In February 1991, striking miners called for Gorbachev's resignation. So did Yeltsin.

In March 1991 there was a referendum on whether the USSR should continue to exist as a single state. The population as a whole voted strongly for the continuation of the Soviet Union. This had no perceptible effect on the fissiparous activities of republic elites. The next month Georgia declared its independence. Soviet politicians were increasingly preoccupied with questions of the integrity of the Soviet state.

In August there was a coup attempt against Gorbachev by a group of traditionalist politicians and officials. This was fuelled by a general distaste for the way things were going, but triggered by the imminence of a break-up of the USSR into fifteen separate states. The coup failed. Gorbachev resigned from the Party leadership (he was still President). Immediately after this, Estonia, Latvia and Lithuania declared their independence. They had been forcibly annexed by the Soviet Union in 1940, under the terms of a deal struck between Stalin and Hitler (more immediately, by Molotov and Ribbentrop). The United States had never formally recognised their incorporation in the USSR, and it was generally understood that they were special cases. Their independence was quickly recognised by foreign states, and the break-up of the USSR had begun – in September 1991.

In December there was a hefty majority for independence in a referendum in the Ukraine. On 8 December Russia, Ukraine and Belarus signed an agreement renouncing the 1922 treaty under which the Soviet Union had been formed. After a short interval, at Christmas 1991, Gorbachev was forced to resign as Soviet President, the USSR ceased to exist, and the Russian leadership occupied the Kremlin.

The period 1989–91 did not provide a political environment in which economic reforms could be calmly discussed, let alone effectively implemented. A great deal happened as part of a struggle to hold the Union together against those who wanted, first, sovereignty, then independence for individual republics.

Above all, Gorbachev's political reforms, starting from 1987, tended to weaken the authority of the Communist Party. In particular, they tended to substitute election from below (to Party posts, as well as to the Congress of People's Deputies) for appointment from above. The Party hierarchy, however, was the basic means by which order was maintained in the country.

(The KGB was an instrument of Party rule.) Not laws and contracts, not custom and practice and not organised crime, but Party instructions got things done.

Two consequences followed that matter greatly to the economic outcome.

First, local, regional and republic Party bosses found they had to cultivate local power bases. They could no longer rely on higher-level patrons. As speech became freer, nationalist sentiments surfaced, and there were the beginnings of nationalist movements: at first in the Baltic States, then in Ukraine and Georgia. To outflank this local competition, republic Party bosses turned nationalist. In Lithuania Algirdas Brazauskas announced in December 1989 that the Lithuanian party was seceding from the CPSU. Rumour had it that in Ukraine Leonid Kravchuk changed his office decorations overnight: out went the bust of Lenin, in came a bust of Taras Shevchenko, the Ukrainian national poet. The crunch came when Russian politicians, led by Boris Yeltsin, began to see Russia as a rival power-base to the Union. What became known as the 'parade of sovereignties' gathered pace in 1990. It was accompanied by a war of laws as differences in economic reforms emerged and were contested.

The second effect was that many middle-level and senior officials, if they had effective control of useful assets, began to see their way clear to doing very nicely out of them: usually by some form of asset stripping. This was not a new activity for Soviet officials, but it rapidly became less risky, as Party control withered away.

These two effects accelerated the economic decline. Output fell, the public finances deteriorated, and inflationary pressure grew. In December 1989 the financier and philanthropist George Soros wrote that the Soviet Union had 'a centrally planned economy with the center knocked out' (*Wall Street Journal*, 7 December 1989).[1]

Economic policies

The policy-making process became chaotic. Different measures were passed that conflicted with one another. A succession of increasingly radical reform proposals was put forward, rejected and diluted, while at a less grand level measures were taken that restricted the development of market institutions.

In the course of 1989 there were developments that amounted to a retreat from the market. There were measures to limit the activities of co-operatives and control their prices. Local food rationing spread. So did local trade wars, as cities (notably Moscow) limited retail sales to people who could show a local residence permit. Some restrictions were introduced on the previous devolution of foreign trade rights (Hanson 1992, Chapter 17).

At the level of grand strategy, however, legislation and policy measures accelerated towards the market. From July 1989 Leonid Abalkin was chairman of a State Commission on Economic Reform and a deputy Prime Minister. The Commission contained senior officials, such as Stepan Sitaryan, the first deputy head of Gosplan, and senior academics. Apart from Abalkin, these included Aganbegyan, Stanislav Shatalin, Vladlen Martynov of the Institute of the World Economy and International Relations, and Ruben Evstigneev from Bogomolov's institute. It had a remit to draft reform measures, including measures on price-determination, taxation, credit, the autonomy of republics and measures based on 'multiple forms of socialist ownership'. (These forms might now perhaps be stretched to include joint-stock companies.) The commission also had a staff of its own and could issue instructions, within its sphere of competence, to ministries (Council of Ministers decree establishing the commission, *Ekonomicheskaya gazeta*, 1989 no. 31, pp. 16–17; for Abalkin's own account see Abalkin 1991).

Anders Aslund, a close observer of events from the Swedish Embassy for much of the Gorbachev period, pointed out that the new reform commission was not under the thumb of Gosplan, as had been the nearest it had to a predecessor, a Commission for the Improvement of Planning and Management, set up in 1985 (Aslund 1989, pp. 63–4).

Grigorii Yavlinskii and Evgenii Yasin, two economists who have featured prominently in post-Soviet Russian politics, drew up for the commission an outline plan for reform measures, which Abalkin approved. Yasin wrote later that the Prime Minister, Nikolai Ryzhkov, trusted Abalkin and took no part in the process at this stage (Yasin in Ellman and Kontorovich 1998, pp. 228–37). Yasin also remarks that the limits of the 'socialist choice' (which Gorbachev declared the Soviet people had made at the Revolution, irrevocably) were understood by all involved. It was already possible to advocate de-stateification (*razgosudarstvlenie*), though not to use the word *privatizatsiya* (privatisation). The report did say, however, that the aim of reform must now be to replace one internally consistent system with a different, internally consistent system, incompatible with its predecessor (*ibid.*).

Three variants of reform were offered: conservative, moderately radical and radical. The authors, attempting to practise the art of the possible, plumped for the moderately radical option. The radical variant later was amplified and revised as the 500 Days programme put out by a group headed by Shatalin in September 1990 (*ibid.*). The moderately radical version had the same end-state in view as the radical one – a mixed economy masked in phoney socialist terminology. The difference was that it envisaged a slower progress towards that state, with state controls removed more gradually.

In November 1989 a conference was held to discuss these reform plans. It took place in the Hall of Columns in Moscow. Outside were demonstrators from one of the newly permitted social movements, the National Salvation Front. Their placards said 'DOWN WITH THE ABALKINIZATION OF THE WHOLE COUNTRY' (Yasin 2001, March, p. 83). The slogan played not only with the word Balkanization but also with a treasured slogan of Lenin's that referred to the electrification of the whole country.

On 1 January 1990 a programme often referred to as 'shock therapy' was introduced in post-communist Poland. This entailed the immediate decontrol of most prices, including the exchange rate of the zloty; the proclamation of tight monetary and fiscal policies to constrain inflation to a once-for-all adjustment of price levels after decontrol; and plans for general privatisation of state assets. Macro-economic stabilisation subsequently proved to be more difficult than the Polish reformers initially expected, and privatisation of large state enterprises took much longer than had been hoped. But the decontrol, together with an acceptance by the population of the general direction of change, allowed a very rapid growth of new private businesses. After the initial fall in officially recorded output, recovery began before the end of 1992.

Developments in Central-Eastern Europe, which had long influenced Soviet thinking, now began to provide new ideas about radical change. Aleksandr Orlov, a deputy chairman of Abalkin's commission, listed the countries whose experience the commission was studying as Germany, Japan, Sweden and Poland, and specifically cited shock therapy as the subject to be studied in Polish experience (*Izvestiya*, 3 April 1990, p. 1).

Meanwhile the Soviet authorities had decided not to be even moderately radical. The commission's report, having been debated at the November conference, was put to the government. The Prime Minister, Ryzhkov, opted for a two-year delay in the start of a 'moderately radical' reform, with the Thirteenth Five-Year Plan to start on more or less traditional lines, and reforms to begin in 1992 (Ryzhkov's speech in *Pravda*, 4 December 1989; decree 'On measures to make the economy healthy . . .', *Pravda*, 22 December 1989). There was a case to be made for this delay. What Ryzhkov and his advisers said they wanted to do was to reduce inflationary pressure before starting to remove controls. Unfortunately, the centre probably could not have imposed financial discipline within the framework of central planning, at a time when output was falling and resistance to control from above was rising.

By the start of 1990, in Yasin's account, a group of reformers in the presidential apparatus (of Gorbachev) and the government had concluded that slowing change would make things worse; the radical option was after all preferable. These, whom he lists as Yavlinsky, Nikolai Petrakov, Boris

Fedorov, Sergei Aleksashenko and himself, were in broad agreement at this stage with people outside the state machinery such as Egor Gaidar and Mikhail Zadornov. To the latter we can add the young economists from Leningrad, later to be part of the Gaidar team in the Russian government, such as Anatolii Chubais and Sergei Vasiliev.

Gorbachev now became more directly involved. His advisers pushed the government to think again about its planned delay of the start of radical reform. Within the government a group of economists and officials finally recommended faster reform. This group was composed of people not generally associated with radical market reform: Leonid Abalkin, Yurii Maslyukov, Valentin Pavlov and Stepan Sitaryan (Yasin in Ellman and Kontorovich 1998, p. 232). In the mid-1990s, Maslyukov held the economic portfolio in the Communist Party of Russia's opposition team.

Yet another reform plan was drafted, more radical than before. Yasin quotes its opening sentences (*ibid.*):

> The economy cannot long function under an artificial combination of the fundamentally incompatible command and market structures. Practically all attempts at transition to economic methods of control run into powerful opposition from a monopolistic non-market environment, which discredits the general idea and concrete goals of reform . . . condemning a country with great potential to chronic shortages and disequilibria.

The new plan envisaged the decontrol of most prices and rapid privatisation of both large and small state enterprises. It also included forecasts of damaging short-term effects: a doubling or tripling of the price level, the closure of inefficient enterprises, a growth of unemployment and a fall in average real incomes of 20–25 per cent. The programme was rejected – this time by Gorbachev's Presidential Council. The reason, in Yasin's view, was that the leadership could not contemplate these dire short-run consequences. Hitherto, Yasin comments, all reform proposals had been accompanied by assurances that there would be immediate benefits for all – something Yasin attributes to 'the incompetence of the majority of Soviet economists, not to mention the leadership' (Yasin in 2001, p. 233).

On 24 May 1990 Ryzhkov made a fateful speech to the Supreme Soviet, outlining for two hours the latest, revised reform plan (*Izvestiya*, 24 May evening edition 1990, pp. 1–2). Part of his plan was to reduce the overhang of excess consumer purchasing power (repressed inflation) by raising prices. He, along with his Finance Minister, Valentin Pavlov, still envisaged price revisions from above rather than a decontrol of prices. The trouble with announcing planned price increases in advance (months in advance, in this case) is well known: it may be admirably transparent, but it does encourage panic buying. Soviet buyers panicked. Any visitor to Moscow in the summer of 1990 saw price tickets in the shops that displayed impressively stable prices. What was lacking was the goods to go with them.

The XXVIII (and last) CPSU Party Congress was to be held in July. Ahead of it, Leonid Abalkin said that transition to the market required a plan for transition, strong state power to implement it and social agreement; the first two were present, but not yet the third, and he hoped that the Party Congress would consolidate 'healthy' forces for change (*Ekonomika i zhizn'*, 1990 no. 21, p. 4).

There were, he said, 30 draft laws ready for consideration to implement the transition. Commodity and capital markets would need to develop. There would still be state orders, but they would be at market clearing prices. The government, he added, is not planning a currency reform (meaning measures to liquidate some or all of people's cash and savings-bank assets, as in 1947). This was probably true when he said it, but this was a time when everyone in authority changed his mind twice a day. Pavlov, who succeeded Ryzhkov as Prime Minister, introduced such a measure the following January.

The Congress in fact achieved nothing in economic policy. Meanwhile the war of laws between the Union and the republics was getting nastier. In July the Russian government, under Boris Yeltsin, issued an invitation to state enterprises subordinate to all-Union ministries to switch their subordination to the Russian authorities, who would give them more freedom.

At the same time, however, there was an attempt, brokered by Yavlinskii and Petrakov, to get the Soviet and Russian leaders to cooperate over yet another economic reform plan. Two plans were being worked on: an in-house government plan, revising what Ryzhkov had put forward in May, and a plan to be thrashed out by a group of radical reformers, chaired by Stanislav Shatalin. The latter, put together at a dacha in Arkhangel'skoe, outside Moscow, became known as the '500 Days Programme' because it included a timetable of measures, of which the crucial ones would be introduced in that length of time. The text was published in August (*Perekhod* 1990; the *Economist* ran an excellent two-page critical analysis of it in its 15 September issue, pp. 125–7; Shatalin and his co-authors gave a brief, spirited account of the gist of it in *Izvestiya*, 4 September 1990, p. 3).

The 500 Days Programme included a plain statement that private enterprise should be allowed and should operate on an equal legal basis with state enterprise. It started with severe budget spending cuts to reduce inflationary pressure, the conversion of some state enterprises into joint-stock companies (corporatisation) and the division of state and collective farms into separate plots – these latter measures preparatory to privatisation. All this was to happen before the end of 1990.

Then most subsidies to producers were to be cancelled, and in the first half of 1991 most prices quasi-liberalised, in the sense that the prices for goods bought by the government from producers would be negotiated. Also small-scale privatisation would get under way. In the second half of 1991 and up to February 1992 the privatisation and decontrol process would continue. The central bank would be made independent of the government and commercial banks would be clearly separated from the central bank, with credit regulated by changing interest rates and minimum reserve requirements.

The authors included most of the usual suspects: Shatalin, Petrakov, Yavlinskii, Aleksashenko, Zadornov, Fedorov and Yasin. Many were in their thirties. Petrakov, Martynov, Yasin and Shatalin himself came from an older generation.

The plan was addressed to both the Soviet and Russian governments. The authors accepted that the nominally federal USSR had experienced such a drainage of authority to its republics that implementation by these two (at least) would be necessary if the entire Soviet Union were to undergo radical reform. Shatalin told the Soviet parliament on 17 September that he and his colleagues did not wish to get involved in politics; they simply took the republics' declarations of sovereignty as given (*Izvestiya*, 17 September 1990, p. 1).

The Russian Federation parliament, still obedient at this stage to Yeltsin, accepted the plan straightaway. The Soviet leadership did not. Again, crucially, Gorbachev temporised. Ryzhkov opposed the 500 Days Programme partly because it accepted what amounted to loose confederation arrangements, which he said would lead to the dissolution of the Soviet Union. Gorbachev called for the USSR to consider a compromise plan that would be put together to bisect the differences between the Ryzhkov and Shatalin (500 Days) plans.

Gorbachev then used his presidential powers to issue two edicts that would hinder implementation of the Shatalin plan: one to raise domestic wholesale prices (still by control from above) in 1991, and one to deploy internal security forces to protect state enterprises from being unlawfully taken over (that is, contrary to Soviet, but not Russian, legislation; *Izvestiya*, 5 and 13 October 1990, respectively).

The new Soviet compromise plan (*Izvestiya*, 17 October 1990, pp. 1, 3) did not differ fundamentally in objectives from the Shatalin plan, but envisaged a longer time-period for implementation and was a great deal more vague on detail. It was easy to make fun of the Shatalin Plan's detailed timetable, and indeed its overall time horizon, but this had the merit of signalling a very clear commitment to the changes set out, which the compromise plan did not.

It was also reported that the Soviet authorities aimed to keep central control of major natural resource exports (Reuter's from Moscow, 18 October 1990). About four fifths of these exports originated in Russia, and this would have greatly hindered, if not wrecked, unilateral implementation of the Shatalin Plan by Russia.

At this point Gorbachev probably still controlled the military and the KGB. His determination to cling on to the Soviet Union, and therefore his power, was now blocking effective reform – however problematic the Shatalin Plan would have been even in more favourable circumstances. (There was considerable doubt about the feasibility both of the planned cuts in state spending and of the revenue projected from sales of state assets.)

A strange situation now existed. Russia was committed to radical market reform. It was still part of the USSR, which was not committed to radical market reform. About half the Soviet population lived in Russia (148.5 million at the end of 1990, out of 290.1 million; *Narkhoz 90*, p. 67). Russia contained just under half the non-collective-farm workforce (*op. cit.*, p. 102). It accounted for around three fifths of Soviet net material product (61.1 per cent in 1988, according to Soviet official data provided to the G7 study; IMF 1990, Appendix Table III).

A large part of Russian industrial production came from plants subordinated to USSR branch ministries. The great bulk of that output was delivered according to USSR state orders or, previously, state instructions from USSR Gosplan. In 1988 the Russian state planning committee (RSFSR Gosplan), Russian officials claimed, coordinated only 4–5 per cent of Russian industrial output and RSFSR Gossnab (the state supply committee at republic level) organised the distribution of only 0.9 per cent of it (*Izvestiya*, 5 September 1990, p. 2).

How could the part reform if the whole did not? For a time, Yeltsin sought a coordinated adoption of the Shatalin plan by the union and all the republics (press conference, Moscow TV, 1 September 1990). But this idea made no headway.

In October 1990 the Russian parliament passed a law that transferred the control of most assets on its territory from Moscow (the Soviet government) to Moscow (the Russian government). The Union government did not accept this, hence the attempts by the Russian authorities to woo industrial enterprises with lower-than-USSR tax rates: there was competition for their allegiance.

While all this was going on, food supplies to the cities were deteriorating. This was nothing to do with shortfalls in production. Official data show grain production well up from 1989, the potato crop down, and meat and milk production almost unchanged (*Narkhoz 90*, pp. 460, 462). But the chronic problem of shortage at controlled prices had been greatly exacerbated. Money earnings rose strongly as central control splintered. Urban workplaces had become less obedient to instructions from above, and sent far less workers off to help with the harvest than usual (this had always been a wasteful arrangement, but it was not easily replaced in a hurry). A steep increase in Soviet state procurement prices for crops increased the budgetary cost of food subsidies without stimulating supply. Also local trade wars developed. These trade wars were rooted in the new phenomenon of (partial) local democracy.

Moscow provided a good example. Gavriil Popov has been mentioned before (in Chapter 5) as an ideologically adventurous reform economist in the Brezhnev era. More recently he had become a *perestroika* TV celebrity. In the first series of competitive and partly open local elections, he had been elected mayor of Moscow. Like other members of the new breed of elected local officials, he had good reason to take notice of his constituents' wishes. Worsening food shortages had created a good deal of discontent even in Moscow – traditionally privileged by the supply system.

Popov introduced a restriction on retail sales to favour his constituents: a purchaser had to show their Moscow residence permit to be served. This angered the many people who habitually travelled from outside Moscow to shop in the capital. Moscow, precisely because it had better food supplies than anywhere else, had always had a lot of out-of-town shoppers. In fact, 'out-of-town' is too mild a term. People would travel all day by train or fly to Moscow just to buy food. Many came from rural areas, from which farm produce had been ruthlessly extracted for the cities.

Many of these people were from Moscow's traditional food-supplying regions. They made their displeasure known to their elected local officials. Those regions retaliated. Deliveries of farm produce to Moscow were held back. The food shortages in Moscow got worse (Hanson 1992, Chapter 19).

Moscow is seldom typical of Russia, and was seldom typical of the Soviet Union. In this respect, however, its experience was representative of that of other large Soviet cities. Leningrad and Chelyabinsk suffered similar fates. The mayor of Leningrad – Anatolii Sobchak, another reformer – appealed to the West in November for emergency food aid.

In December the study of the Soviet economy commissioned by the G7 was published (IMF 1990). It noted that Soviet output and employment had begun to fall, and there were growing imbalances. 'The old planning system has broken down but has not been dismantled; meanwhile the structures vital to the functioning of a market have yet to be put in place' (p. 1). Soros had said the same thing more vigorously a year before, when he described the Soviet Union as having a centrally planned economy with the centre knocked out.

In the economics of post-communist transition the phrase 'systemic vacuum' is sometimes used, with exactly the meaning conveyed by this quote from the G7 report. The Soviet Union could be said to have been in a systemic vacuum for the last two years of its existence – perhaps a little longer.

The Soviet systemic vacuum was all the more damaging because it coincided with a political vacuum. In 1990 and 1991 Yasin and Yavlinsky worked on a project for an economic union. The idea was to preserve a single economic space and therefore common rules of the economic game even if politically the republics all seceded from the USSR. This was important, because the Soviet economy was regionally highly integrated. It was not an efficiently organised economic space, but it was one in which producers in one republic were likely to be highly dependent on suppliers or users or both in other republics. They could (and eventually did) adjust to other geographical patterns of activity, but an enforced, rapid adjustment was going to be highly disruptive, lowering production levels at least for a time. Hence the urgency of arrangements for cooperation. Yasin, however, recalls Yavlinsky wondering already in early 1990 who was going to implement whatever proposals they came up with (Yasin 2001, April, p. 50).

An economic agreement of sorts was signed in Almaty in October 1991. But Yasin observes that there was an immediate impasse over who would be responsible for Soviet sovereign debt, and in what amounts. (The Baltics had by then escaped; they had consistently argued that the problems of their erstwhile invaders were nothing to do with them.) Nobody then knew, observes Yasin, who was feeding whom; each thought they were being exploited by the others (pp. 51–2).

If nobody knew 'who was feeding whom', it was not for want of efforts by the Union authorities to provide an answer. As the parade of sovereignties moved along, making ever more noise, previously unissued statistics began to appear about inter-republic flows of goods and about Soviet exports and imports by republic of origin and destination (*Narkhoz 90*, pp. 636–44, for instance). Regional input–output tables had been published earlier, but not in a form that addressed the who-whom question so clearly. One particularly telling calculation, or so the Soviet authorities supposed, was how the flows would look if conducted at world market prices.

The initial aim of these publications was to show the Estonians, Latvians and Lithuanians that leaving the Soviet Union would make them impoverished orphans. This did not stop them, partly because the Baltic nationalists already considered their nations to be impoverished prisoners, and partly because such calculations by no means told the whole story about the economic consequences of secession (see the UN Economic Commission for Europe, *Economic Bulletin for Europe*, vol. 43 [1991], pp. 74–87, for a discussion with further calculations).

The arithmetic offered by the Soviet state statistics committee did under-line an obvious point: Russia was the origin of a disproportionally large share of Soviet hard currency exports, and these, resting heavily on oil, gas and raw materials, were especially underpriced in the domestic economy. If any one republic – given available resources and technologies and the inherited pattern of production capacities – was being exploited by the rest, it could be argued that it was Russia.

A belief that Russia was the provider for the whole of the USSR assisted the break-up of the Soviet federation. The issue was seldom described as one of Russian secession. For ethnic Russians, Russian and Soviet identity were hard to disentangle. For many, they still are. An indecisive, unpopu-lar, unelected Soviet leadership should step aside and communism should be overthrown: that seems to have been the thrust of Yeltsin's policies in 1991. If Russia could rid itself of a colonial burden in the process, so much the better.

During 1991 the struggle between republics and the centre played itself out. It had great immediate costs. The confusion over who was in charge blocked further reform. Producers did not have legally grounded profit incentives, but they also had little incentive to obey instructions from above in the traditional way. Output continued to fall.

Inflationary pressure increased. Monetary and fiscal control disintegrated: republic budgets ceased to be controlled by the Union (they had previously been mere allocations within the Union budget; the Soviet Union was nominally a federation but had in practice been, up to 1990, a unitary state). The 1990 budget deficit was officially reported at 58 billion roubles (*Ekonomika i zhizn'*, 1991 no. 5, p. 9; a lower figure was given in *Narkhoz 90*, p. 17; the general government deficit was certainly higher than either of these).

The figure of 58 billion roubles was equivalent to 6 per cent of the Soviet GNP as estimated by the Soviet statistical authorities (*Narkhoz 90*, p. 5). Even though this is an understatement, the reported deficit was already large enough to be a problem.

A Soviet budget deficit of any size could be financed only by printing money or borrowing from abroad. A small deficit, such as had been run for many years (though not publicly admitted) could be financed by borrowing from the state banking system, in effect from the State Savings Bank (Sberbank). That meant that increments of household savings were financing the budget. Even this was not entirely straightforward. Part of that incre-ment of savings was involuntary: the overhang of frustrated spending power, reflecting repressed inflation. When budget deficits grew as a percentage of GNP in the late 1980s, both borrowing and monetary emission increased. Officially reported internal state debt rose from 20.3 per cent of GNP at the end of 1986 to 56.6 per cent at the end of 1990 (*Narkhoz 90*, p. 19). Ellman argues that part of this reported internal debt was probably the rouble counterpart of external debt, and points out that Soviet external borrowing had been increasing (Ellman 1992, p. 120). Meanwhile rouble currency in circulation also rose steeply, increasing by 24.3 per cent in 1990 (*Narkhoz 90*, p. 29). Real output had fallen (see Table 8.1 below), so inflationary pressure was intensifying.

For 1991 Soviet Gosplan had at one stage projected an overall government deficit of 197 billion roubles, or more than three times the level acknowledged for 1990 (*Variantnyi* . . . , 1990, Table 1.4). The published plan 1991 deficit was only 26.7 billion roubles, but that excluded off-budget funds and republic budgets.

Use of external borrowing was precarious. Soviet external borrowing was all explicitly or implicitly sovereign borrowing, since all economic entities dealing with the outside world were state-owned. So long as the Soviet state maintained its impeccable record of political stability and timely debt service, both foreign banks and (embargoes and sanctions apart) foreign governments lent to it on good terms. In 1990 the banks began to reduce their exposure to Moscow. Western governments had only taxpayers' money at stake, plus a belief in supporting Gorbachev the reformer. They behaved less prudently. Still, foreign borrowing was becoming more difficult.

The Soviet government scrambled during 1991 to control the budget problem. There were attempts to negotiate agreements with republic governments about the sharing of revenue and limitations on spending. These broke down. Yeltsin said Russia would cut its contribution to the Union budget, and spend more (Yasin in Ellman and Kontorovich 1998, p. 298). Inflationary pressure threatened to grow out of control.

Valentin Pavlov, who had been in charge of the State Prices Committee and then of the Ministry of Finance, took over as Prime Minister when Ryzhkov resigned. He undertook two measures for which *bien pensant* Moscow intellectuals and most Western commentators derided him.[2] The measures were not, under the circumstances, as daft as they were made out to be.

Pavlov freed 40 per cent of wholesale prices from 1 January 1991, and imposed a 5 per cent sales tax. He cut the money supply by withdrawing large denomination notes (the usual instrument of large-scale black market activity) and froze deposits in Sberbank. Then, with effect from 2 April, he moved to raise the retail price level: prices for what were defined as luxury goods were, with qualifications, freed; other prices remained centrally controlled but were raised. The free prices of consumer goods were free in the sense that they could be negotiated between producers and the distributive network, subject to monitoring and the threat of regulation (*Ekonomika i zhizn'* 1991 no. 14, p. 6). Increments in profits resulting from the price increases mostly accrued in the first instance to the republic budgets, but not proportionally with population. There was to be a special inter-republic redistribution fund to reallocate the funds both among republics and between republics and the centre (*ibid.*). Compensating payments would be made to lower-income families to cushion the effect of the price rises. Net of those, there was supposed to be an increase in both Union and republic budget incomes.

This was not a market-friendly set of measures, but as a short-term expedient to moderate inflationary pressure it had its merits. It was undermined by two things. The republics did not cooperate with the centre. The widespread presence of local monopoly power often led to very large increases in 'free' prices and considerable bending of the definitions of a luxury good, and the state (especially at local level) lacked the means to monitor and regulate (see Eduard Gonzal'es in *Izvestiya*, 5 April 1991, p. 1). To these two impediments it must be added that the sequencing was bad. Raising wholesale prices three months ahead of retail prices generated a surge of subsidies to retail prices in the interim, weakening the budget. This delay between the two price rises was probably enforced by difficulties in centre-republic negotiations.

In the second quarter of the year both the Soviet and republic governments were tinkering with economic programmes and holding inter-republic and union-republic meetings to agree on the way ahead. Their visions of the near future differed. The most important difference was between the Soviet and Russian programmes.

The Soviet Union had an Anti-Crisis Programme. This contained an awkward mix of liberal remedies and controls. Prices were to be largely freed, but not until 1 October 1992. Macro-stabilisation was to be pursued by financial tightening. Interest rates should be set so as to allow for inflation – meaning presumably that nominal interest rates should exceed inflation. Enterprises and individuals should be free to trade in foreign currency. At the same time, enterprises should for a time at least be allowed to dispose of only 30 per cent of their output at free prices. A special administrative regime should be introduced to protect and control the activities of enterprises in electricity supply, transport and communications. And there should be special legislation requiring subordinate enterprises to obey their superior organisations. This last provision was aimed at enterprises that the Soviet authorities deemed to be subordinate to All-Union (USSR-level) branch ministries. (See Tass in Russian, 9 April 1991 for the draft; *Izvestiya*, 16 May 1991, pp. 1, 2 for a report of the government consideration of the draft.)

Russia had, before the Gaidar team was installed late in the year, an economic programme covering the period from mid-1991 to end-1993. It was drawn up by a group headed by a junior minister, Evgenii Saburov, and presented by the Russian Prime Minister, Ivan Silaev. This emphasised early price liberalisation and an early start to privatisation. It accepted that inflation would be high through 1992, and envisaged a monetary squeeze delayed until the start of 1993 (*Komsomolskaya Pravda*, 23 April 1991, p. 4; *Kommersant*, 1991 no. 26, pp. 2–3).

Silaev, introducing the Russian programme, said he expected that Pavlov, the Soviet Prime Minister, would not oppose it. This may have been correct in the sense that Pavlov would not engage in public denunciations. But conflicts can take other forms. For a start, the Soviet programme contained provisions to underline traditional subordination of production units – most large units being subordinate to Soviet authorities. Russia, repeating its attempted legislation of October 1990, sought to 'nationalise' (declare as Russian) all the All-Union property in Russia, except that belonging to the Soviet Defence Ministry, the KGB and the Ministry of Internal Affairs (MVD) (*Izvestiya*, 3 July 1991, p. 1). Pavlov and Gorbachev were not about to agree to that. Disputes continued especially over who was to control defence-industry (VPK) enterprises (*Guardian*, 6 July 1991). The speed of price liberalisation and the question who would control foreign trade licensing and quotas were other contentious issues, both between Russia and the USSR and among republics (*Izvestiya*, 1 July 1991, p. 2).

Ten republics agreed to an anti-crisis programme. Those governments that had the decency not to pretend to agree were those of the three Baltic states, Georgia and Moldova (Reuters from Moscow, 9 June 1991). As the other ten were only pretending to agree, this was not a deal with consequences.

Public finances remained a major battleground. The Soviet Finance Minister, Vladimir Orlov, claimed, quite possibly correctly, that the RSFSR (Russia) had remitted to the Union budget in the second quarter of the year only 4.7 per cent of the tax revenue it should normally have remitted (*Kommersant*, 1991 no. 26, p. 1). The figure is so small it suggests that the Russian authorities had meant to remit nothing, and slipped up.

With the attempted coup against Gorbachev in August, Soviet economic policy-making came to an end. The republics now made the running. Yeltsin reshaped the Russian government, bringing in a team of young reformers headed by Acting Prime Minister Egor Gaidar. After the final collapse of the Soviet Union, Russia introduced its own attempt at radical reform at the start of 1992. By then, shops had emptied and shortages were pervasive. Gaidar has consistently maintained that the general decontrol of prices from 2 January 1992 was carried out not as a matter of free-market doctrine but as the only way out of a crisis characterised by a ferocious shortage of everything. Anyone who was in Russia in November or December 1991 will know what he means.

Breaking up a single economic space

There was a strong economic logic to the Soviet break-up, but it sprang from political conflict. Partly repressed inflation got out of control in 1991 because the Soviet Union remained a single currency area but its fifteen republics were pursuing incompatible fiscal policies.

The emission of roubles was something for which the Soviet central bank was responsible. That is to say, it had the immediate responsibility for rouble cash creation. Government spending was no longer controlled in the centre. Credit could also be expanded at the republic level. If a republic ran a budget deficit, this increased aggregate demand in that republic. If another republic tried to run a tight fiscal policy, controlling the aggregate demand of its households and firms, output would flow from the second republic to the first: there would be an outflow of resources. Firms and households in the spendthrift republic would be bidding resources away from those in the would-be prudent republic. As long as some republics behaved as spendthrifts, it made no sense for any other republic to attempt fiscal prudence.

So long as the republic leaderships were not prepared to cooperate for the long-term benefit of rouble stabilisation for the whole federation, this monetary union was doomed. Yeltsin, for one, was not prepared to cooperate. In a speech to the Russian Congress of People's Deputies, he declared that the communist order was a powerful political system that maintained a monstrous economic system that ignored Russian people. The 1990 elections of republic leaders had displayed the people's desire for liberty. A 'coalition government of the people's trust' was needed at Union level, presiding over a Union of Sovereign States. But not (he implied) the present leadership (*Izvestiya*, 30 March 1991, p. 3). Whether that is a full account of his reasons for opposing Gorbachev so relentlessly, is beside the point here. Cooperation was ruled out. Especially financial cooperation: the chairman of the (new) Russian central bank, Georgii Matyukhin, called for the Soviet central bank to be abolished (*Financial Times*, 1 May 1991, p. 3).

In this situation, a single Soviet currency area was incompatible with financial stabilisation. Oleh Havrylyshyn and John Williamson saw this early on, and spelt out the argument: only if each republic (or possibly each of a few clusters of republics) bore the economic costs of fiscal irresponsibility, would policies improve. In the absence of a readiness to coordinate fiscal policies, this would come about only if each had its own currency (Havrylyshyn and Williamson 1991). With uncoordinated fiscal policies and a single currency, the attraction for each republic of free riding would prevent macro-stabilisation. The IMF, advising the post-Soviet states, clung for some time to the idea of preserving the rouble area. Estonia re-established its own kroon currency in June 1992 against IMF advice, and soon started its economic recovery. In 1993 Russia effectively brought the shared rouble currency area to an end. The financial mess of 1991 took a long time to sort out.

Economic outcomes; Western assistance

A country can have poor government policies and still prosper, if the private sector is strong. It cannot have a systemic vacuum and prosper. Figures for the last two years of the Soviet Union are particularly problematic, but there is no doubt that the deterioration was sharp. Table 8.1 assembles some data.

If these figures are any guide (and they are, in a rough and ready way), Soviet output as normally measured (real GDP or GNP) fell during these two years by nearly a fifth (17.1 per cent, and 18.0 per cent on a per capita basis). Yet it cannot be emphasised too strongly that this was not the 'old Soviet system' failing but the old Soviet system being abandoned. It was the

Table 8.1   *Selected Soviet economic indicators, 1990–91 (% p.a. change year-on-year unless otherwise specified)*

	1990	*1991*
GNP (Soviet official)	−2.3	
GDP (Maddison)	−2.4	−15.1
NMP produced	−4.0	−8.5
Numbers employed	−0.6	
Population	0.5	0.6
Retail price index, state shops	5.0	
Prices on kolkhoz markets	21.5	
Government deficit (% GNP/GDP)	6.0	26

Notes: the figure for the government deficit as a percentage of GNP in 1990 is almost certainly an understatement. It may have been 8–9 per cent.
Sources: 1990 figures except Maddison GDP from *Narkhoz 90*, pp. 6, 7, 67, 166, 174 and derived from pp. 5 and 17. Maddison GDP and 1991 population from Maddison 1995, tables C-16c and A-3c. 1991 NMP and 1991 govt deficit/GDP from Ellman and Kontorovich 1998, p. xxii.

product of a collapse of the rules of the economic game and of economic warfare between the Soviet republics and the Union.

Opinion surveys at the time showed widespread shortages of food. In April 1991 only 12 per cent of respondents said they saw meat and sausages on open sale in their local shops; only 23 per cent saw dairy products on sale. Three months later, in July, only 8 per cent of respondents said they were in areas where there was no rationing. Those who had ration cards seem to have gained little protection from them. Only 11 per cent said they could convert their ration coupons into the goods specified on them (Soviet coupons were usually product-specific); 34 per cent said they could convert only some of their coupons into the items specified; 36 per cent said they could not get anything for their coupons (cited in Mau and Starodubrovskaya 2001, p. 144).

The administrative inefficiency of local Soviet rationing is striking. When ration coupons are issued, they need to be backed by supplies of the relevant items such that the coupons can be traded for those items at the ration price. In India the system of ration shops, designed to help the poor, works well in that sense (information from Professor Ramnath Narayanswamy in Bangalore, 1999).

Calling this period a time of economic vacuum is not the same as saying that there were no economic institutions, or even that there was no development of economic institutions. The earlier development of cooperatives and the beginnings of Russian private commercial banks have already been mentioned in the previous chapter. These continued, with the modification that cooperatives tended to transform themselves into overtly private companies. New legislation allowed joint-stock companies to be formed. Auctions of foreign currency were developed, which would evolve into a currency market later. The currency black market expanded. The rouble was still inconvertible, with an official rate during 1991 of about $1.7 to the rouble, while the very limited open trading, such as foreign currency auctions by the Bank of Estonia, were yielding rates like 75 roubles to the dollar in early July (*Izvestiya*, 11 July 1991, p. 3). Commodity exchanges sprang up. In late 1991 there were as many as 200 of them. Exportable items like coal and oil traded on these exchanges at much higher prices for lots with an export licence attached than for lots that could be sold on only within the USSR (e.g. *Kommersant*, 1991 no. 26, p. 6).

The anomalies that would haunt the Russian economy later in the decade were already apparent. Legislation allowing workers and managers to lease state enterprises was parlayed by some, at least, into asset grabbing (*prikhvatizatsiya*, as distinct from *privatizatsiya*, privatisation). The Ministry of the Machine-Tool Industry turned itself into a joint-stock company, Stankoinstrument, headed by the former minister. Arkady Volskii, an adviser to Chernenko, surfaced at the head of an association called the Scientific-Industrial Union (NPS). This evolved later into the (Russian) Union of Industrialists and Entrepreneurs. Volskii advocated the formation of holding companies in which the state would have a leading role (*Ekonomika i zhizn'*, 1991 no. 22, p. 5). Aslund maintained that the NPS represented the old Party *apparat* and the state-enterprise managers, with a large representation from military industry (*New York Times*, 19 April 1991).

There had been calls for Western food aid to the USSR in 1990, and a review by the G7 nations of how the West might help more generally (see above). In 1991 the Western debate about assistance got under way. Yavlinskii, from the Russian government, along with Shcherbakov from the Soviet government, visited the US seeking financial assistance. Yavlinskii found intellectual advocates of large-scale, up-front assistance. The Harvard economist Jeffrey Sachs argued that the West could and should come up with a package of assistance to the USSR, to assist rapid economic transformation, of the order of $30 billion a year over five years (*Economist*, 25 May 1991, pp. 41–2). When Western assistance did come, it was later, smaller and conditional, with assistance policy led by the IMF. The meagre results of the aid that was eventually given to Russia and other former Soviet states do not necessarily discredit this earlier and grander idea.

Public opinion

When momentous things happen to nations, the people have seldom been consulted in advance. In the case of the Soviet collapse and the abandonment of communism, they were, and it did them no good at all.

The referendum on the continuation of the USSR has already been mentioned. When asked, the great majority of the Soviet population expressed a view, and it was against breaking up the country. The Baltic states apart, separatism was driven largely by republic elites.

On radical market reform, the Soviet public, when asked, gave confusing answers. This was not surprising. They were, for good reasons, confused. A survey of Muscovites in late 1989 asked respondents to say whether they responded negatively or positively to certain words. The word 'capitalism' elicited a 34 per cent positive, 38 per cent negative response; 28 per cent were smart enough to admit they didn't know or were ambivalent. The word 'socialism' did much better: 61, 17 and 12, respectively (*Moscow News*, 1990 no. 1, p. 9). A nationwide poll would probably have shown a larger negative balance. A few months later 801 Muscovites were polled on whether the country should go over to market relations: 58 per cent were for, 26 per cent against (*Moscow News*, 1990 no. 20, p. 10). A survey with a broader geographical respondent base asked whether land should be freely bought and sold. In Moscow and Leningrad there was a clear majority for a land market: 64 to 12 per cent. In rural areas there was only a plurality, and much more opposition: 46 per cent for and 42 per cent against (*Izvestiya*, 12 November 1991, p. 2).

In July 1991 a nationwide survey had found that 64 per cent of respondents favoured 'transition to a market economy'. This was not surprising in view of the prevailing shortages at the time. But only 23 of those 64 per cent favoured *rapid* transition to the market (cited in Mau and Starodubrovskaya 2001, p. 145).

These questions about a desirable economic order are not matters on which opinion polls or referenda would provide much guidance in any country. Fortunately, most nations never have even to consider them. Capitalism evolves; change is incremental, and irrational answers do only marginal damage (wanting lower taxes and better public services at the same time, for example). The Soviet people had two changes of economic order inflicted upon them: by the 1917 revolution and by the 1991 collapse of the USSR. Neither was consciously chosen by the people; nor could it have been.

Notes

1   This was no mere outsider's comment. In 1988 and 1989 Soros had led a team of Western economists in meetings in Moscow and elsewhere with Soviet officials up to and including the Prime Minister, in an effort to advise on a strategy for market reform. The meetings were secret at the time, so everyone in Moscow knew all about them. I was a member of that team and have described the abortive mission elsewhere (Hanson in Ellman and Kontorovich 1998, pp. 238–57; see also Soros 1990).

2   Apart from anything else, he is not their kind of person. A shrewd, droll man, he exemplifies classic Soviet machismo. At meetings with the Soros group in 1988, he constantly rolled an unlit cigarette beneath his nose. When I asked him what this was about, he said, 'A man gives up three things before he dies: alcohol, tobacco and women. I've started with tobacco. But I like to remember.'

CHAPTER NINE

The Soviet Economy in Retrospect

The Soviet economic system, like the dinosaurs, ceased to exist. If survival denotes success, it failed. With dinosaurs, we look for the change in their environment that brought about their extinction. In the case of the Soviet economy, there is a temptation to look instead for fundamental defects that would have brought about the economy's downfall eventually, under any circumstances. This temptation exists because of the fundamental issues of social doctrine that surround our judgements on Soviet history. The dinosaurs have less chance to engage our deepest social and political beliefs.

It is not only dinosaurs that are treated differently. The Inca civilisation collapsed, and that collapse is seldom blamed on its internal contradictions – and this despite the fact that the Incas also had a centrally planned economy. A rather more obvious explanation is to hand: the Conquistadors, and their superior military technology.

To argue that the Soviet economic system came to an end because comprehensive state ownership and central planning were inherently unworkable is difficult. Soviet central planning worked after a fashion for sixty years, from 1928 to 1988. It coped with all-out war, and it left Soviet citizens somewhat better off in the late 1980s than they had been in the late 1920s. Those who argued in the 1920s and 1930s that socialist production was not possible were wrong.

The more moderate arguments of Hayek and von Mises have been supported by the historical evidence. When they argued that socialist production was doomed to be more inefficient than capitalist production, they were surely right. And when they argued that the market and state ownership, as general characteristics of a whole national economy, were incompatible, they were on to something. The Hungarian economy for twenty years after 1968 did display a mixture of predominant state ownership and regulated product markets, but the incompatibility of state ownership with capital markets, and therefore with hard budget constraints on producers, remained a great weakness. China, since the late 1970s, has developed a strange dual economy, in which a *de facto* capitalist, market economy co-exists with a planned, state-owned economy – and growth comes mainly from the former.

The questions to ask about Soviet post-war economic experience, therefore, concern comparative economic performance and the reasons for the deterioration over time. How did Soviet economic performance compare with that of the capitalist world? Why the growth slowdown? Why, at the end, the collapse?

Soviet post-war economic performance in comparative perspective

Soviet output, as assessed by the CIA using Western definitions and standards of measurement, increased in almost every year from 1946 to 1991. The exceptions are 1963, 1979, 1990 and 1991 (Maddison 1995, Table B 10 c, showing a CIA-based series revalued in 1990 international dollars, also shows a slight fall in 1959, which is hard to square with the CIA *Growth* 1990). Particularly bad harvests account for the 1963 and 1979 downturns. The output falls in 1990 and 1991 constitute the collapse as the system disintegrated (see Chapter 8). Figure 9.1 shows the Soviet growth trajectory.

Inspection of Figure 9.1 suggests no regular cyclical fluctuations. There is an abundant literature about alleged cyclical patterns in output in Central-Eastern Europe under central planning, but a careful reconsideration by Peter Mihalyi (1992) concludes that the evidence of a cyclical mechanism in growth there does not stand up. In the Soviet case, it has not even been suggested.

One thing, therefore, that did not afflict Soviet citizens was the more-or-less regular cycle of boom and recession that is part of capitalist experience. More broadly, unemployment was not a problem. What unemployment there was amounted to about 0.5 per cent of the workforce, and was almost entirely short-term and frictional (Lane 1986).

People's lives in the Soviet Union were characterised by a secure, humdrum poverty. There was a general regime of job security – that is, of security of tenure in existing jobs – as well as a very low level of unemployment. This job security was the product of labour hoarding in a shortage economy, by enterprises whose managers had nothing to gain from reducing

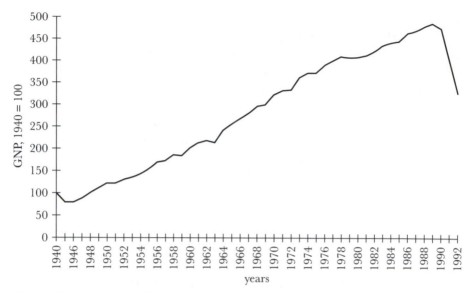

Figure 9.1 Soviet GNP, 1940–92

their payrolls (Hanson 1986). This was inefficient, but comfortable. It is much missed in post-Soviet Russia.

Money incomes were less unequal than in the West but the dispersion of money incomes understated material inequality (Wiles 1974). The latter rested on access to often unobtainable items in a shortage economy. 'To each according to his official rank' was the principle, modified by another principle – to each according to the official rank of his or her place of residence: Moscow was better supplied than anywhere else, provincial capitals better supplied than other provincial towns, and so on (see Chapter 5).

The growth of the Soviet economy was impressive up to about 1960, and thereafter decreasingly so. Maddison's figures of per capita GDP show the Soviet Union never coming close to 'catching up and overtaking' the US, as Table 9.1 shows.

Comparison with the US makes sense for two reasons. First, the United States was the rival superpower; Soviet policy-makers sought both to match the US militarily and to catch up with the US economically. Second, in the twentieth century the US was the leading capitalist country. Switzerland or Kuwait might sometimes show higher per capita output, but the US was consistently at or near the top of the tables of per capita production. Above all, more nearly than any other country, it represented the leading edge of world technology and productivity. It served as a benchmark for judging all other countries' development levels, not just that of the USSR.

Table 9.2 shows how the forlorn Soviet catch-up attempt flickered and died. The time periods chosen roughly reflect the chapter divisions in this

Table 9.1   *Soviet and US per capita GDP compared, selected years, 1946–91 (% and 1990 international dollars)*

	Soviet per cap GDP as % US	Absolute gap ($)
1946	20.8	7,294
1950	31.7	6,120
1953	27.8	7,806
1960	35.2	7,258
1964	34.9	8,257
1973	34.0	10,967
1985	33.5	13,335
1991	27.1	15,573

Source: derived from Maddison 1995, Table D-1.

Table 9.2   *Soviet and US per capita GDP: growth rates for selected periods, 1950–91 (% p.a., based on data in 1990 international dollars)*

	USSR	US
1950–53	2.0	6.5
1953–60	3.9	0.5
1960–64	3.0	3.2
1964–73	2.7	3.0
1973–85	1.5	1.6
1985–91	−2.1	1.1

Source: as Table 9.1.

book. This produces some occasionally anomalous figures on the US side of the comparison. Sometimes the end-years of a period correspond to a trough-to-peak period in US business cycles (e.g. 1950–53) or peak-to-trough (1953–60), giving a misleading picture on the American side. Still, the picture that emerges is of a falling behind from the 1960s.

In Figure 9.2 the catching-up or lagging behind is shown graphically, year by year, once more in Maddison's 1990 international dollar terms. The contrast between American cyclical development and the smoother Soviet growth is clear. So is the size of the absolute gap, and its widening over time.

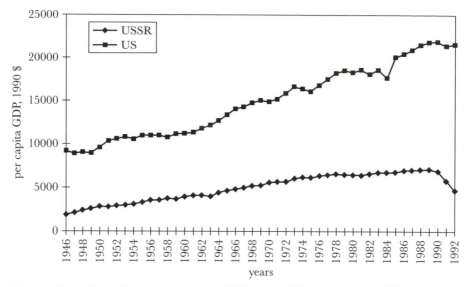

Figure 9.2 Catching up overtaking: USSR and US per capita GDP, 1946–92

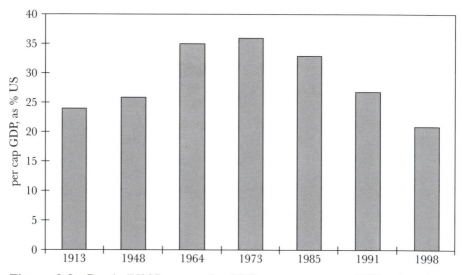

Figure 9.3 Russia/USSR per capita GDP as a percentage of US, selected
years, 1913–98

Figure 9.3 is intended to place the post-war Soviet performance in a
longer time-frame. The post-Soviet decline (continuing the output fall of
1990–91) brings the Russian economy back in 1998 close to its relative
standing vis-à-vis the US in 1913. The middle years of the Brezhnev period
are the high point of Russian and Soviet attempts to join the developed

Table 9.3 *Selected countries: rates of divergence from (–) and convergence to (+) the per capita GDP level of the US over the period 1950–92 (% p.a. average)*

USSR	−0.74	France	1.01	Japan	3.70
Bulgaria	0.21	Germany	1.67	China	1.94
Czechoslovakia	−0.34	Italy	1.79	Argentina	−0.93
Hungary	0.02	UK	0.05	South Korea	3.85
Poland	−0.37	Spain	2.02	Ghana	−2.31

Source: Maddison 1995, Table 1–4.

world. They were also the time when Moscow achieved strategic parity with the US. The measurement is again in 1990 dollars.

The fact that Soviet production levels did not catch up those of the US might not in itself be so important, if the same was true of all or most other countries. What happened in the forty years after the Second World War, however, was that a large cohort of other countries did narrow the gap between their levels of per capita output and that of the US. This ought in general to have been possible, since followers can apply leading-edge technology already introduced and debugged in (mainly) the leading country, usually at lower cost than the innovator. Stages in technological development may even be skipped by countries that are behind the leader. If innovations are diffused fairly readily across national boundaries, followers have an advantage and ought to be able to narrow productivity gaps over time. Table 9.3 shows Maddison's estimates of this process for a number of countries.

What is striking here is that the leading West European nations and a cluster of Asian countries did greatly reduce their per capita output lags behind the US. Late-developing capitalist countries that began this process (Italy, Spain, Japan, South Korea) show particularly rapid convergence rates. This reflects the particularly large technology gaps they faced in 1950. But even the weary old United Kingdom, which has never grown fast, slightly reduced its lag behind the US.

The capitalist countries that failed to converge are of interest. In Table 9.3, which contains only selected countries, two have been picked to represent rather different kinds of comparative failure. Argentina was quite wealthy in the early post-war period and lost ground under Peronist and post-Peronist regimes of intervention and protectionism. Ghana stands here for the general failure of wealth creation in Africa, associated both with high levels of state intervention and perhaps also with a lack of the minimum levels of trust and civic engagement outside kinship networks that may be needed to build the social foundations of a well-functioning market. (Ghana is treated here as capitalist despite the episode of quasi-socialism under

Nkrumah; the predominantly rural economy was little touched by Nkrumah's socialism.)

The Soviet-bloc countries shown in Table 9.3, with the exception of Bulgaria and Hungary, failed to converge. (Romania and Yugoslavia, not shown here, also diverged rather than converged.) That is the sense in which Soviet-type economies failed. China is the one country shown in the table that defies easy classification. It shows successful convergence, almost certainly because of the reforms starting in 1978 that created a special kind of mixed economy.

The divergence occurred in the second half of the period. This is a distinctive characteristic of the Soviet bloc and of Latin America, but not of Western Europe and Asia. Here the evidence is to do with labour productivity. Table 9.3 shows convergence and divergence with respect to GDP per head of population. A different, though obviously quite closely related, measure is labour productivity (GDP per hour worked). In the Soviet Union this was converging on US levels in 1950–73 and then diverging in 1973–92 (Maddison 1995, Table 2–8). The same pattern holds for Czechoslovakia, Poland and Hungary. China, interestingly, exhibits divergence (that is, comparative failure) in 1950–73 and then convergence in 1973–92, the latter period coming mostly after the creation of a large private sector. On this criterion, West European countries exhibited convergence in both sub-periods. So did most Asian countries, though Bangladesh, China, India and Indonesia moved from divergence in the earlier sub-period to convergence in the later sub-period (*ibid.*).

Soviet output growth per head of population in 1960–89 was poor by international standards if factors shown to influence growth in that period in 102 countries are taken into account. Easterly and Fischer (1995, especially Table 2), show that if initial (1960) level of per capita GDP and schooling, population growth and investment:GDP ratios over the same period had had the same effect on Soviet output growth as regression analysis identifies (on average) for 102 countries, Soviet growth would have been 2.3 per cent a year higher than it actually was.

Judged by international comparisons, then, the Soviet economy performed poorly over the entire post-war period, and this comparative failure was concentrated in the latter half of the period. This was a failure not only to catch up with the US but also to catch up with Western Europe. In any comparison with Japan and the Asian newly industrialising countries, the Soviet Union trails badly. The same could be said about most of the Soviet-bloc countries. This is *prima facie* evidence that the comparative failure was systemic.

Gross national product and gross domestic product figures are not ends in themselves and not very good measures of human welfare more broadly. Per capita GDP figures, however, are well, though not perfectly, correlated

Table 9.4 *World and selected countries and groups of countries: years of life expectancy in 1960–65 and 1985–90 (years at birth, male and female together)*

	1960–65	*1985–90*
World	52.4	63.1
Developed countries	69.8	74.1
Soviet Union + Central-Eastern Europe	69.2	70.1
Russia	69.0	69.2
Ukraine	70.7	70.5
Less developed countries	47.7	60.5
Least developed countries	39.7	49.2

Source: Kontorovich 2001, citing 1999 UN data.

with more direct measures of welfare, such as mortality and morbidity rates. Table 9.4 shows one very summary health measure: life expectancy at birth. It can be seen that almost the whole world enjoyed a substantial improvement in life expectancy between the early 1960s and the late 1980s. The Soviet bloc, starting with quite high levels, also displays an improvement, but, in comparison with developed, less developed and least developed countries – that is, with the rest of the world – only a very modest one.

This fits, very loosely, with the the per capita GDP evidence: life improved (and lengthened) in the USSR, but by much less than in the capitalist world. Again, this picture holds for the Soviet bloc as a whole.

Through 1989, it could be said, the Soviet economy was not failing in an absolute sense. Per capita GDP was almost stagnant in the 1980s (see Figure 9.2) but it was not falling. It was failing only in a comparative sense. Much the same could be said about Central-Eastern Europe. The comparative failure looks systemic.

But who cares about failure that is merely comparative? The international economy is not, after all, an athletics championship. Merely comparative economic failure will matter politically in the following circumstances: when you are in military competition with other countries and have to be able to counter their military threats; when your citizens know about conditions in more successful countries and become disaffected and perhaps even rebellious because you are falling behind, or the ruling elite fears (perhaps mistakenly) that this may happen; and when you are proclaiming to the world at large the superiority of your social system, and the credibility of your government is therefore at stake (or the elite mistakenly fears that it is).

Under Stalin, these conditions were not met. US military technologies for nuclear warfare (atomic warheads and intercontinental missiles) were developed in a military technology enclave somewhat apart from the rest of the US economy (spillovers from space technology to civilian applications notwithstanding). This was the sort of thing the Soviet Union could, just about, match. It did so by throwing resources at its own special military-industrial enclave and starving the rest of the economy. Soviet citizens who had had the temerity to witness the luxury of foreign life as German prisoners of war were packed off to the gulag. Travel even to other communist states was restricted to very few, trusted people. And growth was at this time still faster in the Soviet Union than in the West.

After Stalin, these conditions began to change. Travel restrictions were relaxed. Soviet citizens saw the comparative prosperity of some of the Central-East European countries, and lived to tell the tale. While Soviet growth remained robust, however, an optimistic view of the Soviet system remained perfectly reasonable. But increased acquaintance with the outside world plus slowing Soviet growth began to change that. The result was almost certainly not a propensity to rebel, but the elite lacked confidence and became very sensitive to the possibility of unrest. The rise of Solidarity in Poland focused this concern (Teague 1988).

Then, from the 1970s, a new generation of weapon systems began to be developed in the US: battlefield control systems, supposedly smart bombs, and so on – up to and including the Strategic Defense Initiative or Star Wars. These had in common a foundation of information technology. This had not been developed in a special military technology enclave, as nuclear weapons and rockets had been, but was a spillover from developments in the civilian economy. That was a kind of military technological development that the Soviet Union had no means of matching.

For all these reasons, I suggest, Gorbachev and a few of his close associates came to believe that radical changes were needed in the Soviet economy. Their search for these, chronicled in the previous two chapters, was confused. It ended up undermining the economy.

This version of events is no more than a series of conjectures that fit the factual narrative. There are some others, and they will be considered in the remaining two sections of this chapter. Those are addressed more closely to the factors producing the growth slowdown and the factors behind the final collapse, in that order.

Why did growth slow down?

Table 9.5 presents a picture of Soviet economic growth between 1950 and 1990, in five-year segments. (The designation of periods reverts here to the

Table 9.5 *A growth accounting exercise for the USSR, 1950–90 (% p.a.)*

	1950–55	1955–60	1960–65	1965–70	1970–75	1975–80	1980–85	1985–90
GDP	4.9	5.4	4.8	4.8	2.9	1.8	1.7	1.3
Labour inputs	1.9	0.6	1.6	2.0	1.7	1.2	0.7	0.2
Capital inputs	7.9	9.2	9.7	7.4	8.0	6.9	5.4	4.9
Combined inputs	4.5	4.4	5.2	4.4	4.6	3.9	3.2	2.3
TFP	0.4	1.0	−0.4	0.4	−1.7	−2.0	−1.5	−1.0

Notes: GNP growth based on Maddison 1995, GDP series in 1990 international dollars. Labour inputs: person-hours as calculated by the CIA through 1985; 1985–90: total employment. Capital inputs: gross capital stock as estimated by the CIA (usually close to Soviet official figures): in 1955 roubles through 1965, in 1973 roubles 1965–85; 1985–90 in Soviet 'comparable prices' (Soviet official capital stock series). Combined inputs: weighted average of labour and capital inputs growth rates, with weights of 0.55 and 0.45, respectively (CIA estimated weights to reflect income shares). TFP: total factor productivity growth, measured as GNP index divided by combined inputs index.
Sources: GDP from Maddison 1995, Table C-16c. Inputs through 1985 from Hanson 1990, Table 10.5 (where original data sources are given). Inputs for 1985–90 from *Narkhoz 90*, pp. 97, 288. TFP: author's calculation.

more normal Western style, including the base-year of each period. Thus 1950–55, rather than 1951–55 [inclusive], as in the usual Soviet style that has been employed earlier.)

Two salient facts are that output growth slows significantly after 1970, and the growth of combined inputs slows significantly after 1975. One hypothesis could be that the Soviet Union enjoyed an unusually extended post-war recovery period to the end of the 1960s, after which growth reverted to a much longer-run trend characteristic of pre-war Russia and the Soviet Union. That interpretation implies, not some deterioration of trend but the end of a favourable, and unusually lengthy, blip. It is not clear, however, why the Soviet Union would have a specially prolonged post-war catch-up compared with, for instance, Germany.

An alternative account fits the facts of the post-war period more economically. The slowdown in output growth begins before the slowdown in input growth. This is (arithmetically) why total factor productivity (TFP) change deteriorates so markedly between 1965–70 and 1970–75. Then GDP growth slows further, in the late 1970s, the additional deterioration being largely accounted for by the slowdown in the growth in both labour and capital inputs. The slowdown in capital inputs follows the deliberate slowing of planned investment growth from 1975. Subsequent deterioration of output growth in the 1980s can again be attributed chiefly to a further slowing of input growth. This implies that something affecting the change in output per unit input occurred around 1970.

These measurements are rather crude. The logic behind them, and a possible alternative measure, are described in the Annex to this chapter.

A number of influences combined in the 1970s, I suggest, to slow Soviet output growth, regardless of the rate of growth of measured labour and capital inputs. Resource reallocation from lower- to higher-productivity sectors slowed as the rate of transfer of labour from agriculture to industry decreased. The shift of the centre of gravity of natural resource exploitation from the European part of the country to Siberia raised infrastructure and transport costs per unit of final output. There is evidence of a deterioration in the rate of introduction of new technologies (within any given sector) (Kontorovich 1986) – though that observation itself calls for explanation. And perhaps also there was a loss of plan discipline and morale as the regime became softer (or people began to grasp how much softer it already was than in Stalin's or even Khrushchev's time).

These points are discussed more fully in Chapter 5. None of them amounts to a change in the system. Rather, the limits of the Soviet planning system begin to emerge. It could and did mobilise additional inputs of labour and capital, and reallocate resources from agriculture to industry. Insofar as aggregate labour productivity lags behind the West narrowed in the first quarter of a century after the war, this was not because technology gaps within each sector were being reduced; they were not (Amann *et al.* 1977). But the composition of output was still shifting quite rapidly towards higher-productivity sectors, and that reallocation could not go on at the same rapid rate.

On top of this, it can be conjectured, the depletion of the most cheaply accessible natural resources and the easing of social control and plan discipline produced an added braking effect.

The special weakness of one particular sector, agriculture, compounded the difficulties. Resource transfer out of a more efficient farm sector could have continued at a higher rate. Given the policy-makers' preference for minimal dependence on foreign trade, a more productive agriculture would have freed more importing capacity for productivity-enhancing technology imports. Windfall gains from oil-price rises had provided the opportunity for this. As things were, the farm sector continued to absorb a large amount of resources directly; indirectly, its deficiencies forced a diversion of hard currency away from machinery and technology imports in favour of food imports.

Meanwhile, the soft, post-Stalin regime could not rely on repression to keep order. Fearful, probably without good cause, of social unrest, the Brezhnev leadership felt unable to increase the investment share of national income; indeed, they moved the other way and slowed investment growth from the mid-1970s. Gorbachev's brief attempt to reverse that policy a decade later encountered an economy whose growth had slowed further, and which simply could not support a rapid growth of investment. For one thing, demographic effects had by then kicked in: the labour force was growing more slowly after 1980.

All of this can be interpreted as a systemic comparative failure, but not so much in the static-efficiency sense of Hayek, as in the sense of another Austrian economic thinker, Joseph Schumpeter: the Soviet system's inability to maintain rapid rates of introduction and diffusion of new products and processes, in the absence of capitalist profit incentives (Schumpeter 1944). A more innovation-friendly system would have sustained a higher rate of technological change and therefore, other things equal, a higher rate of TFP growth or a slower rate of TFP decline.

A somewhat different interpretation, stressing a 'resource curse' element in the Soviet slowdown, has been put forward by Mau and Starodubrovskaya (2001). This interpretation is part of an ambitious exercise in seeking to understand the transformation of the Russian economy in the light of the historical evidence of other revolutions. They see the basic Soviet economic difficulties originating in the 1960s and 1970s, as a system designed for extensive, resource-absorbing growth proved to be poor at handling technological change (*op. cit.*, pp. 73–9). The oil-price rises of the 1970s promised a way out, but only by tying the Soviet economy more closely to international markets, leaving it hostage to energy-price declines without addressing domestic barriers to growth (pp. 91, 93).

Mau and Starodubrovskaya agree with the view put forward here: that there was a creeping, *de facto* decentralisation of economic control in the USSR in the 1960s and 1970s. This phenomenon, however, is one they link, not with the general post-Stalin softening of social control, but with a proliferation and fragmenting of economic bureaucracies designed (unsuccessfully) to coordinate an increasingly complex economy (p. 80).

Perhaps their greatest disagreement with the account given here, however, concerns the role of perestroika. They imply that policies pursued in 1985–91 did not precipitate the output collapse; that it was due to happen anyway. For the reasons given here (see below) and in Chapter 8, I do not find this convincing. However, disagreements about what might have been are not easily resolved.

Imperial over-reach is sometimes adduced to account for the deterioration of Soviet economic performance. If this is taken to mean the burden of defence spending, there are two fundamental objections to it as an explanation. First, there was a high defence burden when the Soviet economy was growing comparatively strongly, as well as when it was slowing down. Second, the defence burden was far lower in the other Warsaw Pact countries throughout the post-war period – lower indeed than in most non-US NATO countries (see the annual *Military Balance* assessments of the International Institute for Strategic Studies). Yet they also suffered a slowdown, and lost ground in international comparisons, in a fashion very similar to that of the USSR (see above). Easterly and Fischer (1995) test statistically (on the basis of cross-section analysis of the effects of defence burden on growth across many countries) for a 'defence burden' influence on Soviet growth, and find only a very small negative effect.

Harrison (2001a) offers a theoretical model to account for the collapse of Soviet output. In it, a loss of powers of coercion plays a central role. He models the Soviet economy as a game played between a dictator (the central authorities) and producers. The dictator employs both rewards and punishments to elicit effort from producers in pursuit of his production targets. Both rewards and punishments are costly to use, and the costs reduce the net output available for the dictator. So does stealing by producers, which punishments are meant to deter. Changes in the mix of rewards and punishment can be made in the light of information about their cost-effectiveness. A relaxation of coercion may be hard to reverse if producers come to expect further relaxation.

Harrison posits that the monitoring costs needed to support coercion rose as the economy became more developed and therefore more complicated.

Ways of relying more on incentives were sought, but the reforms ended up weakening plan discipline without improving incentives (from the dictator's point of view). See Chapter 4 above for a discussion of the 1965 Kosygin reform which is consistent with this view.

In the game played between dictator and producers, various stable equilibria are possible. Harrison argues that the output collapse from 1989 was triggered by the undermining of one such equilibrium: it became clear that the centre simply could not enforce its penalties or come through with its rewards. The 'dictator' gave up. Output collapsed.

This is an intellectually powerful account, much neater and less baggy than the one presented here. But it focuses attention on the abrupt, final output collapse, not on the preceding, gradual deterioration of perform-ance. What is suggested here is that a gradual weakening of discipline, that is, of the power credibly to threaten punishment, played a part, along with the other factors discussed above, in the slowdown from the early 1970s.

The circumstantial evidence for this view has, I hope, emerged in earlier chapters. More direct evidence would be hard to identify. The general sense is concisely captured by Max Hayward: 'Stalin was right in his under-standing of the fact that an untenable formula for social change can be maintained only by terror' (Hayward 1963, p. 16).

If this interpretation is right, the tragedy is that the weakening of plan discipline can be traced back to de-Stalinisation, and de-Stalinisation was in part prompted by decent impulses. The desire of Khrushchev and others to make Soviet socialism more humane contributed to a softening of the sys-tem. Improved incentives, particularly in the farm sector, yielded real im-provements for a time, but the long-term economic effects of a softer regime were insidious.

The final output collapse

Harrison's modelling of the final output collapse is consistent with the story told in Chapter 8. The traditional Soviet system depended on a chain of command, and Gorbachev destroyed that chain of command. This, as Chapters 7 and 8 show, was an unintended economic side-effect of policies pursued in the cause of political reform.

There is however a sharp break between the prolonged slowdown and the abrupt collapse. Ellman and Kontorovich (1992, 1997 and 1998) have shown very persuasively that the final output collapse was not predeter-mined by (say) 1985. Bungled policies in 1985–87 of accelerating invest-ment growth, accelerating the growth of the defence effort and abruptly reducing alcohol consumption damaged the public finances and greatly increased inflationary pressure. But even in 1987–88 a political leader unin-terested in political liberalisation and more prepared than Gorbachev was to use or threaten violence (in Poland, in the Baltic states and in the Transcaucasus) would have maintained the Party system. With it, the chain of command on which the economy functioned would have survived. There would have been no reason to expect an improvement in the Soviet cent-rally planned economy, but it could probably have limped on.

ANNEX

Measuring changes in productivity

The TFP calculations in Table 9.5 are based on a very simple characterisa-tion of the relationship between inputs and outputs, known as a Cobb-Douglas production function. This is not the only possible approach (see below).

As the notes to Table 9.5 indicate, the growth of combined inputs is measured with weights for capital and labour that follow the CIA's assess-ments (for the same purpose) of shares in national income – such shares being appropriate weights in a Cobb-Douglas estimate. A 70:30 weighting, which would be more conventional for Cobb-Douglas production function estimates for market economies, would of course alter the measure of com-bined inputs change and therefore of TFP change. But it does not much affect the order of magnitude and direction of the changes in those rates of change. On either weighting, the big deterioration in TFP comes around 1970 (for the calculations, using a slightly different series for total output, see Hanson 1990, Table 10.5).

This Cobb-Douglas approach to measuring changes in total factor pro-ductivity, whatever the weights used for labour and capital, rests on strong assumptions about the relationship between inputs and output: that is, about the aggregate production function for the whole economy. In the calcula-tions presented in Table 9.5 it is implicitly assumed that changes in the amounts of labour and capital used will, other things equal, affect output in certain ways: in particular, that if capital inputs available increase more rapidly than labour inputs, capital can always be substituted for labour fairly readily (the elasticity of substitution between the two inputs is equal to one), and that there are constant returns to scale (if capital and labour inputs both increase by 10 per cent then, in the absence of technological change, so will total output). There are also implicit assumptions about the nature of technical change: that it is not capital-saving biased or labour-saving biased, but neutral as between the two inputs.

Alter these assumptions specifying a Cobb-Douglas production function with constant returns to scale, and measures of the rate of change in TFP may alter. And it is not easy to discriminate between one specification of the production function and another by statistical testing on the data: the choice of production function cannot in general be settled in that way.

It is therefore only fair to add that the same Soviet data on output, labour inputs and capital inputs can be analysed in a rather different way: that is, with different assumptions about the character of the production function. Easterly and Fischer (1995), following earlier work starting with Weitzman (1970), adopt a constant-elasticity-of-substitution (CES) production function approach to the Soviet slowdown. Their interpretation is somewhat different from the one developed here. They find rates of TFP change, 1950–87, altering little; growth slows, in their analysis, because the Soviet Union accumulates capital at a very high rate (by international standards) but exhibits an exceptionally low elasticity of substitution between capital and labour, so that sharply diminishing returns to capital set in.

This is a very different picture from the one presented in Table 9.5. But their conclusions about the origins of the slowdown are the same as those drawn here: there was something about the nature of the centrally planned economy that impeded capital–labour substitution, so that the planners' chosen route of extensive growth of inputs, particularly capital inputs, was not sustainable. They find similar patterns in Central-East European growth. Therefore, they conclude, the roots of the Soviet slowdown are embedded in the Soviet economic system – the same conclusion as that offered here.

One reason why I find the simple Cobb-Douglas approach more appealing is precisely that it does show productivity growth slowing in the 1970s. Total factor productivity change, or the change in output not accounted for by changes in labour and capital inputs, must logically contain many elements – not just technological change but the arithmetical effects of resource shifts between sectors, changes in returns to scale and the discovery or depletion of natural resources, among other sources of growth. And we know that several of these things did change in ways that were adverse for the USSR in the 1970s.

BIBLIOGRAPHY

Abalkin, Leonid (1991), *Neispol'zovannyi shans*, Moscow: Politizdat.

Abramov, Fedor (1963), *The Dodgers*, (*Vokrug da okolo*), translated by David Floyd, London: Flegon Press.

Aganbegyan, Abel (1965/1982), 'The real state of the economy', in Stephen F. Cohen (ed.), *An End to Silence. Uncensored Opinion in the Soviet Union*, New York: W.W. Norton, 1982, pp. 223–8. (Also published in *samizdat* in Roy Medvedev's *Politicheskii dnevnik* no. 11, 1965 [in Russian] and in *Socialist Commentary*, October 1965.)

Aganbegyan, Abel (1986) 'Perelom i uskorenie', *EKO*, no. 6, pp. 3–25.

Amalrik, Andrei (1970), *Involuntary Journey to Siberia*, Boston: Harcourt, Brace, Jovanovich.

Amann, R., J.M. Cooper and R.W. Davies (eds) (1977), *The Technological Level of Soviet Industry*, New Haven: Yale University Press.

Amann, R. and J.M. Cooper (eds) (1982), *Industrial Innovation in the Soviet Union*, New Haven: Yale University Press.

Amann, R. and J.M. Cooper (eds) (1986), *Technical Progress and Soviet Economic Development*, Oxford: Blackwell.

Artemova, M. (1969), 'O fonde potrebleniya v natsional'nom dokhode', *Planovoe khozyaistvo*, no. 12, pp. 45–50.

Aslund, Anders (1989), *Gorbachev's Struggle for Economic Reform*, London: Pinter.

Ausch, Sandor (1972), *Theory and Practice of CMEA Cooperation*, Budapest: Akademiai Kiado.

Axelrod, Seth (1994), *The Soviet Union, the IMF and the World Bank, 1941–1947: from inclusion to abstention*, Ph.D. thesis, The University of Birmingham.

Baibakov, Nikolai (1993a), 'Mnenie' (interview), *Segodnya*, 20 November, p. 10.

Baibakov, Nikolai (1993b), *Sorok let v pravitel'stve*, Moscow: Respublika.

Barber, John and Mark Harrison (1991), *The Soviet Home Front, 1941–1945: a Social and Economic History of the USSR in World War II*, London: Longman.

Baryshnikov, N.N. and B.L. Lavrovskii (1982), 'Moshchnosti i rezervy', *Ekonomika i organizatsiya promyshlennogo proizvodstva (EKO)*, no. 3, pp. 31–51.

Bauer, Tamas (1988), 'Economic reforms within vs. beyond the state sector', paper presented at conference at Gyoer, Hungary.

Belotserkovsky, Vadim (1979), 'Workers' struggles in the USSR in the early sixties', *Critique*, nos. 10–11, pp. 37–50.

Belousov, Andrei (2000), 'Stanovlenie sovetskoi industrial'noi sistemy', *Rossiya XXI*, no. 2, pp. 28–78 and no. 3, pp. 20–70.

Bergson, Abram and Hans Heymann (1954), *Soviet National Income and Product, 1940–48*, New York: Columbia University Press.

Bergson, Abram (1961), *The Real National Income of Soviet Russia*, Cambridge, MA: Harvard University Press.

Bergson, Abram and Simon Kuznets (eds) (1963), *Economic Trends in the Soviet Union*, Cambridge, MA: Harvard University Press.

Bergson, Abram (1983), 'Technological Progress', in Bergson and Herbert S. Levine (eds), *The Soviet Economy: Towards the Year 2000*, Winchester, MA, pp. 34–79.

Berliner, Joseph (1976), *The Innovation Decision in Soviet Industry*, Cambridge, MA: MIT Press.

Berliner, Joseph (1984), 'Economic measures and reforms under Andropov', in Philip Joseph (ed.), *The Soviet Economy after Brezhnev*, Brussels: NATO, pp. 55–69.

Berry, M.J. (1987), 'Science, technology and innovation', in McCauley 1987a, pp. 71–95.

Birman, Igor (1981), *Secret Incomes of the State Budget*, Boston: Martinus Nijhoff.

Bogomolov, Oleg T. (2000), *Moya letopis' pewrekhodnogo vremeni*, Moscow: Ekonomika.

Bornstein, Morris (1959), 'A Comparison of Soviet and United States National Product', in US Congress JEC 1959, pp. 377–97.

Bornstein, Morris and Daniel R. Fusfeld (1962), *The Soviet Economy. A Book of Readings*, Homewood, IL: Irwin.

Brackett, James W. and John W. De Pauw (1966), 'Population policy and demographic trends', in US Congress JEC, 1966, pp. 593–703.

Bradley, M.E. and M. Gardner Clark (1972), 'Supervision and efficiency in socialised agriculture', *Soviet Studies*, vol. XXIII no. 3, pp. 465–74.

Braithwaite, Rodric (2002), *Across the Moscow River. The World Turned Upside Down*, New Haven: Yale University Press.

Bronson, David W. and Barbara S. Severin (1973), 'Soviet consumer welfare: the Brezhnev era', in US Congress JEC, 1973, pp. 376–404.

Brown, Archie (1996), *The Gorbachev Fractor*, Oxford: Oxford University Press.

Brus, Wlodzimierz (1988), 'The East European economic reforms: lessons from experience', paper presented at a conference at Gyoer, Hungary.

Bush, Keith (1973), 'Resource allocation policy: fixed investment', in JEC 1973, pp. 39–45.

Bush, Keith (1975), 'Soviet living standards: some salient data', in NATO Colloquium, *Economic Aspects of Life in the USSR*, Brussels: NATO, pp. 49–65.

Bushnell, John (1980), 'The "New Soviet Man" Turns Pessimist', in Stephen F. Cohen, Alexander Rabinowitch and Robert Sharlet (eds), *The Soviet Union Since Stalin*, London, pp. 179–200.

Butler, Nick (1983), 'The New US-Soviet Grain Deal', *The World Today*, November, pp. 411–12.

Buzhinskii, A.I. and S.A. Kheinman (1983), 'Ob intensifikatsii i investitsiyakh', *EKO* no. 10, pp. 144–9.

Carey, David W. and Joseph F. Havelka (1979), 'Soviet agriculture: progress and problems', in JEC 1979, vol. 2, pp. 55–87.

Chapman, Janet G. (1963), 'Consumption', in Bergson and Kuznets 1963, pp. 235–83.

Chawluk, Anthony (1974), 'Economic policy and economic reform', *Soviet Studies*, January, pp. 98–120.

Chernyaev, A.S. (1993), *Shest' let s Gorbachevym*, Moscow: Kul'tura.

CIA 1946–76, Paul Kezaris (ed.) (1982), *The Soviet Union 1946–1976. CIA Research Reports*, Frederick, MD (5 microfilm reels).

CIA (1983), 'USSR: economic trends and policy developments', US Congress Joint Economic Committee Briefing Paper, 14 September.

CIA Budget (1988), 'USSR: sharply higher budget deficits threaten *perestroyka*', SOV88–10043U (September).

CIA (1990), *Measures of Soviet Gross National Product in 1982 Prices*, Washington, DC.

CIA *Oil* (1977), *Prospects for Soviet Oil Production* (ER77–10270), April.

CIA *Oil Supplementary* (1977), *Prospects for Soviet Oil Production: A Supplementary Analysis* (ER77–10425), July.

Clarke, Roger and Dubravko Matko (compilers) (1983), *Soviet Economic Facts 1917–81*, London, 2nd edn.

Cohn, Stanley H. (1973), 'Economic burden of defense expenditure', in JEC 1973, pp. 147–63.

Conquest, R. (1986), *The Harvest of Sorrow. Soviet Collectivisation and the Terror-Famine*, London: Hutchinson.

Cooper, Julian (1982), 'Innovation for innovation in Soviet industry', in Amann and Cooper 1982, pp. 453–514.

Cooper, Julian (1989), *The Defense Sector and Change in the Soviet Economy*, Washington DC: Kiser Research and Center for Strategic and International Studies.

Copetas, Craig A. (1991), *Bear Hunting with the Politburo*, New York: Simon and Schuster.

Crankshaw, Edward (1959), *Khrushchev's Russia*, Harmondsworth: Penguin.

Dalrymple, D.G. (1964), 'The Soviet famine of 1932–34', *Soviet Studies*, January, pp. 250–85.

Davies, R.W. (1957), 'Industrial planning reconsidered', *Soviet Studies*, vol. VIII, no. 4, pp. 426–37.

De Long, J.B. and B. Eichengreen (1992), 'The Marshall Plan: history's most successful structural adjustment program', Centre for Economic Policy Research Discussion Paper Series, no. 634.

Diamond, Douglas B. and Constance B. Krueger (1973), 'Recent developments in output and productivity in Soviet agriculture', in JEC 1973, pp. 316–40.

Diamond, Douglas B. and W. Lee Davis (1979), 'Comparative growth in output and productivity in US and USSR agriculture', in JEC 1979, vol. 2, pp. 19–55.

Djilas, Milovan (1963), *Conversations with Stalin*, Harmondsworth: Penguin.

Dudintsev, V.S. (1957), *Not by Bread Alone*, London: Hutchinson.

Dunham, Vera (1979), *In Stalin's Time*, Cambridge: Cambridge University Press.

Dyker, David (1984), 'The fate of Andropov's industrial planning experiment', Radio Liberty RL 154/84 (16 April).

Eason, Warren W. (1963), 'Labor force', in Bergson and Kuznets 1963, pp. 203–35.

Easterly, William and Stanley Fischer (1995), 'The Soviet economic decline', *The World Bank Economic Review*, vol. 9, no. 3, pp. 341–71.

Edwards, Imogene U. (1973), 'Automotive trends in the USSR', in JEC 1973, pp. 291–316.

Edwards, Imogene, Margaret Hughes and James Noren (1979), 'US and USSR: comparisons of GNP', in US JEC 1979, vol. 1, pp. 369–402.

EIU QER, Economist Intelligence Unit, *Quarterly Economic Review of the USSR* [written in 1975–85 inclusive by the present author].

Ekonomika na pereput'e (1987), *Literaturnaya gazeta*, 3 June.

Ellman, Michael (1969), *Economic Reform in the Soviet Union*, London: Political and Economic Planning.

Ellman, Michael (1992), 'Money in the 1980s', in Ellman and Kontorovich 1992, pp. 106–37.

Ellman, Michael (2000), 'The 1947 Soviet famine and the entitlement approach to famines', *Cambridge Journal of Economics*, vol. 24 no. 5, pp. 603–30.

Ellman, Michael and Vladimir Kontorovich (eds) (1992), *The Disintegration of the Soviet Economic System*, London: Routledge.

Ellman, Michael and Vladimir Kontorovich (1997), 'The collapse of the Soviet System and the memoir literature', *Europe-Asia Studies*, vol. 49 no. 2, pp. 59–79.

Ellman, Michael and Vladimir Kontorovich (eds) (1998), *The Destruction of the Soviet Economic System. An Insiders' History*, Armonk NY: M.E. Sharpe.

Ericson, Paul and Ronald S. Miller (1979), 'Soviet foreign economic behavior: a balance of payments perspective', in JEC 1979, vol. 2, pp. 208–44.

Eucken, Walter (1948), 'On the theory of the centrally administered economy: an analysis of the German experiment', *Economica*, vol. XV no. 58 (May), pp. 79–100, and vol. XV no. 59 (August), pp. 173–93.

Fal'tsman, V.K. and A. Kornev (1984), 'Rezervy snizheniya kapitaloemkosti moshchnostei promyshlennosti', *Voprosy ekonomiki*, no. 6, pp. 36–46.

Fal'tsman, V.K. (1985), 'Mashinostroenie: puti peremen', *EKO*, no. 12, pp. 3–21.

Farrell, John T. (1973), 'Soviet payments problems in trade with the West', in JEC 1973, pp. 690–714.

Fedorenko, Nikolai P. (1983) (chief ed.), *Voprosy optimal'nogo planirovaniya i upravleniya sotsialisticheskoi ekonomiki*, Moscow: Nauka (10 vols).

Filtzer, Donald (1992), *Soviet Workers and De-Stalinisation, the Consolidation of the Modern System of Soviet Production Relations*, Cambridge.

Filtzer, Donald (1993), *The Khrushchev Era. De-Stalinisation and the Limits of Reform in the USSR, 1953–1964*, London.

Filtzer, Donald (1999), 'The standard of living of Soviet industrial workers in the immediate postwar period, 1945–1948', *Europe-Asia Studies*, vol. 51 no. 6, pp. 1013–39.

Frankland, Mark (1966), *Khrushchev*, Harmondsworth: Penguin.

Gorbachev, Mikhail (1985), *Nastoichivo dvigat'sya vpered*, Moscow: Politicheskaya literatura.

Gorbachev, Mikhail (1995), *Zhizn' i reformy*, 2 vols, Moscow: Novosti.

Gorlizki, Yoram (2001), 'Stalin's Cabinet: the Politburo and decison making in the post-war years', *Europe-Asia Studies*, vol. 53 no. 2 (March), pp. 291–313.

Grayson, John (1982), 'Innovation at the Soviet plant level: the case of Group Technology (1950–70)', in Amann and Cooper 1982, pp. 101–27.

Greenslade, Rush V. and Wade E. Robertson (1973), 'Industrial production in the USSR', in JEC 1973, pp. 270–83.

Gregory, Paul (1987), 'Productivity, slack and time-theft in the Soviet economy', in Millar 1987, pp. 241–79.

Gregory, Paul (2001), *Behind the Façade of Stalin's Command Economy*, Stanford CA: Hoover Institution Press.

Gregory, Paul and Robert C. Stuart (1995), *Comparative Economic Systems* (5th edn), Boston: Houghton Mifflin.

Grossman, Gregory (1987), 'Roots of Gorbachev's problems: private income and outlay in the late 1970s', in JEC 1987, vol. 1, pp. 213–31.

Grossman, Gregory (1989), 'Private and cooperative economic activities', in *Soviet Economic Reforms: Implementation Under Way*, Brussels: NATO, pp. 115–30.

Hahn, Werner G. (1972), *The Politics of Soviet Agriculture, 1960–1970*, Baltimore, MD: Johns Hopkins University Press.

Hanson, Philip (1968), *The Consumer in the Soviet Economy*, London/Evanston, IL: Macmillan/Northwestern University Press.

Hanson, Philip (1981), *Trade and Technology in Soviet-Western Relations*, London/New York: Macmillan/Columbia University Press.

Hanson, Philip (1983), 'Success indicators revisited: the July 1979 decree on planning and management', *Soviet Studies*, vol. XXXV, no. 1, pp. 1–14.

Hanson, Philip (1986), 'The serendipitous Soviet achievement of full employment', in Lane 1986, pp. 83–112.

Hanson, Philip (1988), *Western Economic Statecraft in East-West Relations. Embargoes, Sanctions, Economic Warfare, and Détente*, London: Royal Institute of International Affairs.

Hanson, Philip (1990), 'The Soviet Union', in Andrew Graham with Anthony Seldon (eds), *Government and Economies in the Postwar World. Economic Policies and Comparative Performance, 1945–85*, London, pp. 205–25.

Hanson, Philip (1992), *From Stagnation to Catastroika. Commentaries on the Soviet Economy, 1983–1991*, New York: Praeger/Center for Strategic and International Studies.

Hardesty, Von (2001), 'Made in the USSR' (Smithsonian) *Air and Space Magazine*, February-March (www.airspacemag.com/ASM/Mag/).

Harrison, Mark (2001a), 'Coercion, compliance and the collapse of the Soviet command economy', University of Warwick, Dept of Economics, draft.

Harrison, Mark (2001b), 'Economic growth and slowdown', draft of February for Edwin Bacon and Mark Sandle (eds), *Brezhnev Reconsidered* (London, forthcoming).

Havrylyshyn, Oleh and John Williamson (1991), *From Soviet DisUnion to Eastern Economic Community?*, Washington DC: Institute for International Economics.

Hayek, Friedrich von (1945), 'The use of knowledge in society', *American Economic Review*, vol. 35 no. 4 (September), pp. 519–30.

Hayward, Max (1963), 'Introduction', in Abramov 1963, pp. 15–19.

Hedlund, Stefan (1989), *Private Agriculture in the Soviet Union*, London: Routledge.

Hersey, John (1986), *Hiroshima*, 2nd edn, London: Penguin.

Hessler, Julie (2001), 'Postwar normalisation and its limits in the USSR: the case of trade', *Europe-Asia Studies*, vol. 53 no. 3 (May), pp. 445–73.

Hewett, Ed (1979), *Foreign Trade Prices in the Council for Mutual Economic Assistance*, Cambridge: Cambridge University Press.

Hewett, Ed, Bryan Roberts and Jan Vanous (1987), 'On the feasibility of key targets in the Soviet Twelfth Five-Year Plan (1986–90)', in JEC 1987, vol. 1, pp. 27–54.

Heymann, Hans (1959), 'Problems of Soviet-United States comparisons', in JEC 1959, pp. 1–11.

Holloway, David (1983), *The Soviet Union and the Arms Race*, New Haven, CN: Yale University Press.

Holzman, Franklyn D. (1963), 'Foreign trade', in Bergson and Kuznets 1963, pp. 283–333.

Holzman, Franklyn D. (1974), *Foreign Trade Under Central Planning*, Cambridge, MA.

Hosking, Geoffrey (1992), *A History of the Soviet Union*, 1917–1991, London: Fontana.

Ignatovskii, P. (1983), 'O politicheskom podkhode k ekonomike', *Kommunist*, no. 12, pp. 60–73.

IMF, World Bank, OECD and EBRD (1990), *The Economy of the USSR. Summary and Recommendations*, report for Group of Seven Countries (December).

Ioffe, Grigory and Tatyana Nefedova (2001), 'The Russian food system's transformation at close range: a case study of two oblasts', [US] National Council for Eurasian and East European Research, Washington, DC, Title VIII Program report (17 August).

Jasny, Naum (1949), *The Socialized Agriculture of the USSR*, Stanford, CA: Hoover Institution.

Jasny, Naum (1957), *The Soviet 1956 Statistical Handbook: A Commentary*, Lansing, MI: Michigan State University Press.

Jasny, Naum (1961), *Soviet Industrialization*, Chicago: University of Chicago Press.

JEC 1959, JEC 1965, etc.: see under US Congress Joint Economic Committee.

Johnson, D. Gale and Arcadius Kahan (1959), 'Soviet agriculture: structure and growth', in JEC 1959, pp. 201–39.

Johnson, D. Gale (1982), 'Prospects for Soviet agriculture in the 1980s', in JEC 1982, vol. 2, pp. 7–23.

Jones, David (1973), 'The "Extra" costs in Europe's biggest synthetic fibre complex at Mogilev, USSR', *Worldwide Projects and Installations*, vol. 7, part 3, pp. 30–35.

Kapitza, Petr. L. (1966/84), *Teoriya, eksperiment, praktika*, Moscow.

Kaser, Michael (1967), *Comecon: Integration Problems of the Planned Economies*, Oxford: Oxford University Press, 2nd edn.

Kaser, Michael (1970), *Soviet Economics*, London: Weidenfeld and Nicholson.

Kaser, Michael and Michael Maltby (1988), 'Perestroika and foreign trade', paper presented at SSEES conference on Gorbachev and Perestroika, London (July).

Kaufman, Richard (1983), 'Soviet defense trends', study prepared for the Sub-committee on International Trade, Finance and Security Economics of the US Congress Joint Economic Committee, September, mimeo.

Khanin, Gigorii I. (1981), 'Al'ternativnye otsenki rezul'tatov khozyaistvennoi deyatel'nosti proizvodstvennykh yacheek proizvodstva', *Izvestuya Akademii Nauk SSSR. Seriya ekonomicheskaya*, no. 6, pp. 62–74.

Khrushchev, N.S. (1971), *Khrushchev Remembers* (ed. Strobe Talbott), London: Deutsch.

Khrushchev, N.S. (1974), *Khrushchev Remembers. The Last Testament*, London: Deutsch.

Khrushchev, Sergei (2000), 'The military-industrial complex, 1953–1964', in Taubman *et al.* 2000, pp. 242–75.

Kokurin, Aleksandr and Yurii Morukov (1999–2000), 'Gulag: struktura i kadry', *Svobodnaya mysl'*, (series of articles) 1999 no.s 8–12, 2000, nos. 1–3, 5–9.

Kontorovich, Vladimir (1985), 'Discipline and growth in the USSR', *Problems of Communism*, vol. 36 (November-December), pp. 18–31.

Kontorovich, Vladimir (1986), 'Soviet growth slowdown: econometric vs. direct evidence', *American Economic Review*, vol. 76 no. 2 (May), pp. 181–6.

Kontorovich, Vladimir (1988), 'Lessons of the 1965 Soviet economic reform', *Soviet Studies*, vol. 40 no. 2 (April), pp. 308–17.

Kontorovich, Vladimir (2001), 'The Russian health crisis and the economy', *Communist and Post-Communist Studies*, vol. 34, pp. 221–40.

Kooperativy g. Zaporozha. Spravochnik (1988), Zaporozhe: Poisk Cooperative and city council.

Kornai, Janos (1958), *Over-centralisation in Economic Administration*, Oxford: Oxford University Press.

Kornai, J. (1986), 'The Hungarian economic reform process: vision, hopes and reality', *Journal of Economic Literature*, 24.

Kosygin, A.N. (1965), 'Ob uluchshenii upravleniya promyshlennostyu, sovershenstvovanii planirovaniya i usilenii ekonomicheskogo stimulirovaniya promyshlennogo proizvodstva', *Pravda*, 28 September, pp. 1–14.

Kozlov, A. (1998), *Kozel na sakse*, Moscow: Vagrius.

Kurashvili, B.P. (1985), 'Kontury vozmozhnoi perestroiki', *EKO*, no. 5, pp. 59–80.

Kusin, Vladimir V. (2001), 'Another Third World', mimeo, February.

Kuznetsov, V.V. (1990), *Predpriyatie vo vneshneekonomicheskikh svyazyakh*, Moscow: Mezhdunarodnye otnosheniya.

Lane, David (ed.) (1986), *Labour and Employment in the USSR*, Brighton: Wheatsheaf, 1986.

Latsis, O. (1983), 'Glavnyi sud'ya', *Literaturnaya gazeta*, 3 August, p. 13.

Lavigne, Marie (1985), *Economie Internationale des Pays Socialistes*, Paris. English version: *International Political Economy and Socialism*, Cambridge: Cambridge University Press, 1991.

Lavigne, Marie (1987), 'Compte rendue de mission effectuée en URSS', mimeo.

Lee, J. Richard and James R. Lecky (1979), 'Soviet oil developments', in JEC 1979, vol. 1, pp. 581–600.

Leggett, Robert (1982), 'Soviet investment policy in the 11th Five Year Plan', in JEC 1982, vol. 1, pp. 129–47.

Leggett, Robert (1987), 'Soviet investment policy: the key to Gorbachev's plans for revitalising the Soviet economy', in JEC 1987, vol. 1, pp. 236–57.

Levikov, A. (1986), 'Remeslo', *Novyi mir*, no. 4, pp. 180–99.

Levine, Herbert S. (1982), 'Possible causes of the deterioration of Soviet productivity growth in the period 1976–80', in JEC 1982, vol. 1, pp. 153–69.

Lushina, N.L. (1984), 'Melkoe proizvodstvo v sotsialisticheskom khozyaistve', *EKO*, no. 5, pp. 147–58.

McAuley, Alastair (1979), *Economic Welfare in the Soviet Union*, Madison,WI: University of Wisconsin Press.

McAuley, Alastair (1987), 'Social policy', in McCauley 1987a, pp. 138–56.

McCauley, Martin (1976), *Khrushchev and the Development of Soviet Agriculture: the Virgin Lands Programme*, London: Macmillan.

McCauley, Martin (ed.) (1987a), *Khrushchev and Khrushchevism*, London: Macmillan.

McCauley, Martin (ed.) (1987b), *The Soviet Union under Gorbachev*, London: Macmillan.

MacDuffie, Marshall (1955), *Red Carpet: 10,000 Miles through Russia on a Visa from Khrushchev*, London.

McIntyre, Joan F. (1987), 'The USSR's hard currency trade and payments position', in JEC 1987, vol. 2, pp. 474–89.

Maddison, Angus (1993), *Explaining the Economic Performance of Nations*, Cheltenham: Edward Elgar.

Maddison, Angus (1995), *Monitoring the World Economy, 1820–1992*, Paris: OECD.

Maddison, Angus (1998), 'Measuring the performance of a communist command economy: an assessment of the CIA estimates for the USSR', *Review of Income and Wealth*, vol. 44 no. 3, pp. 307–23.

Maksimova, Margarita (1974), 'Vsemirnoe khozyaistvo; mezhdunarodnoe ekonomicheskoe sotrudnichestvo', *Mirovaya ekonomika i mezhdunarodnye otnosheniya*, no. 4, pp. 3–21.

Mau, Vladimir and Irina Starodubrovskaya (2001), *The Challenge of Revolution. Contemporary Russia in Historical Perspective*, Oxford: Oxford University Press.

Mihalyi, Peter (1992), *Socialist Investment Cycles. Analysis in Retrospect*, Dordrecht: Kluwer.

Millar, James R. (ed.) (1987), *Politics, work and daily life in the USSR. A survey of former Soviet citizens*, Cambridge: Cambridge University Press.

Moorsteen, R.H. and R.P. Powell (1966), *The Soviet Capital Stock 1928–1962*, Homewood, IL: Irwin.

Morton, Henry W. (1979), 'The Soviet quest for better housing: an impossible dream?' in JEC 1979, vol. 1, pp. 790–811.

Narkhoz 60, Narkhoz 70, etc.: Tsentral'noe statisticheskoe upravlenie SSSR, *Narodnoe khozyaistvo SSSR v . . . [year] . . . godu*, Moscow: TsSU, annual (statistical handbook).

Naumov, Vladimir (2000), 'Repression and Rehabilitation', in Taubman *et al.* 2000, pp. 85–113.

Noren, James (1986), 'Soviet investment strategy under Gorbachev', paper presented at the annual AAASS conference, New Orleans (November).

Nove, Alec (1953), 'Rural taxation in the USSR', *Soviet Studies*, vol. V, no. 2, pp. 159–67 (October).

Nove, Alec (1987), 'Industry', in McCauley 1987a, pp. 61–71.

Nove, Alec (1992), *An Economic History of the USSR, 1917–1991*, 3rd edn, Harmondsworth.

Ofer, Gur (1988), *Soviet Economic Growth: 1928–1985*, Santa Monica, CA: RAND/ UCLA Center for the Study of Soviet International Economic Behavior (also published in the *Journal of Economic Literature*, December 1987).

Pasternak, Boris (1958), *Dr Zhivago*, London: Collins.

Pavlov, Valentin (1995), *Upushchen li shans?*, Moscow: Terra.

Perekhod k rynku (1990), *Chast' 1: kontseptsiya i programma*, Moscow: Arkhangel'skoe.

Pipes, Richard (1984), 'Can the Soviet Union reform?', *Foreign Affairs*, Fall, pp. 47– 62.

Pitzer, John (1982), 'Gross National Product of the USSR, 1950–80', in JEC Growth 1982, pp. 3–169.

Popkova, L. (1987) (Larissa Piyasheva), 'Gde pyshnee pirogi?' *Novyi mir*, no. 5, pp. 239–41.

Poznanski, Kazimierz (1987), *Technology, Competition and the Soviet Bloc in the World Market*, Berkeley, CA: University of California at Berkeley, Institute of International Studies.

Poznanski, Kazimierz (1988), 'Opportunity cost in Soviet trade with Eastern Europe: discussion of methodology and new evidence', *Soviet Studies*, vol. XL no. 2 (April), pp. 290–308.

Problemy sobstvennosti v real'nom sotsializme (1987), Moscow: IEMSS.

Rabkin, Yakov (1977), 'Science studies as an area of scientific exchange', in J.R. Thomas and U. Kruse-Vaucienne (eds), *Soviet Science and Technology*, Washington, DC: George Washington University, pp. 69–83.

Rapawy, Stephen (1987), 'Labour force and employment in the USSR', in JEC 1987, vol. 1, pp. 187–213.

Rice, Condoleezza (1987), 'Defence and security', in McCauley 1987b, pp. 192–210.

Rimmington, Anthony (2000), 'Invisible weapons of mass destruction: the Soviet Union's BW programme and its implications for contemporary arms control', *The Journal of Slavic Military Studies*, vol. 13 no. 3 (September), pp. 1–46.

Robbins, Greg S. (1991), *The Soviet Banking System Within the Context of Change*, Oxford University M.Phil. dissertation.

Roberts, Frank K., 'Encounters with Khrushchev', in McCauley (1987a), pp. 211– 29.

'Samostyatel'nost' (1984), Round-table discussion, 'Klub direktorov. Samostoyatel'nost': idei i voploshchenie', *EKO* 1984 no. 12, pp. 33–72.

Schoonover, David M. (1979), 'Soviet agricultural policies', in JEC 1979, vol. 2, pp. 87–116.

Schroeder, Gertrude E. (1975), 'Consumer goods availability and repressed inflation in the USSR', in NATO Colloquium, *Economic Aspects of Life in the USSR*, Brussels: NATO, pp. 37–49.

Schroeder, Gertrude E. (1979), 'The Soviet economy on a treadmill of reforms', in JEC 1979, vol. 1, pp. 312–41.

Schroeder, Gertrude E. (1982), 'Soviet economic "Reform" decrees: more steps on the treadmill', in JEC 1982, vol. 1, pp. 65–89.

Schroeder, Gertrude E. and M. Elizabeth Denton (1982), 'An index of consumption in the USSR', in JEC Growth 1982, pp. 317–402.

Schumpeter, J.A. (1944), *Capitalism, Socialism and Democracy*, 1st edn, London: Allen and Unwin.

Schwarz, Solomon (1952), *Labor in the Soviet Union*, New York: Praeger.

Selkhoz 60 (Soviet statistical handbook on agriculture, 1960, etc.), Tsentral'noe statisticheskoe upravlenie SSSR, *Sel'skoe khozyaistvo SSSR*, Moscow: TsSU, 1960.

Selyunin, Vasilyi (1985), 'Eksperiment', *Novyi mir*, no. 8, pp. 173–95.

Sen, Amartya K. (1981), *Poverty and Famines*, Oxford: Clarendon Press.

Service, Robert J. (1981), 'The road to the Twentieth Party Congress: an analysis of the events surrounding the central committee plenum of July 1953', *Soviet Studies*, vol. XXXIII no. 2 (April), pp. 232–46.

Severin, Barbara and Margaret Hughes (1982), 'An index of agricultural production in the USSR', in JEC Growth 1982, pp. 245–317.

Shatalin, Stanislav (1986), 'Sotsial'noe razvitie i ekonomicheskii rost', *Kommunist* no. 4, pp. 59–71.

Shmarov, A. and N. Kirichenko (1989), 'Inflatsionnyi vsplesk: masshtaby i prichiny', *Ekonomicheskaya gazeta*, no. 13, p. 12.

Shtromas, Alexander (1988), 'How the end of the Soviet Union may come about', in Alexander Shtromas and Morton A. Kaplan (eds), *The Soviet Union and the Challenge of the Future*, New York: Paragon House, pp. 201–301.

Silk, Leonard (1983), 'Andropov faces difficulties in attempts to revive Soviet economy', *New York Times*, 12 June.

Smelyakov, Nikolai S. (1973), 'Delovye vstrechi', *Noviy mir*, no. 12, pp. 203–40.

Smith, G.A.E. (1987), 'Agriculture', in McCauley 1987a, pp. 95–117.

Smith, Hedrick (1976), *The Russians*, London: Sphere Books.

Solnick, Steven (1999), *Stealing the State*, Cambridge MA: MIT Press.

Solzhenitsyn, Alexander (1963), *One Day in the Life of Ivan Denisovich*, Harmondsworth: Penguin.

Solzhenitsyn, Alexander (1971), *Cancer Ward*, Harmondsworth: Penguin.

Solzhenitsyn, Alexander (1976), *The Gulag Archipelago*, vol. 3, London: Penguin.

Soros, George (1990), *Opening the Soviet Economy*, London: Weidenfeld and Nicholson.

Stern, J. (1987), *Soviet Oil and Gas Exports to the West: Commercial Transactions or Security Threat?*, Aldershot: Gower.

Streliannyi, Anatolii (1986), 'Raionnye budni', *Novyi mir*, no. 12, pp. 231–41.

Strelianyi, Anatolii (2000), 'Khrushchev and the countryside', in Taubman, Khrushchev and Gleason, pp. 113–38.

Sutela, Pekka (1984), *Socialism, Planning and Optimality. A Study in Soviet Economic Thought*, Helsinki: Societas Scientiarum Fennica.

Sutela, Pekka (1991), *Economic Thought and Economic Reform in the Soviet Union*, Cambridge, UK: Cambridge University Press.

Sutton, A.C., *Western Technology and Soviet Economic Development*, Stanford, CA: Hoover Institution, vol. 1 (1968), vol. 2 (1971), vol. 3 (1973).

Taubman, William, Sergei Khrushchev and Abbott Gleason (eds) (2000), *Nikita Khrushchev*, New Haven, CN: Yale University Press.

Teague, Elizabeth (1983), 'Draft Law on Workers' Collectives', Radio Liberty RL 160/83 (20 April).

Teague, Elizabeth (1987), 'Gorbachev's human factor policies', in JEC 1987, vol. 2, pp. 224–40.

Teague, Elizabeth (1988), *Solidarity and the Soviet Worker*, London: Croome Helm.

Tenson, Andreas (1982), 'Food rationing in the Soviet Union', *Radio Liberty Research Bulletin*, RL 321/82 (11 August).

Tikhonov, Aleksei and Paul Gregory (2001), 'Stalin's last plan', in Gregory 2001, pp. 159–93.

Tompson, William (1995), *Khrushchev: A Political Life*, London: Macmillan.

Tompson, William (2000), 'Industrial management and economic reform under Khrushchev', in Taubman, Khrushchev and Gleason 2000, pp. 138–60.

Treml, Vladimir G. (1982a), *Alcohol in the USSR. A Statistical Study*, Durham, NC: Duke Press Policy Studies.

Treml, Vladimir G. (1982b), 'Subsidies in Soviet Agriculture: Record and Prospects', in JEC 1982, vol. 2, pp. 171–87.

Treml, Vladimir G. (1983), 'Soviet dependence on foreign trade', in *External Economic Relations of CMEA Countries*, Brussels, pp. 35–53.

Treml, Vladimir G. (1986), 'Soviet foreign trade in foodstuffs', *Soviet Economy*, vol. 2 no. 1, pp. 95–109.

Treml, Vladimir G. (1987), 'Gorbachev's anti-drinking campaign: a "Noble Experiment" or a costly exercise in futility?', in JEC 1987, vol. 2, pp. 297–312.

Treml, Vladimir G., Barry L. Kostinsky and Dimitri M. Gallik (1973), 'Interindustry structure of the Soviet economy: 1959 and 1966', in JEC 1973, pp. 246–70.

Tret'yakova, Albina and Igor Birman (1976), 'Input-output analysis in the USSR', *Soviet Studies*, vol. XXXVIII, pp. 157–86.

US Congress Joint Economic Committee (1959), *Comparisons of the United States and Soviet Economies*, Washington, DC (JEC 1959).

US Congress Joint Economic Committee (1965), *Current Economic Indicators for the USSR*, Washington, DC (JEC 1965).

US Congress Joint Economic Committee (1966), *New Directions in the Soviet Economy*, Washington, DC (three volumes) (JEC 1966).

US Congress Joint Economic Committee (1979), *Soviet Economy in a Time of Change*, 2 vols, Washington, DC (JEC 1979).

US Congress Joint Economic Committee (1982), *USSR: Measures of Economic Growth and Development, 1950–80*, Washington, DC: US Government Printing Office (JEC Growth 1982).

US Congress Joint Economic Committee (1982), *Soviet Economy in the 1980s: Problems and Prospects*, 2 vols, Washington, DC (JEC 1982).

US Congress Joint Economic Committee (1987), *Gorbachev's Economic Plans*, two vols, Washington, DC (JEC 1987).

Val'tukh, K.K. (1982), 'Investitsionnyi kompleks i intensifikatsiya proizvodstva', *EKO*, no. 3, pp. 4–31.

Variantnyi 1990, Variantnyi prognoz razvitiya SSSR v period stanovleniya rynochnykh otnoshenii, Moscow: Gosplan (n.d., but late 1990).

Venzher, V.G., Ya. V. Kvasha, A.I. Notkin, S.P. Pervushin and S.A. Kheinman (1965), *Proizvodstvo, nakoplenie, potreblenie*, Moscow.

Vishnevskaya, Galina (1984), *Galina. A Russian Story*, London: Hodder and Stoughton.

VT SSSR 60 (annual statistical handbook of foreign trade), *Vneshnyaya torgovlya SSSR v 1960 godu*, Moscow, annual. This source was renamed in the Gorbachev period *Vneshnye ekonomicheskie svyazi SSSR*, when the responsible ministry was renamed the Ministry for External Economic Relations instead of Ministry for Foreign Trade. In references in the text the VT acronym is used throughout.

VT SSSR 22–81 (historical compendium of foreign trade data), *Vneshnyaya torgovlya SSSR 1922–1981*, Moscow, 1982.

Wädekin, Karl-Eugen (1973), *The Private Sector in Soviet Agriculture*, Berkeley, CA: University of California Press.

Wädekin, Karl-Eugen (1989), 'The re-emergence of the Kolkhoz Principle', *Soviet Studies*, vol. XLI no. 1 (January), pp. 20–39.

Weitzman, Martin L. (1970), 'Soviet postwar economic growth and capital-labor substitution', *American Economic Review*, vol. 60 no. 5, pp. 676–92.

Welihozkiy, Toli (1979), 'Automobiles and the Soviet consumer', in JEC 1979, vol. 1, pp. 811–34.

Wheatcroft, S.G. (1990), 'More light on the scale of repression and excess mortality in the Soviet Union in the 1930s', *Soviet Studies*, vol. 42, no. 7, pp. 355–67.

Whitehouse, Douglas and Joseph F. Havelka (1973), 'Comparison of farm output in the US and USSR – 1950–1971', in JEC 1973, pp. 340–76.

Wiles, P.J.D. (1962), *The Political Economy of Communism*, Oxford: Blackwell.

Wiles, P.J.D. (1974), *Distribution of Income, East and West*, Amsterdam: North-Holland Publishing Company.

Yakovlev, Aleksandr (1992), *Predislove. Obval. Posledstvie*, Moscow: Novosti.

Yasin, Evgenii (2001), 'Besedy ob ekonomike' (interviews originally on Ekho Moskvy radio), *Znanie-sila*, February, pp. 62–9, March, pp. 78–85, April, pp. 50–55.

Yevtushenko, Ye. (1963), *A Precocious Autobiography*, Harmondsworth: Penguin.

Zaleski, Eugene (1967), *Planning Reforms in the Soviet Union 1962–1966*, Chapel Hill, NC: North Carolina University Press.

Zal'tsman, I. and G. Edel'gauz (1984), 'Vospominaya uroki Tankograda', *Kommunist*, no. 16, pp. 76–88.

Zaslavskaya, Tatyana [authorship deduced from internal evidence; the title page was removed from the leaked copy], 'Doklad o neobkhodimosti bolee uglublennogo izuchenie v SSSR sotsial'nogo mekhanizma razvitie ekonomiki', reportedly presented at a seminar in Moscow, April 1983, Radio Liberty Arkhiv Samizdata vypusk 35/83, AS 5042 of 26 August 1983.

Zima, V.F. (1996), *Golod v SSSR 1946–1947 godov: proiskhozhdenie i posledstviya*, Moscow: Institute of Russian History, Russian Academy of Sciences.

Zinoviev, Alexander (1976), *Ziyayushchie vysoty*, Lausanne: L'Age d'homme.

Zinoviev, Alexander (1981), *Kommunizm kak real'nost'*, Lausanne: L'Age d'homme.

Zoeter, Joan Parpart (1982), 'USSR: hard currency trade and payments', in JEC 1982, vol. 2, pp. 479–507.

Zubkova, Elena (2000), 'The rivalry with Malenkov', in Taubman, Khrushchev and Gleason 2000, pp. 67–85.

INDEX